100 Activities for Teaching Study Skills

Sara Miller McCune founded SAGE Publishing in 1965 to support the dissemination of usable knowledge and educate a global community. SAGE publishes more than 1000 journals and over 800 new books each year, spanning a wide range of subject areas. Our growing selection of library products includes archives, data, case studies and video. SAGE remains majority owned by our founder and after her lifetime will become owned by a charitable trust that secures the company's continued independence.

Los Angeles | London | New Delhi | Singapore | Washington DC | Melbourne

100 Activities for Teaching Study Skills

Catherine Dawson

Los Angeles | London | New Delhi
Singapore | Washington DC | Melbourne

Los Angeles | London | New Delhi
Singapore | Washington DC | Melbourne

SAGE Publications Ltd
1 Oliver's Yard
55 City Road
London EC1Y 1SP

SAGE Publications Inc.
2455 Teller Road
Thousand Oaks, California 91320

SAGE Publications India Pvt Ltd
B 1/I 1 Mohan Cooperative Industrial Area
Mathura Road
New Delhi 110 044

SAGE Publications Asia-Pacific Pte Ltd
3 Church Street
#10-04 Samsung Hub
Singapore 049483

Editor: Kirsty Smy
Editorial assistant: Jasleen Kaur
Production editor: Martin Fox
Marketing manager: Catherine Slinn
Cover design: Shaun Mercier
Typeset by: C&M Digitals (P) Ltd, Chennai, India
Printed in the UK

Library of Congress Control Number: 2018941565

British Library Cataloguing in Publication data

A catalogue record for this book is available from the British Library

ISBN 978-1-5264-4130-0
ISBN 978-1-5264-4131-7 (pbk)

At SAGE we take sustainability seriously. Most of our products are printed in the UK using responsibly sourced papers and boards. When we print overseas we ensure sustainable papers are used as measured by the PREPS grading system. We undertake an annual audit to monitor our sustainability

Contents

Activity level index

This index helps tutors to find activities that are aimed at the right level for the courses they are teaching. It is not ideal: some may be uncomfortable with the terms (in particular, the term 'elementary', which was felt to be preferable to 'beginner'). Others may feel that it is impossible to categorise learners in this way or that the categories do not translate to a higher education context. However, this simple categorisation is necessary to help tutors to find the right activities for their particular student cohort. It is important to note, also, that these categories are only included in tutor's notes and, therefore, will not be seen by, or discussed with, students.

DEFINITION OF CATEGORIES

- Elementary level: this level includes students who need help with their study skills and learner development so that they feel comfortable with, and progress on, their course. It can include, for example, students at further education level, students in their first year of an undergraduate degree, adult returners, access course students, some Non-English Speaking Background (NESB) students and some international students who may be unfamiliar with study requirements and teaching methods in the United Kingdom.
- Intermediate level: this level includes students who are progressing with their course but need further help with specific study skills and learner development. This

can include students in their first or second year of an undergraduate course, for example.

- Advanced level: this level includes students who are progressing with their course but need help with specific skills and personal development so that they can complete their course and progress on successfully. This can include help with research and enquiry skills, or data analysis skills, for example. They tend to be students in the third year of an undergraduate course. However, it can also include postgraduate students in cases where they have had some time away from education before returning to their studies and they need a recap (or methods of teaching and learning have evolved since they have been away).

Some activities presented in this book are suitable for all three levels outlined above. In these cases the complexity of activity, exercise or discussion will reflect the level of study. The majority of activities, however, are presented at elementary level as this is when students tend to need most help with study skills and learner development.

ACTIVITIES AT ELEMENTARY LEVEL

ACTIVITIES AT INTERMEDIATE LEVEL

ACTIVITIES AT ADVANCED LEVEL

Activity type index
(in alphabetical order)

This index helps tutors to choose the type of activity that most suits their students, course, subject area and teaching and learning preferences. Some activities are listed in more than one category: this is because these activities can be run in more than one way. Alternatives are provided so that tutors can choose a different activity if the main activity type is inappropriate for a particular course, subject or student cohort.

BRAINSTORM FOLLOWED BY TUTOR-LED DISCUSSION

BRAINSTORM WITH TUTOR-LED DISCUSSION AND INDIVIDUAL EXERCISE

BRAINWAVE

COLLABORATIVE DIALOGUE

DIGITAL RESOURCE AND SUPPORT NETWORK

DIGITAL STORYTELLING

ESSAY (WRITTEN ASSIGNMENT)

GAME

ONLINE DIRECTORY

PEER SUPPORT GROUP

PEER TEACHING

PERSONAL LEARNING JOURNAL AND DIARY

SCENARIOS FOR GROUP DISCUSSION

SELF-GUIDED EXERCISE IN PAIRS

SELF-GUIDED INDIVIDUAL EXERCISE

SELF-GUIDED INDIVIDUAL EXERCISE FOLLOWED BY ROLE PLAY

SELF-GUIDED INDIVIDUAL EXERCISE FOLLOWED BY STUDENT PRESENTATION

SELF-GUIDED INDIVIDUAL EXERCISE FOLLOWED BY TUTOR-LED DISCUSSION

SELF-GUIDED INDIVIDUAL EXERCISE WITH ASSIGNMENT AND ASSESSMENT

SELF-GUIDED INDIVIDUAL EXERCISE WITH PROGRESS AND EVALUATION SESSION

SELF-GUIDED INDIVIDUAL EXERCISE WITH STUDENT-CENTRED DIGITAL RESOURCE

SPECIALIST TOUR, TALK AND DEMONSTRATION

STORYTELLING IN CLASS

STRUCTURED SUPPORT GROUP

STUDENT-CENTRED DIGITAL RESOURCE

STUDENT-DEVELOPED QUESTION AND ANSWER SESSION

STUDENT-DEVELOPED SCENARIOS FOR CLASS DISCUSSION

STUDENT-DEVELOPED SCENARIOS FOR DIGITAL DISCUSSION

STUDENT REVIEW

STUDENT WORKSHEET

TIP EXCHANGE (STUDENT-CENTRED DIGITAL RESOURCE)

TUTOR-LED CLASS DISCUSSION FOLLOWED BY INDIVIDUAL EXERCISE

TUTOR-LED EXERCISE AND CLASS DISCUSSION

TUTOR-LED INFORMATION AND SUPPORT NETWORK

VIDEO/PODCAST PRODUCTION (IN GROUPS DURING INDEPENDENT STUDY)

VIDEO/PODCAST PRODUCTION WITH TUTOR-LED VIEWING AND DISCUSSION

VLOG AND BLOG

VOLUNTARY PEER MENTORING PROGRAMME

WHOLE CLASS, PHYSICAL EXERCISE

WORKSHOP

Online resources

Head online to **https://study.sagepub.com/dawsonstudyskills**
to download and print all the student activities from the book and use them as
handouts in your lessons!

Activity • • • • • • • • • • • → 1

Bringing learning to life

STUDENT HANDOUT

Please read the following two paragraphs:

Learning is concerned with the whole person and can include our physical, mental, emotional and psychological development. Learning helps us to think about our identity, who we are, what we do (or want to do) and helps us to find our place in the world. It helps us to think about our past, present and future lives and reflect on how this is interconnected with our past, present and future learning.

Learning helps us to think about, develop and express our attitudes, values and ideals. It helps us to overcome problems, succeed in times of crisis and manage long-term difficulties. It can provide support, encouragement, companionship and increase independence, self-esteem and confidence. New skills are learnt and developed, helping us to work, socialise, improve relationships, improve health and well-being, and develop hobbies. What we learn can be captivating, tantalising and fascinating. Learning involves passion, intrigue and excitement and takes place throughout our lives.

Once you have read these two paragraphs, complete the following exercise:

1. Provide some examples of how learning has helped you to develop. Try to include your 'physical, mental, emotional and psychological' development.
2. Give examples of how learning has helped you to overcome a problem, deal with a crisis and/or manage long-term difficulties.
3. How can learning provide 'support, encouragement and companionship'?
4. How can learning increase 'independence, self-esteem and confidence'?
5. Provide examples of instances where your personal learning has been 'captivating, tantalising and fascinating'. Think about formal learning that has taken place in the classroom, and informal learning that has taken place in your life, perhaps over many years and in many different situations.
6. Provide examples of instances where your personal learning has involved 'passion, intrigue and excitement'. Again, consider both formal and informal learning.

Complete this exercise as fully and honestly as possible. Thinking about your learning in this way will help you to get more from your studies, help you to stay motivated, remain enthusiastic and enjoy your learning. This exercise is for your personal benefit: it will not be assessed or seen by your tutor or peers, unless you wish to discuss the issues that have been raised with someone after you have completed the exercise.

Learning outcome: By the end of this activity you will have an increased understanding of the benefits, improvements and personal development that can be gained from learning, and be able to relate this understanding to your past, present and future learning on your course and in your personal and professional lives.

About the author

Dr Catherine Dawson studied at university in the UK for an undergraduate degree in Combined Humanities, a master's degree in Social Research and a PhD researching the learning choices of adults returning to education. She has worked as a research assistant, research associate and tutor at various UK universities and as a research and training officer in both the public and private sectors. Over the years she has developed and taught courses covering study skills, research methods and learner development for undergraduate and postgraduate students and has designed and delivered bespoke study skills and learner development sessions to employees at all levels in the private sector. Catherine currently works as a freelance researcher and writer, concentrating on study skills, research methods and student finance.

Introduction

This book is a collection of 100 pre-prepared, easy-to-use activities for lecturers, tutors and support staff (referred to as 'tutors' from now on) who facilitate learner development or teach study skills. It is a sourcebook of games, scenarios, role plays, self-guided individual exercises and group exercises that encourage interactive, experiential and reflective learning to help motivate and engage students. These activities can be used by both early-career tutors and more experienced tutors to complement existing course materials and teaching strategies, help with the design of new courses and add to existing learner development and study skills programmes.

Many of the activities presented in the book are relevant to, or can be connected with, course content, enabling students to learn through subject teaching. They are inclusive and are intended for the whole student cohort. Others are standalone activities that can be used where students feel that they need additional help with specific study skills or learner development. In these cases, tutors are advised to spend a little time ensuring that those students who could benefit most are invited to attend. Some activities run throughout the length of a course or module and follow course content, whereas others take only 50 minutes to one hour of contact time to help with specific skills and development. Individual, pairs, group and whole-class activities are offered: some are student-centred or student-developed, whereas others are tutor-led or tutor-developed.

There are a wide variety of activities presented in the book, including collaborative dialogue, reflective journals, brainstorms, storytelling, group presentations, digital resource development, scenario development, one-to-one support sessions, workshops, vlogs and blogs and podcast production. Some activities present a problem for students to work through, reflect and act upon; others place students in the position of educator, asking them to teach about the topic; some encourage collaboration, sharing of ideas and learning from experiences. Tutor and/or peer feedback, support and encouragement are central to most activities.

The activities are aimed at three levels of study, providing continuous learning opportunities throughout an undergraduate course and for some postgraduate courses. This enables students to develop their learning progressively and helps to encourage the development and understanding of transferable and lifelong skills, which will be of benefit to their studies and to their personal and professional lives when their course has finished. The levels of activity are elementary, intermediate and advanced, and these are discussed in detail in the 'activity level' index (this categorisation may be controversial for some: a justification for its use is given in the index). Tutors can use the index to choose the activities that are most suited to the level at which their students are studying. Some activities are suitable for all three levels and when this occurs the level of study will be reflected in the complexity of discussion or exercise and in the topics covered.

An 'activity type' index is also included so that tutors can choose the type of activity that most suits their students, course and subject area. An 'alternative type' is provided, where possible, if tutors are interested in a particular topic but do not think that the activity type would be suitable for their students. It is also possible for tutors to mix and match type of activity with topic (in cases where an activity is of interest, but the specific topic is not relevant, for example).

The activities have been divided into 13 sections for ease of navigation. Tutors can skim and scan the contents to find relevant activities quickly, or choose to use the activity or type index. It is intended that the book should be used as a flexible 'pick and mix' resource: tutors can skip within and between the sections to draw together the activities that are useful and relevant to their particular student cohort (with pointers given to related activities). The flexible nature of this sourcebook enables tutors to use the most relevant and useful activities in the order that they deem most appropriate.

Each activity is divided into tutor's notes and student handouts and includes the following categories:

- purpose;
- type;
- alternative type(s);
- level;
- duration;
- equipment/materials;

- learning outcome;
- description;
- key issues;
- preparatory reading;
- further reading.

These categories enable tutors to choose the most relevant activities for their student cohort and level of study, follow them with related activities and access further information (books, journals and online resources) quickly and efficiently.

Part 1   Tutor Notes

Section 1 Study preparation

Activity · · · · · · · · · · · → 1

Bringing learning to life

Student
handout
page 289

TUTOR NOTES

Purpose: This activity brings learning to life for students by asking them to think about, and reflect on, the benefits, improvements and personal development that can be gained from learning. It provides structured guidance by asking them to read a couple of paragraphs that describe what can be said about learning, and then answer a series of related questions about their personal learning. It is a personal exercise that does not take up contact time and can be used at the start of your course.

Type: Student worksheet.

Alternative type(s): Workshop.

Level: Elementary.

Duration: Up to one hour during independent study or 50 minutes to one hour of contact time, if the workshop option is chosen.

Equipment/materials: None required.

Learning outcome: By the end of this activity students will have an increased understanding of the benefits, improvements and personal development that can be gained from learning, and be able to relate this understanding to their past, present and future learning on their course and in their personal and professional lives.

The activity

Ask your students to undertake the exercise contained in the Student Handout. This requests them to read a couple of paragraphs that describe the positive benefits of learning and then work through a series of exercises and questions that relate this to their own past, present and future learning. Although this activity tends to work best as an individual exercise during independent study, it is possible to run it in a workshop, if this suits your student cohort (if they are happy, willing and able to share personal experiences with group members, for example).

Key issues

Some students are quite surprised by the content of the two paragraphs, having never thought about their learning in this way. These students see themselves as empty vessels to be filled with information given by their tutors, which they can then use to gain qualifications and, hopefully, obtain a good job in the future. This activity helps them to think more deeply about learning and encourages them to see the relevance of their learning not just in instrumental and/or economic terms, but in whole-life terms. Those students who take time with this activity often report feeling more motivated, enthusiastic and interested in their studies because they have a deeper understanding of the relevance of learning. They report that it 'brings learning to life', which provides a useful title for this activity.

➜ Cautionary note

When this activity was first run a list of questions was produced for students to work their way through. However, this was ineffective because many of the students were unable to move beyond the instrumental motivation described above. Once the two descriptive paragraphs were added the exercise worked much better, encouraging students to think more deeply about their learning.

You may find, however, that some students do not agree with the sentiments expressed in the paragraphs and find it difficult to answer the questions. Some have had negative learning experiences, where their self-worth has been damaged, family relationships have suffered or expectations have been raised but not met, for example. In these cases it is useful to discuss the issues with the student, perhaps on a one-to-one basis if time permits. In most cases, with further advice and guidance, they begin to see that learning may have potential, even if their personal experiences, so far, suggest otherwise.

➜ Related activities

Activity 2: Becoming a reflective learner

Activity 3: Learning to learn

Activity 4: Developing metacognition

Activity 8: Becoming part of a learning community

Activity 58: Reflecting, thinking and making connections

➜ Preparatory reading

Reiff, M. and Ballin, A. (2016) 'Adult graduate student voices: good and bad learning experiences', *Adult Learning*, 27 (2): 76–83, published online before print 23 February 2016, http://doi.org/10.1177/1045159516629927. This paper provides interesting preparatory reading for tutors.

Schuller, T. (2004) *The Benefits of Learning: The Impact of Education on Health, Family Life and Social Capital*. London: Routledge. In its entirety this provides useful preparatory reading for tutors (if time is short, part C provides a useful summary).

➜ Further reading

All three books listed below provide relevant reading for tutors and for students who wish to follow up some of the issues raised in this activity.

Feinstein, L., Budge, D., Vorhaus, J. and Duckworth, K. (eds) (2008) *The Social and Personal Benefits of Learning: a Summary of Key Research Findings*. London: Centre for Research on the Wider Benefits of Learning, Institute of Education.

McMahon, W. (2009) *Higher Learning, Greater Good: The Private and Social Benefits of Higher Education*. Baltimore, MD: Johns Hopkins University Press.

Schuller, T. (2004) *The Benefits of Learning: The Impact of Education on Health, Family Life and Social Capital*. London: Routledge.

Activity 1

Activity •••••••••••••• ➜ 2

Becoming a reflective learner

Student
handout
page 290

TUTOR NOTES

Purpose: This activity helps students to become reflective learners by asking them to consider what is meant by this term, think about how it can be of benefit to their learning and life in general, work out how to become a reflective learner and develop a personal plan of action that will help them to become reflective learners as their course progresses.

Type: Self-guided individual exercise.

Alternative type(s): Workshop; group exercise followed by group presentation; personal learning journal.

Level: Elementary, intermediate and advanced (the level of study will be reflected in answers and personal plans of action).

Duration: One to two hours of work for students during independent study, followed by regular reflection throughout their course. Fifty minutes to one hour of contact time for the workshop, followed by regular reflection throughout their course. Up to two hours of contact time if the group exercise followed by group presentation option is chosen, again, with regular reflection throughout their course.

Equipment/materials: None required.

Learning outcome: By the end of this activity students will understand what is meant by reflective learning, know about the benefits that can be gained and will have developed a personal plan of action that will help them to become reflective learners as their course progresses.

The activity

Give the Student Handout to your students. This asks them to consider what is meant by the term 'becoming a reflective learner', think about how this will benefit their studies and life in general, and think about how they might go about becoming a reflective learner. It goes on to ask them to develop a personal plan of action that will help them to become a reflective learner as their studies progress. Suggestions for action are given in the handout because, in the past, some students have needed guidance on how to go about developing a plan of action. However, if you feel that your students should work this out for themselves you can delete this section of the handout.

There are several ways in which this activity can be run and these depend on your student cohort and the amount of contact time that you have available. If you feel that your students can work through this activity individually and can develop a useful plan of action that can be implemented with no tutor or peer input, you can run this activity as a self-guided individual exercise during independent study. If you choose to do this you may find it useful to check that your students have completed the activity and are happy with their reflection activities and plan of action (see 'cautionary note', below). This can be done for a few minutes in class, via email or face-to-face.

Alternatively, this activity can be run as a workshop. Divide your students into small groups and ask them to work though the questions on the Student Handout. You do not need to provide the suggestions for action given in the handout as groups usually work this out for themselves. Wind up the group activity with a discussion on the issues raised (this usually takes about 15 minutes: you can use the list of action in the handout as a basis for discussion if these have not already been raised by student groups). If you prefer, and if you have the contact time available, you can ask that the groups present their findings to their peers, again, leaving enough time for a summary discussion, questions and answers.

It is also possible to ask students to keep a reflective diary that will enable them to become a reflective learner, or combine this activity with Activity 4, which asks students to keep a learning diary that helps them to develop their meta-cognition. Alternatively, you can combine this activity with Activity 58, which asks students to reflect on, think about and make connections with their learning and everyday life as their course progresses.

Key issues

This activity asks students to work out for themselves what is meant by becoming a reflective learner and think about how this can be of benefit to their studies and life in general. Some students are more reflective than others, finding this an easy and useful task to complete, returning to reflective thought throughout their course. When personal plans for action have been discussed they have included a variety of plans and methods, including lists of tasks to complete, flow diagrams of how they wish to proceed and visual representations of how they perceive their personal reflection process. Others, how-ever, find this task difficult, and it is for this reason that information about making contact for further discussion is included on the handout. A short discussion, related to their personal experiences, often helps them to move forward with this task.

→ Cautionary note

Some students may need monitoring during this activity. On occasions, students have suggested that this is a 'pointless' activity, in particular, because it is a personal endeavour that is not seen by the tutor and, as such, they do not take it seri-ously. If you feel that your students may react in this way, you can suggest that you will monitor their progress through a short class discussion or by email as the course progresses. This tends to make them take the activity a little more seriously, enabling them to gain greater understanding into why the activity is run and deeper insight into the personal benefits that can be gained.

→ Related activities

Activity 1: Bringing learning to life

Activity 3: Learning to learn

Activity 4: Developing metacognition

Activity 8: Becoming part of a learning community

Activity 58: Reflecting, thinking and making connections

→ Preparatory reading

Fook, J. and Gardner, F. (2007) *Practising Critical Reflection: a Resource Handbook*. Maidenhead: Open University Press. This book provides useful preparatory reading for tutors as it covers both theory and practical considerations for critical reflection.

→ Further reading

Moon, J. (2004) *A Handbook of Reflective and Experiential Learning: Theory and Practice*. Abingdon, Oxon: Routledge Falmer. This is an informative book for tutors who are interested in reflective learning, containing both theory and practical tools and activities.

The Open University in the UK has a free course available called *Learning to Learn: Reflecting Backward, Reflecting Forward* (http://www.open.edu/openlearn/education/learning-learn-reflecting-backward-reflecting-forward/content-section-0). This course can be recommended to students who wish to follow up the issues raised during this activity, or for those who might struggle with the idea of reflective learning.

Activity 2

Activity · · · · · · · · · · · · · ➔ 3

Learning to learn

Student handout page 291

TUTOR NOTES

Purpose: This activity is a workshop that promotes and encourages learning. It uses group discussion to explore barriers to learning and the issues that promote effective and successful learning. It goes on to explore these issues in relation to students' personal learning, and discuss how this learning can become more effective and successful (illustrating that 'success' should not be seen as purely achieving good grades).

Type: Workshop.

Alternative type(s): One-to-one support session; student worksheet.

Level: Elementary. It is also possible to run this activity with students studying at advanced level if they need a recap after having been away from their studies for some time.

Duration: Fifty minutes to one hour of contact time for the workshop. Up to one hour will be required if the one-to-one support session option is chosen. Students need to spend one or two hours during independent study, if the worksheet option is chosen.

Equipment/materials: None required.

Learning outcome: By the end of this activity students will understand what is required to promote effective and successful learning and will be able to relate this understanding to their personal learning on their course and in their personal and professional lives.

The activity

Invite students to attend a workshop called 'Learning to Learn', trying to ensure that those who would most benefit from the workshop are able to attend. Divide your students into small groups (or pairs if you only have a small number of attendees) and give them a copy of the Student Handout. Ask them to work through the questions in their groups, discussing each as fully as possible. Five questions are provided to encourage your students to think more deeply about issues such as barriers to learning, the factors that promote effective learning and their personal experiences of successful learning. Once they have completed this task (usually after about 20 minutes) lead a discussion to expand on the issues raised.

This activity can, alternatively, be used with individual students on a one-to-one basis if you need to offer specific support and guidance, or as a student worksheet during independent study if contact time is limited (the Student Handout will need to be amended accordingly).

Key issues

The following list provides examples of points that can be raised and discussed during this activity.

- Barriers to learning:
  - Internal influences such as lack of motivation, interest and enthusiasm; lack of self-confidence and self-esteem; perfectionism; stress; illness; a feeling of 'not fitting in' or feelings of alienation; not having enough money to pay for courses (some of these could be considered to be external barriers).
  - External influences such as family and commitments; lack of course provision in the area; courses are too expensive; poor teaching; lack of affordable childcare; disturbances and distractions beyond your control.
- Effective learning can be promoted by:
  - excellent teaching;
  - good relationships with fellow students and with the tutor (including good and timely feedback);
  - collaboration and cooperation with peers, rather than competition;
  - increased self-confidence and self-esteem;
  - interest in the course;
  - positive and constructive support from family and friends.
- Successful learning includes:
  - mastering a skill that can be used for work, hobbies or life in general;
  - learning that promotes a positive change in attitudes or behaviour;

- acceptance of limitations and the development of self-worth, self-respect and self-confidence.
- Examples of successful learning include:
  - passing a driving test;
  - learning to swim;
  - passing exams and gaining academic qualifications;
  - getting a new job or promotion;
  - producing something to be proud of;
  - overcoming a personal difficulty.
- Ways to increase effective learning and promote success:
  - approach learning with the right attitude;
  - make the right learning choices (see Activity 9);
  - foster cooperation and collaboration (see Activity 7);
  - seek help when required;
  - recognise and address problems with perfectionism that can limit learning and enjoyment of learning;
  - listen to and take note of feedback (see Activity 48);
  - negotiate, delegate and compromise when required (with family, work colleagues, fellow students and tutors);
  - maintain health and well-being;
  - create a good working environment or find a place that aids study (avoid disturbances);
  - encourage others (and yourself) to respect and appreciate learning;
  - juggle other commitments successfully (develop time-management and organisational skills: see Activities 11 and 13).

During the class discussion you may need to discuss what is meant by success. Students often need to move beyond success as measured by good grades and examination passes. Instead, they can discuss other dimensions such as increased confidence and self-worth, feelings of satisfaction and self-fulfilment and positive changes in attitudes and behaviour.

➔ Related activities

Activity 1: Bringing learning to life

Activity 4: Developing metacognition

Activity 7: Fostering collaborative learning and interaction

Activity 8: Becoming part of a learning community

Activity 46: Learning through storytelling

➔ Preparatory reading

Chapters 6, 7 and 8 of Gould (2012) provide useful preparatory reading for tutors and Chapter 6 of Pritchard (2014) provides some interesting material on difficulties with learning that is also useful preparatory reading for tutors.

Activity 3

➜ Further reading

The books listed below provide useful further reading for tutors.

Gould, J. (2012) *Learning Theory and Classroom Practice in the Lifelong Learning Sector*, 2nd edition. London: Sage.
Jarvis, M. (2005) *The Psychology of Effective Learning and Teaching*. Cheltenham: Nelson Thornes Ltd.
Pritchard, A. (2014) *Ways of Learning*, 3rd edition. Abingdon, Oxon: Routledge.
The Open University in the UK has a free course available called *Learning How to Learn* (http://www.open.edu/openlearn/education/learning-how-learn/content-section-0). This six-hour introductory course can be recommended to your students if you feel they could benefit from more instruction on this topic

Activity 3

Activity · · · · · · · · · · · · 4

Developing metacognition

Student handout page 292

TUTOR NOTES

Purpose: This activity helps students to develop their metacognition through the use of a personal learning journal (paper or digital, according to student preference). Students are given a number of statements that can be made about metacognition, to which they can refer as they keep their journal (students studying at intermediate and advanced level can be asked to research what is meant by metacognition instead). They are also asked to develop a personal plan of action, using the list as a guide.

Type: Personal learning journal.

Alternative type(s): None.

Level: Elementary, intermediate and advanced (the level of study will be reflected in the journal content).

Duration: No specific duration: students will make entries throughout their course and the number, length and type of entries depends on personal preference, motivation and engagement.

Equipment/materials: A learning journal (paper or digital).

Learning outcome: By the end of this activity students will have produced a personal plan of action and kept a learning journal that will help them to become more aware of, and develop, metacognition, which will be of benefit to their studies, relationships and life in general.

The activity

Give the Student Handout to your students. This provides a list of statements about metacognition and then asks students to think about how they can develop these skills and abilities through the use of a personal learning journal. They are to keep this journal throughout their module or course. For their first entry they are asked to produce a personal plan of action that will help them to develop metacognition, using the statements for guidance.

The Student Handout tends to work best with students studying at elementary level, in particular, with adult returners. If your students are studying at intermediate or advanced level you might prefer not to give them the Student Handout, but instead ask them to research what is meant by metacognition before asking them to produce a learning journal that will help them to develop metacognition.

Key issues

Some students are more metacognitive than others. Some find this an easy, beneficial and worthwhile activity, making relevant entries throughout their course and finding the journal a useful tool for personal development. Others, however, struggle with this activity, finding it difficult to move beyond their view of learning in instrumental terms, usually to improve employment prospects. In these cases you may need to hold a one-to-one session, or a group session, to help these students gain a deeper understanding of metacognition. A discussion about transferable skills and how these can help in the job market is a good way to introduce the session. Students can relate to this and are usually interested to find out more so that the discussion can then move on to deeper issues. Another option is to ask these students to work through Activity 58: Reflecting, thinking and making connections.

➜ Related activities

Activity 1: Bringing learning to life

Activity 2: Becoming a reflective learner

Activity 3: Learning to learn

Activity 33: Engaging in reflective writing

Activity 58: Reflecting, thinking and making connections

➜ Preparatory reading

Benson (2016) provides interesting preparatory reading for tutors, with Chapter 2 of particular relevance. Chapter 4 of Kolencik and Hillwig (2011) provides interesting information about 'thinking journals', which is useful for tutors who are interested in running this activity.

➜ Further reading

The following books provide useful further reading for tutors for this activity (they can also be recommended to students studying at advanced level, if they are interested in finding out more about metacognition).

Benson, J. (ed.) (2016) *Metacognition: Theory, Performance and Current Research*. Hauppauge, NY: Nova Science Publishers, Inc.

Desoete, A. and Veenman, M. (eds) (2006) *Metacognition in Mathematics Education*. Hauppauge, NY: Nova Science Publishers, Inc.

Kolencik, P. and Hillwig, S. (2011) *Encouraging Metacognition: Supporting Learners through Metacognitive Teaching Strategies*. New York: Peter Lang Publishing, Inc.

Activity 4

Activity · · · · · · · · · · · · ➔ 5

Improving concentration and memory

The activity

Divide your students into groups at the end of a teaching session and introduce this activity. Ask them, in their groups, to invent a game that will help their peers to improve their concentration, memory or both. The game that they invent is their choice: they should ensure that it is original, useful and easy to run as they are going to test the game on their peers when you next meet. Their peers should be able to learn something new from the game and/or it should generate a constructive and informative discussion about the topic. Explain that they will be allocated up to 20 minutes for each group to introduce their game and test it on their peers (this timing can be flexible, depending on the number of groups and the contact time available). They can use any materials, props and devices that they choose and these should be made available for their use, if possible.

Students can vote on the best game at the end of the session, if you are happy to turn this activity into a competition. Voting in this way also leads to an interesting discussion that can include the following questions (these can be adapted if you decide not to turn this into a competition):

1. Are they voting for the most effective, entertaining, memorable or informative game, or the game that best relates to their studies, for example?
2. How do they know that the game will be effective in achieving what it has set out to do?
3. Does the game need to be repeated to get the full effect?
4. Have they learnt anything from the game? If so, what?
5. Will it help them to improve their concentration, memory or both?
6. Can they relate the game to their learning? In what way?

Allocate up to 20 minutes for class discussion or, if contact time is limited, you can ask that the discussion continue using a relevant digital platform. Ensure that the discussion relates to their learning so that students can understand the relevance and usefulness of this activity.

Key issues

This activity works well because students must first of all discuss, and get to grips with, issues concerning concentration and memory before they can go on to invent a suitable game. They must also understand how to find valid and reliable sources (see preparatory reading). It is useful to mix students with different experiences and understanding in each group as this leads to an informative and constructive discussion, usually resulting in an inventive game. A fruitful discussion takes place at each stage of this activity, including during the introduction, development, testing and voting.

Students invent a wide variety of games for this activity. Although the games are about memory and concentration, they also highlight other study issues. Examples of games and relevant study issues that have been invented include:

- a quiz based on peer-reviewed journal articles that ask students to consider aspects of their diet that will improve concentration and memory such as proteins, carbohydrates, omega-3, blueberries and rosemary (highlighting the importance of scientific evidence);
- a 'spot the quackery' buzzer game illustrating that there are myths, superstitions and delusions peddled about how to improve concentration and memory (highlighting the importance of source evaluation and critical appraisal);
- a board game containing specific memory exercises when a particular space is landed on;
- a memory game that requires students to memorise more and more items, while someone tries to distract them or make them lose their concentration, including giggling, a mobile phone ringing and a friend knocking on the door (highlighting the importance of a distraction-free study space);
- an adaption of a memory game that uses objects on a tray that students must memorise and repeat: students placed relevant course books and journals on the tray, gave a minute for students to memorise them, then covered them and asked students to list as many as they could, with correct bibliographic details (highlighting relevant books and referencing details).

➜ Cautionary note

It is important to stress that games should be original (adaptions of originals are fine: see above). On occasions, groups have merely copied an online game or test. Usually, other students act as good quality control because they will have come across such games when they carried out research on concentration and memory for their own game. However, it may be prudent for you to spend a little time searching for online games that could be used by students in this activity.

....

➜ Related activities

Activity 14: Maintaining motivation

Activity 52: Evaluating sources

Activity 57: Developing thoughts and imagination

Activity 58: Reflecting, thinking and making connections

Activity 89: Revising effectively

....

Activity 5

➜ Preparatory reading

There are some outlandish, peculiar and misleading books and websites about how to improve concentration and memory. These tend to be self-published, lack quality control of any sort and are not based on scientific evidence. If you feel that your students need this pointed out to them before undertaking this exercise, ask them to perform a simple search of 'memory games' or 'improving concentration and memory' to find relevant sites and books. They should discuss all sources they find with their group members and work out whether they are valid and reliable sources, before moving on to find and use reputable sources of information to help them invent their game. You may find it useful preparatory work to become familiar with some of these sources before you run this activity.

Schrier, K. (2016) *Knowledge Games: How Playing Games can Solve Problems, Create Insight, and Make Change*. Baltimore, MD: Johns Hopkins University Press. This book provides useful preparatory reading for tutors who are interested in using games in teaching and learning.

➜ Further reading

Merriam, S. and Bierema, L. (2014) *Adult Learning: Linking Theory and Practice*. San Francisco, CA: Jossey-Bass. Chapters 8 and 9 of this book cover relevant issues for tutors such as motivation and learning, memory, intelligence and cognitive development and wisdom.

Terry, W. (2017) *Learning and Memory: Basic Principles, Processes, and Procedures*, 5th edition. Abingdon, Oxon: Routledge. This is a comprehensive book on the psychology of learning. It is useful for tutors who would like an in-depth understanding of core methods and research insights.

Activity 5

Activity · · · · · · · · · · · 6

Recognising and overcoming imposter syndrome

The activity

Invite together a group of students who feel that they suffer from imposter syndrome. You may need to provide a definition of what is meant by this term as some students may feel that they are a 'fraud', lack the ability to study at the required level, or feel that they will be 'found out' without being able to relate these feelings to the term imposter syndrome (see key issues).

The students that join the group could be from one course and one level or from a range of courses and levels. The group should not be too large: seven to nine participants is ideal. Explain the purpose and format of the structured support session: first, you will meet in a 50 minute to one hour session to discuss what is meant by imposter syndrome and how it manifests in students; second, students will work on an action plan that will help them to overcome these worries and concerns; third, students will implement their action plan over the next few weeks (the time-scale depends on your timetable and that of your students: four or five weeks is usually a good length of time); fourth, the group will reconvene for another 50 minutes to one hour session to evaluate the action that has been taken and to set long-term goals based on the outcome of the structured support group. Students can also meet on an informal basis as the activity progresses, if they feel that support and encouragement from group members would be of use.

It is possible to run this activity as a one-to-one support session with individual students, if you have the time available and it better suits your students. You will need to be available to offer support throughout the activity if this option is chosen.

Key issues

'Imposter syndrome' (or imposter phenomenon: Clance and Imes, 1978) is the term that has been given to a range of worries, concerns and feelings that people have about their personal ability to complete tasks successfully during study, at work and in everyday life. It can manifest in various ways including perfectionism, fear of failure, over-working, feelings of being out-of-their depth despite evidence to the contrary, personal doubt, excessive criticism and an inability to accept praise and compliments. Imposter syndrome might manifest in postgraduate students who feel that they are a fraud and that they will be found out by saying or writing something 'stupid'. Adult returners may feel that they are not clever enough to go to university and that university study is for other people who are very different and much cleverer than themselves. They feel that they do not belong among 'genuine' students.

Structured support groups work well for feelings of imposter syndrome because:

- Students can discuss worries and concerns with peers and gain support and encouragement from each other.
- Students soon discover that their feelings are not unique: the realisation that others are experiencing similar feelings helps them to recognise, address and overcome their own feelings.
- Group members can pool experiences, knowledge and understanding so that they can develop and implement a constructive and effective plan of action.
- Group members are available for support and encouragement throughout the activity (and often throughout their course).

Examples of action that students can take to overcome imposter syndrome include:

- Recognise that the problem exists. Understand the signs and work out what triggers symptoms.
- Talk to others when symptoms get bad. Be available if group members want to talk. Seek support when required.
- Record feelings in a personal journal. Analyse them. Think about why the feelings occur, looking at past, present and future experiences. Write down ways to tackle feelings and strategies to overcome them. Keep a record that can be returned to when required. Note progression and make sure that 'eureka moments' are recorded.
- Read up on the subject. Read academic articles and personal blogs. See how other people cope and work out whether any of these strategies would work for you.
- Don't compete with others: foster cooperation and collaboration. Don't be a perfectionist. Recognise when you are putting on too much pressure to succeed and/or compete. Recognise when expectations are too high or you are being too hard on yourself.
- Recognise successes. Keep a list of successes, including passing exams, passing tests and getting good grades. Take note of positive feedback (see Activity 48) and when people enthuse about your work. Engage with lecturers and tutors (see Activity 47).
- Find out about famous people and scientists who have struggled with imposter syndrome. See how they deal with and overcome their problems.

→ Related activities

Activity 7: Fostering collaborative learning and interaction

Activity 9: Making the right learning choices

Activity 48: Getting the most from tutor feedback

Activity 93: Coping with stress

→ Preparatory reading

Clance, P. and Imes, S. (1978) 'The impostor phenomenon in high achieving women: dynamics and therapeutic intervention', *Psychotherapy: Theory, Research and Practice*, 15 (3): 241-247, http://doi.org/10.1037/h0086006. The term 'imposter

Activity 6

phenomenon' was first discussed in this paper, which provides useful preparatory reading for tutors. More information is available on Clance's website (http://paulineroseclance.com/impostor_phenomenon.html).

....

➜ Further reading

The following papers provide further reading for anyone interested in this topic.

Hutchins, H. and Rainbolt, H. (2017) 'What triggers imposter phenomenon among academic faculty? A critical incident study exploring antecedents, coping, and development opportunities', *Human Resource Development International*, 20 (3): 194-214, published online 2 November 2016, http://doi.org//10.1080/13678868.2016.1248205.

Lige, Q., Peteet, B. and Brown, C. (2016) 'Racial identity, self-esteem, and the impostor phenomenon among African American college students', *Journal of Black Psychology*, 43 (4): 345-57.

Sakulku, J. (2011) 'The impostor phenomenon', *International Journal of Behavioral Science*, 6 (1): 73-92. This paper gives a good overview of research that has been carried out into imposter phenomenon since 1978.

Relevant articles can be found on the Harvard Business Review website, including a useful article titled 'Overcoming imposter syndrome' (https://hbr.org/2008/05/overcoming-imposter-syndrome).

Activity 6

Activity · · · · · · · · · · · → 7

Fostering collaborative learning and interaction

The activity

Divide your students into groups at the end of a teaching session. Ask them, in their groups, to design a learning space or environment that will encourage them to foster collaborative learning and interaction with their peers and tutors. Once they have done this they must present their design ideas (and reasons for their design) to their peers when you next meet. Explain that they will be given up to ten minutes for their presentation and up to five minutes for questions from their peers. There will also be a few minutes at the end of the presentations to sum up the findings and relate the activity to their course. The amount of time you spend on this activity depends on the number of student groups and the contact time you have available. The groups will need to be larger in size if less contact time is available. If contact time is not available you can ask that groups post their design ideas and justification on the relevant digital platform instead.

It is possible to run this activity over a shorter period of time in a workshop setting. If you choose this option, divide your students into three groups and ask them to design a learning space or environment that will encourage them to foster collaborative learning and interaction with their peers and tutors. They should discuss their ideas in their groups for up to 20 minutes, before presenting their design ideas, and justification for their design, to the rest of the students (allocate up to ten minutes per group). Conclude the workshop with a short discussion about the relevance of this activity to their studies. Design ideas are not as detailed if you choose this option, yet a fruitful and interesting session still takes place.

Key issues

This is a creative, practical and entertaining way to encourage students to think about how they can foster collaborative learning and interaction with their peers and tutors. Students need to think about how spaces and environments can help them to work together and, in doing this, consider what is meant by collaboration and interaction and how this can be of benefit to their studies. This activity provides interesting and memorable design ideas that help students to remember the activity and think more about collaboration and interaction as their course progresses.

Three summaries of design ideas and their justifications are given below. The first two are from the group work and presentation activity, whereas the final example is from the workshop activity (it is shorter and less detailed because less time is available if you choose this option).

1. Design: informal areas with comfortable seating, coffee machine and multiple docks for devices such as smartphones, tablets and laptops. Whiteboards are available to write down ideas and discussion is encouraged. Students agree to use devices only for studies (the particular assignment, group work or project that is required). Checking and sending texts, social media and micro-blogging are banned in this learning space. A 'code of behaviour' is agreed on before sessions commence. This includes issues such as respecting others' views, listening to peers, courtesy and concentrating on the task at hand. It is written or posted somewhere for all to see. Justification: technology helps students and tutors to work together but it must not become a distraction. Students need to agree on rules together: they will take more notice if these rules are student-led. Students and tutors can collaborate and interact well in an informal space that has all the required facilities (including coffee). Collaboration will be successful if everyone respects each other, listens to each other and works together to achieve their goals.

2. Design: a transforming space that can be used for different collaboration projects, depending on subject and level of study. Chairs and desks can be moved into different positions such as small group seating when a small group of students need to work closely together, or larger group seating for bigger groups. Different seating options are available for different projects (e.g. stools of different heights, chairs of different designs and beanbags). The seating can be folded away or removed completely if students need to move around to stimulate thought or demonstrate techniques or equipment. Dividing walls can be moved into place when spaces need to be intimate, or removed when larger spaces are required. Glass walls can be used to open spaces further, with blinds, curtains or drapes used when privacy is required. Justification: Lecture theatres do not help students to collaborate or interact, especially with the tutor. Smaller spaces are required, but this will change, depending on the size of student group and the type of project work required. Different types of seating encourage different types of interaction (formal or informal, for example). This transforming space will save money and can be used across all disciplines and levels of study.

3. Design: an outside space away from the classroom, with comfortable seating and places to charge and use mobile devices. Plants, landscaping, views and shaded areas create a calm and tranquil atmosphere for informal collaboration. If the university is in a place where the climate is not conducive to such an outside space, a learning atrium with glass ceiling to let in light and sun can be built instead. Justification: if informal collaboration and interaction is required it can work well away from the classroom as students might feel more relaxed, open and able to share with their peers. Competition can be avoided and cooperation encouraged.

➜ Related activities

Activity 8: Becoming part of a learning community

Activity 40: Becoming an active listener

Activity 65: Getting the most out of group work

Activity 98: Collaborating and cooperating effectively

....

➜ Preparatory reading

You may find it useful preparatory work to visit YouTube (www.youtube.com) to find examples of different types of collaborative learning spaces and environments (a simple search of 'collaborative learning environments' finds some

Activity 7

interesting videos). This enables you to get a good overview of the different types of collaborative learning environments that are being adopted across a variety of sectors (you can also check that students do not merely copy an environment from YouTube).

....

Further reading

Barkley, E., Major, C. and Cross, K. (2014) *Collaborative Learning Techniques: a Handbook for College Faculty*, 2nd edition. San Francisco, CA: John Wiley & Sons, Inc. This is a useful book for tutors who want to find out more about collaborative learning techniques in higher education.

Hartley, P. and Dawson, M. (2010) *Success in Groupwork*. Basingstoke: Palgrave Macmillan. This is a simple, down-to-earth guide that can be recommended to students who want more information about how to work successfully in groups.

Palloff, R. and Pratt, K. (2005) *Collaborating Online: Learning Together in Community*. San Francisco, CA: Jossey-Bass. This is a good book for students and tutors who are interested in online collaboration. There are some useful collaborative activities described in part two of the book.

Activity 7

Activity • • • • • • • • • • • → 8

Becoming part of a learning community

TUTOR NOTES

Purpose: This activity helps students to become part of a learning community through the establishment of a tutor-led information and support network that provides information, guidance, encouragement and support at the beginning and throughout their course. It is of particular use for students who have entered higher education through non-traditional routes who may feel that they do not belong at university or who are nervous about their ability to study at the required level.

Type: Tutor-led information and support network (face-to-face and online).

Alternative type(s): None.

Level: Elementary.

Duration: Fifty minutes to one hour for an informal introductory session. Additional tutor time depends on student requirements (see below).

Equipment/materials: It is useful to have an informal meeting space, away from the classroom.

Learning outcome: By the end of this activity students will have become part of a learning community, which will enable them to feel more comfortable with, and get the most out of, their studies.

The activity

This activity has been designed for students who have entered university through non-traditional routes, such as through access courses, vocational routes or through the recognition of prior experience. These students tend to be adults who are returning to education as a way to rebalance their lives, perhaps after a major life transition (children going to school, divorce or redundancy, for example), or as a way to rectify a perceived emotional or life imbalance (a sense of not being fulfilled, boredom at work or a feeling that they could do more in life, for example). These students often feel that they are different from other students, that they do not belong, or that they will have difficulty fitting in and studying at the required level.

This activity, therefore, is a little different from others described in this book. It is not a specific activity, but instead is a list of suggested activities that help to develop your tutor-led information and support network that can be used by students over the duration of your course. The number of activities, or the combination that you use, will be your own choice and depend on the type of institution and course, the past experiences of your students and their support needs and requirements. It also depends on the facilities and support that are provided by student services at your institution.

Activity A

Introduce the idea of a 'learning community' when you first meet with your students. Explain what is meant by the term and discuss how it will be of benefit to their studies. Encourage students to meet on an informal basis to build networks and communities to offer support and encouragement (face-to-face or online). See Quinn (2011) for a discussion of how adult learners can gain the most benefit from this type of community and network and Buch and Spaulding (2011) for a discussion about how becoming part of a learning community can improve success and involvement. If time is available you can discuss student worries and concerns about their learning or run Activity 3, which asks them to explore barriers to learning.

Activity B

Help students to feel 'at home'. Arrange informal gatherings with other students and tutors. Invite in other adult returners who have succeeded on the course so that students can talk to them and learn from their experiences (you can arrange for some of these students to become volunteer mentors, if they are happy to do so). Show them informal spaces where they can meet, including cafés and bars, if appropriate.

Activity C

Ensure that students receive a good induction. Take students to the learning resource centre/library and introduce them to staff and facilities. Arrange for a tour and demonstration of library facilities (see Activity 49) so that students will feel comfortable visiting and using the facilities. Help them to gain confidence with IT for academic studies, if required (see Activity 72) and make the most of IT facilities and support (see Activity 73). Invite in second- and third-year students who have entered through non-traditional routes so that they can give a student-centred induction and help to reassure students that they will fit in and will be able to succeed.

Activity D

Ensure that all required information is readily available (or that students know how to access the information). Introduce them to your VLE/intranet and help them to find and access relevant information. Introduce the communication system that you intend to use for your course, explain how it works and discuss courtesy and respect when emailing and arranging face-to-face meetings. Ensure that students know what support services are available and how to access these, if required (learning development units, medical centres, counselling and student welfare, for example).

Activity E

Invite in a member of the students' union to talk about clubs, societies, student representatives and paid employment opportunities within the students' union. Again, if possible, ask a second- or third-year adult returner to talk to students about the extra-curricular opportunities that are available and how it is possible to fit these in to busy adult lives.

Activity F

As your course progresses encourage collaborative learning and interaction (see Activity 7), help students to engage with lecturers and tutors (see Activity 47) and encourage them to get the most from feedback (see Activity 48). Group work also helps students to become part of a learning community, with study groups providing help, encouragement and support for those who might struggle with academic work (see Activity 64).

Activity G

Let students know what research is being carried out in the department and encourage them to become part of the research community through undertaking group research projects or by becoming involved in real world research. You can send a regular email alert informing students of research progress and completed research carried out by staff and students.

Activity H

Meet on an informal basis each term or semester, in small groups, to give students the opportunity to discuss their course so far and discuss any concerns or worries they may have. You may need to meet on a one-to-one basis if you feel that a particular student is struggling on their course (in addition to their usual meetings with their personal tutor).

Activity 8

Activity I

Finish your course with a focus group to discuss whether students feel they have become part of a learning community and to ask about suggestions for improvement for the next student intake. You can also find out whether any students would be happy to return to talk to students in the new intake.

Key issues

The activities described above are aimed at adult returners. If you work with students who are more comfortable with university study, who have entered through more traditional routes, omit and adapt the activities described above, depending on student requirements. If your student cohort is mixed, with students from a variety of backgrounds, it is useful to encourage them to mix together in group work and group assignments as they can help, support and encourage each other to become part of a learning community.

➜ Related activities

Activity 1: Bringing learning to life

Activity 7: Fostering collaborative learning and interaction

Activity 47: Engaging with lecturers and tutors

Activity 48: Getting the most from tutor feedback

Activity 65: Getting the most out of group work

....

➜ Preparatory reading

Benjamin, M. (ed.) (2015) *Learning Communities from Start to Finish: New Directions for Student Services*, no. 149. San Francisco, CA: Jossey-Bass. This volume provides a collection of papers about learning communities, including the history of learning communities and a summary of research illustrating the benefits of participation.

....

➜ Further reading

Buch, K. and Spaulding, S. (2011) 'The impact of a psychology learning community on academic success, retention, and student learning outcomes', *Teaching of Psychology*, 38 (2): 71-7. This paper illustrates how becoming part of a learning community can improve rates of success and involvement.

Palloff, R. and Pratt, K. (2007) *Building Online Learning Communities: Effective Strategies for the Virtual Classroom*. San Francisco, CA: Jossey-Bass. This book is aimed at tutors who want to encourage students to develop and participate in online communities (it could do with a little updating, but still has useful and interesting guidance).

Quinn, J. (2011) *Learning Communities and Imagined Social Capital: Learning to Belong*. London: Continuum International Publishing Group. This book discusses how adult learners can benefit from creating their own 'symbolic communities and networks'.

Yee, A, (2016) 'The unwritten rules of engagement: social class differences in undergraduates' academic strategies', *Journal of Higher Education*, 87 (6): 831-58, first published online 3 November 2016, http://doi.org/10.1080/0022154 6.2016.11780889. This paper provides interesting research on the different learning strategies of people from poorer backgrounds, and how this leads to disadvantage in their studies.

Activity 8

Section 2

Organisation and time management

Activity ⋯⋯⋯⋯⋯⋯ ➔ 9

Making the right learning choices

Student
handout
page 293

TUTOR NOTES

Purpose: This activity encourages students to think about, and make, the right learning choices by asking them to imagine that they are applying for a job as a student guidance worker. As part of the job interview they must role play a guidance interview with one of their peers as client.

Type: Self-guided individual exercise followed by role play.

Alternative type(s): Workshop.

Level: Elementary, intermediate and advanced.

Duration: Students need one or two hours to research and prepare for the role play during independent study. Fifty minutes to one hour of contact time is required for the role play and discussion. If the workshop option is chosen you need 50 minutes to one hour of contact time.

Equipment/materials: None required.

Learning outcome: By the end of this activity students will have a deeper understanding of the issues involved in making the right learning choices and will be able to apply this understanding to their own choices, where relevant.

The activity

This activity needs to take place before significant learning choices are made by students. This could be during an outreach programme to local sixth form or further education colleges, during pre-registration programmes at university, on access courses, before students decide on their second- or third-year modules or before choosing postgraduate study, for example.

Give the Student Handout to your students. This asks them to imagine that they are applying for a job as a student guidance worker, specialising in helping students to make the right learning choices. As part of their job interview they must hold a guidance session with one of their peers as 'client' in which they must help their client to make the right learning choices. To do this effectively students need to think about what is meant by the 'right' learning choices. They need to consider the factors that influence choice, think about the personal circumstances and motivation of their client, consider suitable local and national provision and think about other issues that may be of relevance such as finance, childcare, travel and accommodation. Students need time to research and prepare for this activity, so give them the Student Handout a day or two before the role play is to take place.

When you next meet divide your students into pairs and ask that one play the role of student guidance worker and the other play the role of client. Allocate up to 15 minutes for the pairs to role play a guidance session, with the guidance worker asking appropriate questions, probing for information, seeking clarification and helping the client to consider the right learning choices. Once this task is complete ask the students to reverse roles and conduct another guidance session for up to 15 minutes. When all students have completed the role play lead a class discussion on the issues raised. You can also evaluate the usefulness of the activity. Questions for discussion can include:

- How useful was the role play?
- Did it help students to think about how they make (or have made) their learning choices? If so, in what way?
- Has the role play helped students to make their learning choices or perhaps consider changing their learning choices?
- Has the role play raised any worries or concerns about learning choices?
- Why is it important to make the right learning choices?
- Do students feel they need more help and advice? If so, do they know where to go for help?

It is possible to run this activity as a workshop. If this option is chosen adapt the Student Handout accordingly. Students will not have so much time to research and prepare for the role play (unless you are able to send the handout to students before the workshop takes place), but you can ensure that important issues are raised after the role play has taken place. Allocate up to five minutes to introduce the activity, up to 15 minutes for students to research and prepare for the role play, 10 minutes for each role play and up to 20 minutes for the discussion.

Key issues

This activity works well because students must think about the issues, concerns, motivation and practicalities associated with making the right learning choices. It also helps them to think about why it is important to make the right learning choices. Some students decide to make up a role as client, whereas others decide to be themselves, using the session to help them consider whether or not they are making the right learning choices. The decision as to whether or not to play a role, rather than be themselves, should be left to students. This is because:

- Some students have already made their learning choices and feel that they do not need any guidance. In these cases the role play would be unproductive unless the student decides to play a role in which they need further guidance.
- Some students are unwilling to share personal information with their peers and feel more comfortable playing a role.
- Some students decide to 'test' the skills and knowledge of the guidance worker during the role play.

➜ **Related activities**

Activity 14: Maintaining motivation

Activity 40: Becoming an active listener

Activity 41: Improving listening skills

....

➜ **Preparatory reading**

There is a wide variety of websites that help students to make their learning choices, including Access to Higher Education (www.accesstohe.ac.uk), UCAS (www.ucas.com), Which? (https://university.which.co.uk) and Prospects (https://www.prospects.ac.uk). These are all relevant for students studying in the UK (similar websites are available in other countries). It is useful preparation for both students and tutors to consult some of these websites before this activity takes place.

You might also find it useful preparatory work to visit a student guidance worker at your institution. Ask about the type of guidance they offer, the sessions they conduct and the issues that they feel are important when helping students to make the right learning choices. Obtain contact details and opening times so that you can recommend the service to students who may need further information and guidance.

....

➜ **Further reading**

Most universities provide information on their website about learning choices, including details of personalised learning (mixing and matching modules to suit personal preference), interdisciplinary modules, work experience and seeking

Activity 9

further advice and guidance about learning choices. Students should be encouraged to read this information as it will help them to make their learning choices.

Dawson, C. (1999) 'Learning choices: a grounded theory study of adult returners', doctoral thesis, Sheffield Hallam University, http://shura.shu.ac.uk/id/eprint/3128. This is my doctoral thesis, which is still relevant today despite being almost 20 years old. It is useful reading for tutors who are interested in the factors that influence the learning choices of adult returners.

Activity 9

Activity •••••••••••• ➔ 10

Preparing a study plan

TUTOR NOTES

Purpose: This activity is aimed at students who feel that they need help in preparing a study plan. Students join a structured support group that provides help, advice, support and encouragement to enable students to prepare, implement and evaluate their study plan. It is a 'structured' support group because specific meeting times are arranged and students are required to undertake a specific project for the duration of the activity.

Type: Structured support group.

Alternative type(s): Self-guided individual exercise.

Level: Elementary, intermediate and advanced. The level of study will be reflected in the type and content of study plan.

Duration: Fifty minutes to one hour of contact time for the initial meeting. Students will then implement their plan as their course progresses. Some tutor time may be required at this stage if students need additional help and support. Fifty minutes to one hour of contact time will be needed at the end of the activity to evaluate the effectiveness of study plans and to develop an action plan for future study.

Equipment/materials: None required.

Learning outcome: By the end of this activity students will have prepared, implemented and evaluated a study plan, and will feel confident about preparing study plans for further study.

The activity

Invite together a group of students who feel that they need help with preparing a study plan. Students could be from one course and one level of study, or could be drawn from a variety of courses and levels. This activity is of particular use to adult returners who have been away from the education system for some time and for those who feel unconfident about studying at the required level (this can include postgraduate students who are returning to education after a time in employment).

The purpose of this first session is to discuss study plans with your students and to help them to prepare their plans with the support, guidance and encouragement of their tutor and peers. The way that you run this session depends on your student cohort and your personal preferences (a brainstorm, class discussion or small group exercises, for example). The following questions can be addressed:

- What is a study plan?
- Why do I need a study plan?
- How do I develop a study plan?
- What should I include in my study plan?

- What constitutes a good study plan?
- Are there any potential pitfalls or problems? If so, how can I avoid these?

Once these questions have been addressed (usually after about 20 minutes), ask your students to prepare an outline study plan. This can be done on an individual basis or in small groups, if you feel students need additional support from their peers. They are to do this for up to 15 minutes (they will not be able to produce a comprehensive study plan in this time, but this exercise helps them to think about specific issues that are involved in preparing their plan and discuss these before the session concludes). Take a further 15 to 20 minutes to discuss the issues raised and to check that everyone is happy to go away and prepare a more comprehensive, personal plan.

Once they have done this, students should implement their plans as their course/module progresses. If you have time available you can offer individual guidance and support if any of your students are struggling with their study plans. Alternatively, you can hold a mid-session group meeting to discuss progress and iron out problems that may have occurred.

Meet again at the end of your course, module or after a specified period of time. This session should be used to evaluate study plans and to improve and expand them so that students feel competent with their ability to prepare an effective plan for future study. Again, the way that you run this session depends on your student cohort and personal preferences. Questions that can be discussed include:

- How effective was the study plan?
- How did it help with your studies?
- Did you encounter any problems with your plan? If so, how did you overcome these problems (or do other students have suggestions about how they could have been overcome)?
- What advice would they offer to their peers about how to develop an effective study plan?

If you do not have time available to run this type of structured activity, it is possible to run this activity as a self-guided individual exercise (this is also a good option if you feel that your students can complete this task without support from their peers or tutor). Ask your students to prepare, implement and evaluate a study plan over the duration of their course/module. You can prepare a Student Handout, using the questions given above, as a guide if you think it will be of use.

Key issues

Although study plans differ, depending on course, level of study and personal preferences, there are certain key elements that students should be encouraged to think about when preparing their plan. Examples of these include:

- Setting personal goals. These are clear statements that describe what a student will be able to do at the end of their course. This will include specific behaviour and clear outcomes. Students should be encouraged to consult their course introductory literature to check that the 'course outcomes' or 'learning outcomes' match their personal goals. If not, they need to decide whether there might be a more appropriate course available (see Activity 9).
- Listing study tasks. This should include all the tasks that students will be required to undertake as part of their course (memorising information, learning facts, reading books, analysing books, evaluating sources, writing assignments and conducting research, for example).
- Highlighting potential study problems. This could include, for example, timetable clashes, lack of motivation, procrastination, fear of failure and perfectionism. Or it could include specific skills that need to be developed, such as learning how to cite and reference correctly (see Activity 30), knowing how to find and evaluate sources (see Activity 52) and producing an effective argument (see Activity 28).
- Addressing potential problems. Some problems may need specific action, whereas others will fade as confidence and experience grows.
- Identifying strengths and weaknesses. Students should be encouraged to feel positive and play to strengths, while addressing and combatting potential weaknesses.
- Developing a semester/term plan. This should include all assignment and project deadlines. Students will need to ensure that all work is completed and handed in on time (see Activity 12).
- Managing time effectively (see Activity 11).
- Addressing potential organisation problems (see Activity 13).

→ **Related activities**

Activity 11: Managing time

Activity 12: Completing coursework and meeting deadlines

Activity 13: Overcoming organisation problems

Activity 10

Activity 14: Maintaining motivation

Activity 15: Becoming an independent learner

···

➜ Preparatory reading

There are a variety of student planner apps available that help students to plan their studies, including My Class Schedule (www.my-class-schedule.com), Timetable (Google Play) and Class Timetable (iTunes). Students can also obtain paper wall-charts and student planners from their students' union (in the UK) or from online bookshops. It is useful for both tutors and students to find out about some of these apps and planners as preparatory work for this activity. You can recommend these if you think they will be of benefit to your students. There are also a wide variety of time management apps that may be of use to students and these are listed in Activity 11.

···

➜ Further reading

Becker, L. (2009) *The Mature Student's Handbook*. Basingstoke: Palgrave Macmillan. This book can be recommended to adult returners who feel they need additional help with their studies. Chapter 4 has some useful information on planning to study.

Cottrell, S. (2018) *The Palgrave Student Planner 2018–19*. Basingstoke: Palgrave Macmillan. This is a useful and practical guide that is published annually and is aimed at students who want help with organising and planning their studies.

···

Activity 10

Activity · · · · · · · · · · · → 11

Managing time

Student handout page 294

TUTOR NOTES

Purpose: This activity helps students to understand more about how to manage their time effectively during their studies by asking them, in their groups, to develop a time management app aimed at students. They must pitch their idea to their classmates in the next teaching session (this can be done using the relevant digital platform, if contact time is limited).

Type: Group exercise followed by group presentation.

Alternative type(s): Self-guided individual exercise followed by student presentations.

Level: Elementary.

Duration: Students need to spend one or two hours working with group members (or individually, if this option is chosen) during independent study. Fifty minutes to one hour of contact time will be required for group (or individual) presentations.

Equipment/materials: Students can choose their presentation equipment and materials and these should be made available for their use.

Learning outcome: By the end of this activity students will have a greater understanding of how to manage their time effectively and will be able to apply this understanding to their studies as their course progresses.

The activity

Divide your students into small groups. Ask each group to develop an idea for a time management app aimed at students. They only need to develop the idea for the app: it is not necessary to design an actual app. The Student Handout can be given to your students, if you feel they need specific information about this task.

   Your students will need to pitch their idea to their classmates in the next teaching session (if contact time is limited, ask your students to pitch their idea on the relevant digital platform instead). You can ask your students to do this in the style of *Dragon's Den* or *The Apprentice* if this appeals to your students (these are television programmes in the UK that ask entrepreneurs or employees to pitch ideas to potential financiers or to their employer). If suitable, you can ask your class to vote on the best pitch and/or the most useful app. Follow the presentations with a tutor-led discussion on the issues that have been raised, if time permits.

   It is possible to run this activity as a self-guided individual exercise, if this better suits your students or if you only have a small number of students. Once they have developed the idea for the app they can either pitch their idea individually in class, or you can ask that they pitch their idea on the relevant digital platform. Again, students can vote on the best idea, if appropriate.

Key issues

Students find this an entertaining way to think about how to manage their time during their studies. They must get to grips with and discuss important aspects of time management before they can develop their ideas for their app. Once they have done this, their pitches tend to be creative and inventive, with students enjoying pitching their ideas to the rest of the group. This activity enables students to pool and develop ideas, discuss the important aspects of time management and think about how to present their ideas to others. They can then take away the salient, relevant and useful ideas, and apply these to their studies.

Ideas that are presented in this activity depend on your student cohort and the subject you are teaching, but can include combinations of the following:

- A calendar to store, highlight and alert students to important dates, such as assignment deadlines and exam times.
- A day-by-day diary that lists all lectures, seminars and tutorials, along with other tasks that have to be undertaken (such as picking children up from school or paid working hours) with alerts to possible clashes.
- A 'deadline looming' alert that counts down to important deadlines, giving information about when different parts of assignment should be completed, for example.
- Notifications when a task should be completed.
- A timing facility for study sessions, including an alarm or alert when the session has gone on for too long. It can contain built-in breaks with ideas for short bursts of exercise to keep the mind and body active.
- A facility that switches off your device when you have spent too long on social media, texting, chatting or gaming.
- A 'kids activity' facility that provides games, quizzes and puzzles to keep children occupied for a certain amount of time while their parent completes an assignment.

- An interactive quiz on time-wasting activities and the methods that can be used to overcome them.
- An interactive facility that enables students to upload details about how they spend their time and then produces an analysis of how they can better spend their time and improve their productivity.
- A 'chat' facility linking to experts and supportive peers who can offer advice and support when students are struggling or beginning to panic because they are running out of time.
- A 'reward' facility when tasks are completed successfully.
- A referencing facility that scans codes on books and journals, produces the reference in the correct format and stores it together with related references. Notifications about previous, related references when a new reference is added. Production of a bibliography in the correct format when required.
- Links to useful and relevant time management software.
- Links to useful training courses and seminars.

Although some of the features described above may not be possible, given technological limitations, and others are already widely available, this activity is useful because it encourages students to think about, and raise, personal and practical issues involved in managing their time.

➜ Related activities

Activity 10: Preparing a study plan

Activity 12: Completing coursework and meeting deadlines

Activity 13: Overcoming organisation problems

Activity 30: Citing, referencing and producing a bibliography

Activity 55: Organising, managing and storing information

➜ Preparatory reading

Both of the books listed in further reading are aimed at students and can be recommended to those who need further help and advice concerning time management. They are simple, introductory texts that provide useful preparatory reading for this activity.

There are a wide variety of apps that help with different aspects of time management for students. It may be useful to view a few of these as preparatory work for this activity (and to check that students have not merely copied an existing app). Examples of relevant apps that are available at time of writing are given below (these change frequently so have a good look around at what is available at the time you run this activity).

Activity 11

- Productivity apps:

  - Evernote: https://evernote.com;
  - Focus Booster: www.focusboosterapp.com;
  - any.do: https://www.any.do.
- To do list apps:

  - Listastic: http://mcleanmobile.com/Listastic;
  - 2Do: www.2doapp.com;
  - Trello: https://trello.com/platforms;
  - Finish: http://getfinish.com.

- Student planner apps:

  - My Class Schedule: www.my-class-schedule.com;
  - Timetable (Google Play);
  - Class Timetable (iTunes).
- Bibliography helper apps:

  - EasyBib: www.easybib.com;
  - EndNote: http://endnote.com/product-details/ipad;
  - Cite this for me: www.citethisforme.com/cite/resources/mobile-app.

➜ Further reading

Cottrell, S. (2018) *The Palgrave Student Planner 2018-19*. Basingstoke: Palgrave Macmillan. This is a useful and practical guide that is published annually and is aimed at students who want help with organising their studies and time management.

Williams, K. and Reid, M. (2011) *Time Management (Pocket Study Skills)*. Basingstoke: Palgrave Macmillan. This is a short, simple book aimed at students in higher education that can be recommended to those who need more help with their time management.

Activity 11

Activity · · · · · · · · · · · → 12

Completing coursework
and meeting deadlines

The activity

Find out whether any of your new students are worried about their ability to complete coursework successfully and meet assignment and project deadlines. If they are concerned, ask if they would like to take part in a volunteer peer mentor programme. Explain that this will involve pairing them with a more experienced student who can offer advice, support and encouragement to help them to complete coursework and meet deadlines. It is useful, at this stage, to find out a little more about students, their experiences, background, hopes and concerns, for example. That way, it will be easier for you to pair students (see below).

Once you have found out how many students would like to be involved in the programme put out a call for volunteer mentors. This can be done in various ways, depending on circumstances and preferences. For example:

- through the relevant digital platform;
- through personal contact with some of your previous students or when you teach students at different levels;
- by asking students who have completed a course successfully whether they would like to take part in a volunteer mentor programme the following year to help other students who are just beginning their course;

- by asking postgraduate students that you teach or supervise (or by contacting your university postgraduate association/committee);
- by recruiting from a mentoring training programme if such a course is run at your institution.

Mentors benefit from this activity in various ways, including gaining in confidence, improving communication skills, consolidating learning and gaining interpersonal skills that will help in studies, employment and life in general.

When you have enough mentors invite together both mentors and mentees to an informal gathering. This should be done at a time and in a place when all can meet. Refreshments can be provided to create an informal and relaxed atmosphere. Introduce the programme by discussing the aims and purpose. Lead a discussion on what students would like to gain from the programme, how they expect their relationship to work and their concerns and worries (usually this is led by the mentees, but some mentors may also be a little concerned about their ability to provide the required support). Ask students to talk about their requirements and expectations from the programme, and what they expect from their mentor/mentee (commitment, dedication, courtesy, respect, good communication and empathy, for example). You will also need to raise the issue of confidentiality (information shared in mentoring sessions will not be passed onto third parties without the agreement of the mentee, except in rare cases where risk of serious harm is suspected) and issues of personal safety (mentoring sessions will take place in public spaces).

Once this discussion has taken place pair students together, based on your understanding of who might work well together. Ask the pairs to have a chat together and get to know each other. Once they have done this, conclude the session with a short discussion and question and answer session to make sure everyone is clear about what is expected of them.

Key issues

This activity uses the experiences and knowledge of peers to help students who are unconfident about their ability to complete coursework and meet assignment deadlines. Students listen, encourage, share experiences, give tips, offer advice and give support when required. If your institution runs peer mentoring sessions mentors should be asked to attend the sessions so that they can get the most out of the programme. You can also recommend Frith et al. (2017). This book provides comprehensive and useful information about peer mentoring when studying at university.

➜ Cautionary note

Not all mentor/mentee relationships work. Some mentors find that the role is not for them, some pairs find that they cannot work together and some mentees find that they are not getting anything out of the programme. On rare occasions the breakdown in the relationship can be quite damaging to one or both students. It is important, therefore, to monitor mentors and mentees on a regular basis (this can be done with a quick email to each student and a follow-up meeting if any issues are raised that need sorting out). You should also let students know when and how you can be contacted if they need to discuss problems with the programme.

Potential problems can be avoided by adopting the following:

- A requirement that all mentors take part in a mentor training programme, if it is available at your institution.
- A written confidentiality agreement that should be signed by mentor and mentee.
- A written peer mentoring agreement that sets out obligations and responsibilities that should be signed by the mentor.
- Regular supervisory meetings with mentors.
- Two separate focus groups sessions at the end of the programme (one for mentors and one for mentees) to evaluate the programme and to discuss improvements for the future programme.

➜ Related activities

Activity 7: Fostering collaborative learning and interaction

Activity 8: Becoming part of a learning community

Activity 41: Improving listening skills

Activity 98: Collaborating and cooperating ethically

Activity 12

➜ Preparatory reading

Frith et al. (2017) is a comprehensive guide to peer mentoring at university. It provides useful preparatory reading for both tutors and students for this activity.

➜ Further reading

Frith, L., May, G. and Pocklington, A. (2017) *The Student's Guide to Peer Mentoring: Get More from Your University Experience*. London: Palgrave.

Zachary, L. (2009) *The Mentee's Guide: Making Mentoring Work for You*. San Francisco, CA: Jossey-Bass. This is the companion guide to the next book listed and can be recommended to students who are being mentored.

Zachary, L. (2012) *The Mentor's Guide: Facilitating Effective Learning Relationships*. 2nd edition. San Francisco, CA: Jossey-Bass. This is a comprehensive guide to mentoring and can be recommended to students who are interested in finding out more about how to be a good mentor.

Activity 12

Activity • • • • • • • • • • → 13

Overcoming organisation problems

Student handout page 295

TUTOR NOTES

Purpose: This activity helps students to overcome organisation problems by introducing them to a number of scenarios that they can work through with their group members to find solutions to the stated problems.

Type: Scenarios for group discussion.

Alternative type(s): Self-guided individual exercise during independent study.

Level: Elementary.

Duration: Fifty minutes to one hour of contact time or up to one hour during independent study.

Equipment/materials: None required.

Learning outcome: By the end of this activity students will have discussed and found solutions to a variety of organisation problems that they can learn from and relate to their own studies, if and when necessary.

The activity

Divide your students into small groups and ask them to discuss the scenarios presented in the Student Handout. They should do this for about 40 minutes (10 minutes for each scenario), after which time you can lead a class discussion on the issues raised. If you prefer, and if it is more suited to your student cohort or to the time you have available, ask that students work through the scenarios on an individual basis during independent study.

Key issues

This activity is of particular use to adult returners who find it difficult to balance their everyday lives with their studies and to students who find it difficult to overcome distractions and organise their learning. It introduces the problems and related anxieties, concerns and worries that students may be experiencing, but does not require them to discuss their own experiences unless they wish to do so. It enables students to discuss these issues with other students in their group, bounce ideas off each other, learn from those with more experience and/or confidence and provide practical and effective solutions to the stated problems, which they can then relate to their own learning.

The following are examples of discussion points and/or solutions that have been given by students during this activity.

Scenario 1

- Convince spouses (and other family members) of the benefits of study and ask them to be more supportive and take more responsibility for the children. Alternatively, ask a relative or friend for help.

- Find out whether the school offers help, such as a breakfast club and/or an after-school club.
- Speak to tutors to find out whether alternative lectures are possible or if they are available digitally (podcasts, audio or written lecture notes). Explain to tutors that it is not feasible to attend lectures at school collection and drop-off times and discuss alternatives.
- Find a more adult/family-friendly course or postpone studies until children are older and can go to school by themselves. Or think about studying online.

Scenario 2

- Attend a time-management or organisational skills training session.
- Use time-management software or apps to help manage time more effectively.
- Seek personal counselling if the problems are really bad. Go to the university/college counsellor for help and advice. Or use relaxation techniques such as yoga or meditation to calm down.
- Seek help and advice from friends. Find out how they organise themselves and their studies and learn from them.
- Find out all assignment deadlines and complete work early to account for unforeseen problems.

Scenario 3

- Draw up a list of personal time-wasting activities. Keep a diary of these so that it is easy to see how much time is wasted on non-essential tasks. Devise an action plan to reduce and eliminate time-wasting activities. Perhaps do this gradually, over time, but start early in the course so that good habits can be developed from the start.
- Understand that a social life and relationships are important, but that they should not be to the detriment of studies. Take a little time to think about what is important: if succeeding on the course is seen to be paramount think about what needs to be done to succeed. Prioritise what is important.
- Don't undertake mammoth study sessions or work continuously through the night. Work in shorter bursts during the daytime when your mind is fresh and you are not tired. Start assignments early so that you have plenty of time to complete them and do not have to rush and cram overnight.
- Find out when all deadlines are due and mark these onto a calendar (paper or digital). Complete all assignments well before the deadline so that you can edit and proofread and still hand them in on time.

Scenario 4

- Ensure that working hours and class contact time will not clash. If they do, try to alter either work hours or study hours so that they are compatible. Make sure that there will be enough hours in the day to work and study.
- Prepare a study plan (see Activity 10).
- Keep a learning journal and reflect on your learning (see Activities 2 and 4).
- Develop a good relationship with your tutor and with fellow students. Seek help and advice from those with more experience. Realise that college and university can be very different to school: tutors want you to do well and will help you as much as they can (see Activity 47). Ignore what your teachers said all those years ago.

➜ Related activities

Activity 10: Preparing a study plan

Activity 11: Managing time

Activity 12: Completing coursework and meeting deadlines

Activity 15: Becoming an independent learner

➜ Preparatory reading

Chapters 8 and 9 of Tefula (2014) cover 'focus and attention' and 'goals and planning' and provide useful preparatory reading for this activity.

Activity 13

→ Further reading

All three books below can be recommended to students who need further help with organising their studies.

Cottrell, S. (2018) *The Palgrave Student Planner 2018-19*, published annually. Basingstoke: Palgrave Macmillan.

Tefula, M. (2014) *Student Procrastination: Seize the Day and Get More Work Done*. Basingstoke: Palgrave Macmillan.

Williams, K. (2011) *Time Management*. Basingstoke: Palgrave Macmillan.

Activity 13

Activity · · · · · · · · · · · ➔ 14

Maintaining motivation

The activity

Ask your students to produce a vlog or blog about maintaining motivation during their studies. Explain that vlogs and blogs are to be uploaded on the relevant digital platform to build a useful resource that can be accessed by students throughout their studies. You can ask students to undertake this activity on an individual basis, in pairs or in small groups, depending on what best suits your student cohort. If, for example, you have students who may feel unconfident with the technological requirements of this activity, it is useful to place them within a small group of students who are familiar and comfortable with the technology.

Students should make their vlog or blog as useful as possible, providing advice, guidance, tips or any other information that will benefit their peers. Their work should be interesting, creative and original so that a useful and informative resource can be developed. You will need to monitor the digital resource from time to time to ensure that the information is constructive, helpful and correct.

A slight variation on this activity is to build a digital resource that does not consist of vlogs and blogs, but instead contains tips, advice, questions and answers, references and information about who to contact if further help is required. This should be student-led, but you can make a few posts to get the resource started (see key issues). Again, you will need to monitor posts to ensure that information is correct, constructive and helpful.

Key issues

This activity is an entertaining way to build a resource of useful, creative and informative vlogs and blogs for students who may struggle with maintaining motivation. All students are asked to contribute to the resource, but not all students will need or use the resource. Some students produce entertaining videos, illustrating through action how students can be disturbed and distracted from their work, or showing how to remain motivated when reading academic texts that are too full of jargon or too basic, for example. One group chose to video different working environments, illustrating how some environments help to increase motivation, whereas others have a detrimental influence on motivation. They also produce informative blogs that concentrate on one particular issue, such as how to remain motivated through the application of learning, or covering a wide variety of tips for maintaining motivation. A summary of these is provided below (you can use this list as a basis for entries in the student-led digital resource, if you choose this option).

- Make the right learning choices (see Activity 9):
  - choose courses that are of personal interest;
  - conduct careful research to find out about all the options;
  - seek advice from experts.
- Create or find a good working environment:
  - comfortable chair and desk;
  - good lighting;
  - good ventilation and suitable temperature;
  - free from distractions and disturbances.
- Become active in the learning process:
  - prepare for lectures and seminars;
  - complete all the required work (whether assessed or non-assessed);
  - read as much as you can;
  - ask questions and seek answers.
- Be clear about purpose, method and outcome:
  - set goals;
  - ensure goals match learning outcomes;
  - take action;
  - challenge yourself;
  - celebrate success.
- Apply learning:
  - apply learning to the real world (internships, work placement, volunteering);
  - process deep ideas and establish relevance;
  - apply learning to new environments.
- Control disturbances:
  - set aside study time and ensure everyone knows you are not to be disturbed;
  - switch off phones and only check email at set times;
  - get control of gaming and social media habits;
  - keep study and play separate.
- Read the right texts:
  - avoid boring and long-winded books: if you have to read them learn to skim and scan (see Activities 16 and 17);
  - choose texts that are of interest;
  - avoid books that are too basic, unless they help to explain something;
  - become active in reading and read more than the reading list;
  - enjoy your reading.
- Tutors must play their part:
  - give constructive and timely feedback;
  - reward hard work;
  - give praise when deserved;
  - encourage collaborative, active and student-led learning.

➜ Related activities

Activity 1: Bringing learning to life

Activity 8: Becoming part of a learning community

Activity 9: Making the right learning choices

Activity 32: Overcoming difficulties with writing

Activity 58: Reflecting, thinking and making connections

....

➜ Preparatory reading

Magnifico, A., Olmanson, J. and Cope, B. (2013) 'New pedagogies of motivation: reconstructing and repositioning motivational constructs in the design of learning technologies', *E-Learning and Digital Media*, 10 (4): 483–511. This paper

Activity 14

discusses motivational constructs and examines them in relation to new media education and technology. It provides useful preparatory reading for tutors who are interested in these issues.

There are a wide variety of videos about maintaining motivation on YouTube (www.youtube.com). It is useful to view some of these as preparatory work for this activity, to check that students are not copying what is already available (a search of 'maintaining motivation for university students' finds a good selection). Links to some of the better videos can be posted on your digital resource, if appropriate.

....

→ Further reading

Evans, P. and Bonneville-Roussy, A. (2016) 'Self-determined motivation for practice in university music students', *Psychology of Music*, 44 (5): 1095–1110, first published 4 November 2015, 10.1177/0305735615610926. This study of needs fulfilment and autonomous motivation of music students in Australia and New Zealand provides interesting reading for tutors.

The Open University on the UK has a free course available called 'Motivation and Factors Affecting Motivation' (http://www.open.edu/openlearn/health-sports-psychology/motivation-and-factors-affecting-motivation/content-section-0?active-tab=description-tab). This course considers what is meant by the term motivation and looks at some influential theories about motivation. It can be recommended to students who are interested in finding out more about these issues.

Activity 14

Activity • • • • • • • • • • • → 15

Becoming an independent learner

Student handout page 297

> **TUTOR NOTES**
>
> **Purpose:** This activity is a workshop that helps students to become independent learners by exploring what is meant by independent learning, addressing personal concerns and developing an action plan that will help students to become independent learners.
>
> **Type:** Workshop.
>
> **Alternative type(s):** Brainstorm with tutor-led discussion and self-guided individual exercise.
>
> **Level:** Elementary and advanced.
>
> **Duration:** Fifty minutes to one hour for the workshop, followed by independent study time to implement action plans. The same amount of time is required if the brainstorm option is chosen. Students need one to two hours of independent study time if the self-guided individual exercise option is chosen.
>
> **Equipment/materials:** None required.
>
> **Learning outcome:** By the end of this activity students will feel more confident in their ability to study independently and will have developed an action plan that will help them to become efficient and effective independent learners.

The activity

Invite together a group of students who are interested in finding out more about becoming an independent learner, ensuring that those students who can benefit most from this workshop are encouraged to attend. These tend to be students who are new to university study (students who have just left sixth form college or school and adult returners) and those who have had a long time away from university study who feel that they need help to get back into studying (postgraduate students who have had a long period of time in employment, for example). You can choose to mix these students together or run separate workshops for different levels of study, depending on student numbers.

Divide your students into small groups and give them a copy of the Student Handout. This poses four questions that they should discuss with their group members. Once they have completed this task (usually after about 20 minutes) lead a discussion on the issues raised. Once this has finished (usually after about ten minutes), ask the students to work individually on an action plan that will help them to become an independent learner. Leave a few minutes at the end of the session for students to ask questions, if required. Conclude the workshop by asking students to implement their action plan as their course progresses.

It is possible to run this activity as a brainstorm with your students at the beginning of the course, rather than inviting students to a workshop. You can use questions 1 and 2 on the Student Handout for two separate brainstorms. Once these are complete, ask your students to work individually on developing a personal action plan that will help them to become an independent learner. If contact time is not available, or if it is better suited to your student cohort, ask students to work through the questions on the Student Handout individually during independent study.

Key issues

The following issues can be raised during this activity.

Question 1

Independent learners:

- think and act autonomously;
- manage their study time;
- organise their studies;
- motivate themselves;
- choose modules, courses and extra-curricular activities;
- engage with their learning and studies;
- appraise and rectify shortcomings;
- remain disciplined and focused;
- carry out the required reading and are interested in additional reading;
- hand in assignments on time;
- revise effectively for exams;
- know where to get help and assistance if required.

Question 2

There is a wide variety of skills, attributes and characteristics of independent learners that can be mentioned, including:

- organisation and time-management skills;
- the ability to meet deadlines/set goals;
- the ability to work under pressure;
- crisis management;
- adaptability and flexibility;
- the ability to work independently, using initiative;
- the ability to reflect;
- problem-solving skills;
- skills of analysis, evaluation and synthesis;
- the ability to review and critique;
- communication skills (verbal and written);
- editing/proofreading skills;
- IT skills;
- numerical skills;
- reading skills;
- research skills;
- presentation skills;
- teamworking skills;
- social skills;
- listening skills;
- the ability to empathise/support others.

Question 3

Students can:

- feel overwhelmed by study demands;
- think that they are not clever enough;
- not know where to start or not know how to seek help;
- worry about overdependence on tutors or significant others;
- think that other students know what to do and find independent study easy.

Problems can be overcome by seeking help when required, building confidence and adopting the strategies listed below.

Question 4

Action includes:

- taking relevant modules or attending relevant workshops;
- learning how to manage time and studies (see Activity 11);
- developing organisational skills (see Activity 13);
- understanding how to remain motivated (see Activity 14);
- ensuring that all coursework is completed on time (see Activity 12);
- reading as much as possible;
- collaborating with others and seeking and offering help to peers (see Activity 7);
- seeking advice when required.

Activity 15

➜ Related activities

Activity 2: Becoming a reflective learner

Activity 3: Learning to learn

Activity 10: Preparing a study plan

Activity 11: Managing time

Activity 12: Completing coursework and meeting deadlines

Activity 13: Overcoming organisation problems

Activity 14: Maintaining motivation

➜ Preparatory reading

The 2016 UK Engagement Survey: Student Engagement and Skills Development, conducted by the Higher Education Academy (HEA) in the UK, found that independent study 'appears to have a stronger link than taught sessions to all types of skills development' (www.heacademy.ac.uk/institutions/surveys/uk-engagement-survey). The final report from this survey provides useful preparatory reading for tutors, illustrating how independent learning can help with developing active learning skills such as innovation and creativity, and with civic skills such as developing values and ethics.

➜ Further reading

Burns, T. and Sinfield, S. (2016) *Essential Study Skills: the Complete Guide to Success at University*. 4th edition. London: Sage. This book can be recommended to students who need further help with study at university.

Moran, P. and Sutton, S. (2000) *Managing Your Own Learning at University: a Practical Guide*, 2nd edition. Dublin: University College Dublin Press. Although this is an older book that could do with some updating, it is a useful reference to recommend to students who wish to follow up the issues raised in this activity.

Activity 15

Section 3

Reading and note-taking

Activity • • • • • • • • • • • ➔ 16

Reading academic texts effectively

Student handout page 298

TUTOR NOTES

Purpose: This activity helps students to understand how to read academic texts effectively by holding a workshop that covers three issues: active reading, improving understanding and improving efficiency.

Type: Workshop.

Alternative type(s): Group exercise followed by poster presentation; self-guided individual exercise during independent study.

Level: Elementary.

Duration: Fifty minutes to one hour of contact time for the workshop. If the group exercise option is chosen students need to spend a few hours preparing their poster presentation during independent study and 50 minutes to one hour of contact time to present their posters. Students will spend one or two hours during independent study on this activity if the self-guided individual exercise option is chosen.

Equipment/materials: None required for the workshop and self-guided individual exercise. If the poster presentation option is chosen, ensure that students have access to the relevant poster production equipment and materials.

Learning outcome: By the end of this activity students will be able to read academic texts more effectively by knowing how to read actively, improve understanding and become more efficient.

The activity

Invite together students who feel that they need guidance about reading academic texts effectively, ensuring that those who could benefit most are encouraged to attend. Divide your students into three groups and allocate one of the tasks in the Student Handout to each group. These tasks ask them to discuss 'active reading', 'improving understanding' and 'improving efficiency'. Allocate up to 20 minutes for the groups to discuss their topics. Once they have completed this task, ask them to present their ideas to their peers in the workshop. Allocate up to ten minutes for each group to present their ideas and answer questions from their peers, and use the remaining ten minutes to sum up the findings of the workshop. You may find it useful to walk among the groups during their discussion, offering advice and guidance where required (see key issues).

It is possible to run this activity as a group exercise followed by a poster presentation if it is better suited to your student cohort. Divide your students into three groups and allocate one task on the Student Handout to each group. If students are unfamiliar with the poster presentation technique, give them a copy of the Student Handout from Activity 28 (this provides information and advice about producing a poster presentation). Introduce the activity at the end of a teaching session and ask that the groups prepare their poster presentation during independent study ready for the next teaching session.

You can also adapt the Student Handout to run this activity as a self-guided individual exercise during independent study, if contact time is limited. If this option is chosen students should work through all three of the tasks provided on the Student Handout, on an individual basis.

Key issues

The following issues can be raised and discussed during this activity.

Active reading:

- reading should not be passive, but should be active: students should be engaged actively and critically with the material;
- it requires students to be observant, perceptive, focused and interested;
- it involves relating reading to past experiences and current interests and knowledge;
- students will need to develop their own thoughts, learn to question and understand how to evaluate, analyse and critique the text (see Activities 21 and 59);

- students can become active readers by:
  - having an interest in the material;
  - maintaining high levels of motivation;
  - reading at the right time (not when tired, busy or distracted, for example);
  - keeping the purpose in mind when reading;
  - practising as much as possible.

Understanding can be improved by:

- starting with simple texts and leaving more complex reading until a deeper understanding is gained (books aimed at the lay-person or at students studying at a lower level, for example);
- compiling a list of things they want to know or questions that they want answered before and during reading; if questions are not answered with one text they can move to another;

- summarising what they have read and returning to the text to check that their summary is correct;
- using a dictionary and thesaurus for complex words;
- discussing their reading with peers and tutors to gain a deeper understanding and overcome difficulties;
- remaining interested, motivated and alert (avoiding distractions).

Efficiency can be improved by:

- breaking down reading into manageable chunks and taking regular breaks;
- using contents and index pages wisely and only reading relevant material;
- skimming and scanning to obtain a general idea of what the text is about, to find relevant information quickly and to dismiss irrelevant information;
- taking correct referencing details of all sources as they read (see Activity 30);
- improving reading speed by:
  - concentrating on key words and meanings rather than sounding out, or reading, each word;

- reading through difficult material and obtaining help or clarification from tutors, peers or other sources;
- reading at a productive time, when there is good light and when students are not tired;
- considering what is important and remembering facts selectively;
- finding a quiet place free from distractions;
- having eyes tested on a regular basis.

→ Related activities

Activity 18: Establishing academic reading groups

Activity 19: Producing a personal reading strategy

Activity 20: Adopting and adapting reading styles and strategies

Activity 30: Citing, referencing and producing a bibliography

Activity 59: Learning how to question

Activity 16

→ Preparatory reading

Godfrey (2014) in its entirety provides a quick and simple introduction to this activity for students.

··

→ Further reading

The following books can be recommended to students if they need further help to develop their academic reading.

Chong Ho Shon, P. (2015) *How to Read Journal Articles in the Social Sciences*, 2nd edition. London: Sage.
Godfrey, J. (2014) *Reading and Making Notes*, 2nd edition. Basingstoke: Palgrave Macmillan.
Metcalfe, M. (2006) *Reading Critically at University*. London: Sage.

Activity 16

Activity · · · · · · · · · · · ➔ 17

Reading scientific material for unconfident adults

Student handout page 299

TUTOR NOTES

Purpose: This activity is for adults who feel unconfident about reading scientific material at the required level. It is a workshop in which students are able to discuss their concerns and worries, talk about solutions to stated problems and develop a plan of action that will help them to feel more confident when reading scientific material. They are asked to read a scientific paper in preparation for the workshop, which gives them specific examples and issues to discuss. Once the workshop has finished students are paired together to offer peer support and encouragement as their course progresses.

Type: Workshop.

Alternative type(s): One-to-one support session; self-guided individual exercise followed by tutor-led discussion.

Level: Elementary.

Duration: Fifty minutes to one hour for the workshop, followed by informal meetings as required between paired students. Half an hour initial contact meeting, plus one or two follow-up meetings will be required if you choose the one-to-one support session option. Students will take one or two hours of time during independent study, and up to half an hour of contact time if the self-guided individual exercise option is chosen (the discussion can take place online if contact time is limited).

Equipment/materials: A copy of a suitable scientific paper (a suggestion is given below).

Learning outcome: By the end of this activity students will understand how to approach scientific material and will feel more confident with their ability to read scientific material as their course progresses.

The activity

Invite together a group of students who feel unconfident about their ability to read scientific material at the required level, ensuring that those who can benefit most are invited to attend. These students tend to be studying at elementary level (in their first year, for example) but can be from different courses as this usually gives a variety of perspectives and enlivens the discussion. Give the students a copy of a scientific paper a few days before the workshop is to take place and ask that they read the paper in preparation for the workshop. You can choose a relevant paper or use the example given in 'preparatory reading', below. As the students read the paper they should answer the questions contained in the Student Handout. Discuss the questions during the workshop, concluding with action that students can adopt and work on as their course progresses. At the end of the workshop pair students together so that they can help, support and encourage each other when they need to read scientific material.

This activity can be run as a one-to-one support session if you feel that a particular student needs specific, individual support. You can ask the student to prepare for the session by reading a paper in advance or, if it is better for the student, you can work through a paper and develop a plan of action together. Alternatively, you can run this activity as a self-guided individual exercise by adapting the Student Handout slightly and asking students to read a paper and work through the questions on an individual basis during independent study. If contact time is available you can discuss issues raised by this exercise when you next meet, or you can ask students to post comments on the relevant digital platform.

Key issues

Examples of issues that can be raised for each question are given below.

1. Initial thoughts and feelings when given a scientific paper to read include:

    a. feeling of being overwhelmed;
    b. it's an impossible task or insurmountable problem;
    c. fear or anxiety about figures, tables and graphs;
    d. maths phobia or anxiety (some students believe that some people are 'naturally predisposed' towards maths, whereas others are perhaps predisposed to anxiety about maths);
    e. fear of failure;
    f. worrying about 'looking stupid'.

2. Students report not understanding:

    a. technical words and phrases;
    b. methods and methodology;
    c. theoretical issues;
    d. figures, equations, graphs, tables, diagrams and/or charts.

3. After having read the paper students report the following thoughts and feelings:

    a. there is even more confusion;
    b. some issues have become a little clearer;
    c. it was not as bad as initially perceived;
    d. they found the paper more interesting than they thought, but are still a little confused;
    e. they feel anxious and overwhelmed;
    f. they are worried about failing.

4. Students would feel more confident if they:

    a. realise that all students have the ability to learn new subjects;
    b. don't let bad school experiences, previous examination results or poor learning environments influence their attitude to learning at higher education level;
    c. embrace the new learning environment, build networks, utilise expert help and seek advice and guidance, when required;
    d. overcome their fear of failure;

    e. utilise help from tutors who are friendly and experienced (students should always seek advice if they are struggling and should not be afraid to admit that they don't understand something);
    f. know about the required level of mathematical or scientific knowledge that is required for the course (this should be made clear from the outset so that students don't enrol on a course that is totally inappropriate for them).

5. Specific action that can be taken includes:

    a. reading around the subject and taking extra maths and science courses, if they are offered and can be incorporated into a student's course;
    b. skimming and scanning scientific material, rather than wading through whole texts (returning to relevant texts to read in more detail, if required);
    c. paying particular attention to the introduction, summary and conclusion;
    d. building up an overview of the information first by scanning the relevant sections and working out how they all fit together;
    e. looking for keywords or phrases that aid comprehension and help to piece together what is being read;
    f. finding definitions of new words and terms within the text or referring to a glossary or dictionary and keeping a note of the definition for future reference;
    g. understanding what is being read rather than memorising facts (understanding aids memory);
    h. paying particular attention to charts and figures as these tend to summarise the major ideas and facts that are being presented;
    i. critiquing and analysing the work of other academics, asking questions about the methodology, methods, results and conclusions;
    j. looking out for researcher bias and problems with validity and reliability, where appropriate;
    k. maintaining interest and motivation;
    l. persevering and realising that understanding comes with reflection and experience.

➜ Related activities

Activity 16: Reading academic texts effectively

Activity 18: Establishing academic reading groups

Activity 19: Producing a personal reading strategy

Activity 20: Adopting and adapting reading styles and strategies

Activity 21: Reading, critiquing and questioning

Activity 17

➜ Preparatory reading

Freeman, S., Theobald, R., Crowe, A. and Wenderoth, M. (2017) 'Likes attract: students self-sort in a classroom by gender, demography, and academic characteristics', *Active Learning in Higher Education*, 18(2): 115-26, published online before print 16 May 2017, http://doi.org/10.1177/1469787417707614. This paper can be given to students for the preparatory reading for this activity. It contains tables, equations, figures and discussion that can appear daunting and complex for those not familiar with scientific reading. However, it is on a topic that students can relate to and it has direct relevance to this activity because students are asked to pair up at the end of the workshop. It also provides useful preparatory reading for tutors who can decide whether or not to let students form their own pairs, in light of the research findings.

➜ Further reading

The following books can be recommended to students who need to follow up some of the issues raised in this activity, depending on their subject of study.

Cheng, E. (2015) *Cakes, Custard and Category Theory: Easy Recipes for Understanding Complex Maths*. London: Profile Books Ltd.
Greenhalgh, T. (2014) *How to Read a Paper: the Basics of Evidence-based Medicine*, 5th edition. Chichester: Wiley-Blackwell.
Rowntree, D. (2000) *Statistics without Tears: an Introduction for Non-Mathematicians*. London: Penguin Books Ltd.
Yudkin, B. (2006) *Critical Reading: Making Sense of Research Papers in Life Sciences and Medicine*. Abingdon, Oxon: Routledge.

Activity 17

Activity · · · · · · · · · · · → 18

Establishing academic reading groups

The activity

Introduce the idea of a reading group to your students. Tell them that they will be given specific academic texts each week (book chapters, journals, research papers, academic blogs, etc.), which they are to read beforehand and then discuss with their group members. The purpose of the group is to help students to become more confident, increase motivation, improve efficiency, develop understanding and enhance enjoyment of academic reading through gaining support, encouragement and help from their peers. Explain that the group is informal (refreshments can be available, if appropriate) and that it is not assessed. If you are running a long course and there are plenty of demands on student time you may find it more appropriate to run the group fortnightly, monthly or remain flexible about when the reading group is scheduled.

It is useful to ask all students to attend the first session so that they can ascertain whether the reading group will be of interest and of use, and then make future attendance voluntary. Some students are able to undertake the required academic reading without the support of a reading group, so these students should not be forced into attendance. Others do not realise that it will be of interest and value until they attend the first session.

Give your students an interesting and relevant text to read in preparation for the first session. When the group meets, lead the discussion yourself. It is useful to prepare a few questions and discussion points to get the conversation started. You should also ask students to discuss and agree a 'code of conduct' or a 'code of behaviour' that includes issues such as courtesy and respect, domination and digression, confidentiality, purpose and expectations, for example. The aim of the first session is to encourage students to return next time (informal, relaxing spaces with access to refreshments help to encourage attendance). Also, try to choose a time of day when all your students can attend. Introduce a new text for the next meeting at the end of the session.

Once the group is up and running, decide whether to continue leading the group or whether to ask your students to run the group. This depends on the abilities, personalities and preferences of students. Also, decide whether you are going to suggest texts for each week (useful for students at elementary level) or whether students are going to choose their own texts (useful for students studying at intermediate and advanced level). Some groups choose, instead, to work their way through their reading list and others branch out to cover texts that are not course-specific.

Key issues

Reading groups can be useful for students who are unconfident about their ability to undertake the required academic reading and for students who find it difficult to build enthusiasm for academic reading. They can be tutor-led groups or student-led groups, depending on your student cohort and their preferences. Reading groups help students to read academic texts with the support, help and encouragement of their peers. Discussions enable students to share knowledge, exchange ideas, overcome problems, raise concerns or offer advice and support to others, in particular, when they have a flash of insight or discover something new.

When establishing reading groups it is important to ensure that:

- all group members are clear about the purpose;
- all group members know how to behave;
- every member of the group has a chance to speak, if they wish;
- reading is manageable and aimed at the right level;
- there is a competent person available to lead, coordinate, facilitate or manage the group;

- all group members are clear about time and dates;
- meetings are arranged when everyone can attend;
- the meeting space is appropriate, informal and free from disturbances and distractions;
- all group members feel that attendance is of personal benefit and that the reading group meets their needs and expectations.

→ Related activities

Activity 16: Reading academic texts effectively

Activity 19: Producing a personal reading strategy

Activity 20: Adopting and adapting reading styles and strategies

Activity 21: Reading, critiquing and questioning

Activity 63: Analysing and critiquing

....

→ Preparatory reading

A useful way to prepare for this activity is to find out what other universities are doing in terms of reading groups so that you can get an idea of structure, content and style. For example, at time of writing, the School of Literatures, Languages and Cultures Graduate School at the University of Edinburgh runs a variety of reading groups ranging from the Creation of Reality Group to the Interdisciplinary Feminism and Gender Reading Group (www.ed.ac.uk/literatures-languages-cultures/graduate-school/news-events/reading-groups). A simple search of 'academic reading groups' finds some good examples.

....

→ Further reading

Laskin, D. and Hughes, H. (1995) *The Reading Group Book*. New York: Penguin. Although this is an old book that could do with updating, it still provides a useful and comprehensive introduction to reading groups, covering issues such as the logistics of running a group, how to deal with non-attendance and choosing appropriate texts.

Peplow, D. (2017) *Talk about Books: a Study of Reading Groups*. London: Bloomsbury. This is an interesting book for tutors who are interested in research on reading groups.

Activity 18

Activity · · · · · · · · · · · → 19

Producing a personal reading strategy

TUTOR NOTES

Purpose: This activity helps students to get the most from academic reading through the production of a personal reading strategy. It is a tutor-led class discussion that helps students to think about reading strategies: what they entail and what should be included in their reading strategy, before asking them to develop a strategy that they can adopt, modify and improve as their course progresses.

Type: Tutor-led discussion followed by individual exercise.

Alternative type(s): Self-guided individual exercise; one-to-one support session.

Level: Elementary, intermediate and advanced (the level of study will be reflected in personal reading strategies).

Duration: Fifty minutes to one hour of contact time for the tutor-led discussion and introduction to the individual exercise. Students will spend several hours during independent study developing, adopting and modifying their strategy as their course progresses. If the self-guided individual exercise option is chosen students will spend several hours during independent study on the activity. For the one-to-one support session you need 50 minutes to one hour for the initial session, with a follow-up session of the same length a few weeks later.

Equipment/materials: None required.

Learning outcome: By the end of this activity students will have developed a personal reading strategy that will help them to get the most out of their reading as their course progresses.

The activity

Lead a class discussion on the topic of personal reading strategies. There are various questions that you can ask and discuss, examples of which include:

1. What is a personal reading strategy?
2. Why should I develop a personal reading strategy?
3. What benefits can be gained from developing a personal reading strategy?
4. How do I go about developing a personal reading strategy?
5. What should I include in my personal reading strategy?
6. How can I test, modify and adapt my personal reading strategy as my course progresses?

Some of the key issues that can be addressed in the class discussion are listed below. Once you have led this discussion ask your students to develop their personal reading strategy during independent study, based on the class discussion and further research. If you think it would be of interest and benefit to your students (and encourage them to complete the task) ask that they post a summary of their personal reading strategies on the relevant digital platform for discussion, comments and peer review and evaluation. If you feel that a more complete coverage of this topic is appropriate for your students, you can also combine this activity with Activity 20, asking students to work through the given scenarios before developing their personal reading strategy.

It is possible to run this activity as a self-guided individual exercise. Ask your students to develop their personal reading strategies based on personal research, or adapt the questions given above into a Student Handout for students to work through before they develop their strategy. You can also run this activity as a one-to-one support session if a particular student needs specific help and guidance. Again, use the questions given above as a basis for this session. Run a follow-up session to evaluate and check on progress.

Key issues

When students are asked to think about developing a personal reading strategy it encourages them to think about how, when, why, where and what they read, instead of merely working their way through their reading list as quickly as possible. Reading strategies can include practical issues such as:

- finding quiet, comfortable places to read that are free from disturbances (reading rooms, libraries or quiet rooms at home, for example);
- reading when you are not tired, feeling under the weather or feeling under undue pressure (start reading in plenty of time for assignments);
- setting aside time for reading and ensuring that others know you are not to be disturbed;
- joining a reading group for support and encouragement (see Activity 18).

Developing a reading strategy is important because it helps students to:

- organise their reading, know how much is required and manage their reading effectively;
- remain motivated, interested and enthused;
- set and meet reading goals that will develop knowledge and intellect and for personal satisfaction;
- read all the set texts, read around a subject when required and decide on further reading to aid understanding.

There are various techniques that students can adopt when reading academic texts and these can be included in personal reading strategies:

- previewing the text and skimming and scanning to obtain an overview (see Activity 16);
- contextualising the text, placing it within historical, social, cultural and biographical contexts;
- recognising the positionality (and potential bias) of author and reader (see Activity 52);
- making connections between experiences and the text (see Activity 58);
- asking questions and seeking answers (see Activity 59);
- evaluating personal reactions and responses to the text and thinking about how personal beliefs, attitudes and values may be challenged or changed;
- evaluating the strength of argument, checking evidence and recognising the difference between statistics, facts, arguments and opinions (see Activity 54);
- taking note of technical terms and definitions and reading around, and coming to terms with, complex issues and arguments;
- summarising what has been read;
- comparing and contrasting related reading.

➔ Related activities

Activity 16: Reading academic texts effectively

Activity 18: Establishing academic reading groups

Activity 20: Adopting and adapting reading styles and strategies

Activity 21: Reading, critiquing and questioning

Activity 52: Evaluating sources

Activity 19

→ Preparatory reading

Majid, F., Azman, N. and Jelas, M. (2012) 'The reading strategies of proficient and less proficient adult readers', *Journal of Adult and Continuing Education*, 16 (1): 21-40. This paper reports on a study carried out with adult learners at university in Malaysia. It has some interesting points to make about reading strategies and how these are adopted and used by different adult learners and, therefore, provides useful preparatory reading for tutors.

→ Further reading

The following books provide further guidance on reading academic texts at university and can be suggested to students if they want to follow up the issues raised in this activity.

Godfrey, J. (2014) *Reading and Making Notes*, 2nd edition. Basingstoke: Palgrave Macmillan.
MacCaw, N. (2013) *How to Read Texts*, 2nd edition. London: Bloomsbury Academic.
Metcalfe, M. (2006) *Reading Critically at University*. London: Sage.
Wallace, M. and Wray, A. (2016) *Critical Reading and Writing for Postgraduates*, 3rd edition. London: Sage.

Activity 19

Activity · · · · · · · · · → 20

Adopting and adapting reading styles and strategies

Student handout page 300

TUTOR NOTES

Purpose: This activity encourages students to think about and discuss how to adopt and adapt reading styles and strategies as their course progresses. They are asked to work through a number of scenarios, in groups, and develop reading strategies for each scenario. This activity can be combined with Activity 19 if you feel it is beneficial to ask students to develop a personal reading strategy after they have completed this activity.

Type: Scenarios for group discussion.

Alternative type(s): Self-guided individual exercise.

Level: Elementary.

Duration: Fifty minutes to one hour. If the self-guided individual exercise option is chosen students will spend one to two hours during independent study on this activity.

Equipment/materials: None required.

Learning outcome: By the end of this activity students will have a raised awareness of different reading styles and strategies and will know how these can be adopted and adapted, depending on reading purpose, subject and level of study.

The activity

Divide your students into groups and give each group a copy of the Student Handout. This asks them to develop a reading strategy for each scenario, using the given list of styles and strategies as a guide. If you think that the list provided on the handout gives too much information to students, delete it and ask the groups to devise their own strategies. However, you may find it useful to provide a list because some students tend to think about reading styles and strategies only in terms of how much reading to complete, rather than think more deeply about how they can adopt and adapt more complex styles and strategies. You can adapt the list, depending on your student cohort, and students should be encouraged to add to the list, where relevant.

Students should discuss the scenarios for up to 30 minutes. Once they have done this, work through the scenarios with the whole class, inviting each group to discuss and provide a rationale for the reading strategies they have developed. This activity can also be run as a self-guided individual exercise during independent study if you do not have the contact time available or it better suits your student cohort (you will need to modify the Student Handout accordingly).

Key issues

This activity helps students to think about how they can adopt and adapt reading styles and strategies as their course progresses and for different reading purposes. It does not require them to develop a personal reading strategy. However, if you think that this would be of benefit to your students, you can run this activity together with Activity 19, which provides advice and guidance about developing a personal reading strategy.

    Some students express surprise that there are so many ways to read academic texts. This activity encourages them to think about these different techniques and discuss possible styles and strategies with their peers. Students learn from each other: some have more experience with reading academic texts than others and this activity provides a supportive environment in which to explore these issues.

➜ Related activities

Activity 16: Reading academic texts effectively

Activity 19: Producing a personal reading strategy

Activity 21: Reading, critiquing and questioning

Activity 52: Evaluating sources

Activity 54: Recognising statistics, facts, arguments and opinions

➜ Preparatory reading

Majid et al. (2012) provide useful preparatory reading for tutors (see Activity 19).

➜ Further reading

The following books provide further guidance on reading academic texts at university and can be suggested to students if they need further information.

Godfrey, J. (2014) *Reading and Making Notes*, 2nd edition. Basingstoke: Palgrave Macmillan.
MacCaw, N. (2013) *How to Read Texts*, 2nd edition. London: Bloomsbury Academic.
Metcalfe, M. (2006) *Reading Critically at University*. London: Sage.

Activity 20

Activity · · · · · · · · · ➔ 21

Reading, critiquing and questioning

Student handout page 302

TUTOR NOTES

Purpose: This activity helps students to find out more about reading, critiquing and questioning academic texts. It asks them to work independently on a critical appraisal exercise that involves reading an academic paper and answering a series of questions. This is followed by a tutor-led discussion to talk about the issues raised.

Type: Self-guided individual exercise followed by tutor-led discussion.

Alternative type(s): None.

Level: Elementary, intermediate and advanced (there is a different Student Handout for those studying at advanced level).

Duration: Students will spend a few hours during independent study undertaking the exercise, followed by up to 50 minutes of contact time for the tutor-led discussion.

Equipment/materials: A suitable research paper for students to read, critique and question (some examples are given below).

Learning outcome: By the end of this activity students will have a deeper understanding of what is involved in critical appraisal and will be able to apply this understanding to academic texts, and to their written work, as their studies progress.

The activity

Give a research paper and the Student Handout to your students and ask that they undertake the task ready for your next session (Student Handout 1 should be given to students studying at elementary and intermediate level and Student Handout 2 should be given to students studying at advanced level). Choose a research paper that is relevant to your course or use one of the suggestions given below.

  Students should work on this exercise during independent study and be prepared to discuss the issues raised when you next meet. The questions contained in the Student Handouts can be used as a basis for discussion, along with more general questions about how easy or difficult students found this exercise and possible concerns they may have about tackling more complex texts in the future. It is important to stress to students that, although this appears as a stand-alone activity, they should reflect on what they have learnt and think about how they can further develop their ability to read, critique and question as their course progresses. They should also understand the importance of relating critical appraisal to their own written work.

  This exercise takes a slightly different approach to that described in Activity 63, which pairs students together to find and critique a research paper related to their course. The handout provides similar questions to those listed below.

However, students are asked to work through the questions on an individual basis before discussing, comparing and contrasting answers with their partner, which provides mutual support and encouragement for students studying at elementary level. Therefore, choose the activity that is most suited to your student cohort and level of study.

Key issues

This activity works best if you choose a recent research paper that is of interest to students and relevant to their course and country of study. If you prefer, you can use one of the suggestions given below. These have been chosen because they should be of interest and relevance to students from a variety of disciplines and will enable you to highlight relevant key issues (sources and citations, interpretation of data, bias, positionality, validity and reliability, generalisability, authenticity and trustworthiness, for example).

Baker, S. (2017) 'Shifts in the treatment of knowledge in academic reading and writing: adding complexity to students' transitions between A-levels and university in the UK', *Arts and Humanities in Higher Education*, first published online 24 July 2017, http://doi.org/10.1177/1474022217722433.

Bell, R. (2016) 'Concerns and expectations of students participating in study abroad programmes: blogging to reveal the dynamic student voice', *Journal of Research in International Education*, 15 (3): 196-207, first published online 10 October 2016, http://doi.org/10.1177/1475240916669028.

Cooper, H. and Hughes, H. (2017) 'First-year international graduate students' transition to using a United States university library', IFLA Journal, first published online 15 August 2017, http://doi.org/10.1177/0340035217723355.

➜ Related activities

Activity 16: Reading academic texts effectively

Activity 52: Evaluating sources

Activity 54: Recognising statistics, facts, arguments and opinions

Activity 59: Learning how to question

Activity 63: Analysing and critiquing

....

➜ Preparatory reading

Tutorials about reading and critiquing can be found on YouTube (www.youtube.com). These are presented by academics from around the world and cover a number of different subject areas and disciplines, at a variety of levels. The search terms 'critiquing and reviewing', 'writing a critique' or 'research critique' find many of these videos. Some of the better videos can be recommended to students as preparatory work for this activity.

....

➜ Further reading

The following books can be recommended to students as both preparatory and further reading, depending on their level and subject of study.

Greenhalgh, T. (2014) *How to Read a Paper: the Basics of Evidence-based Medicine*, 5th edition. Chichester: Wiley-Blackwell.
Harris, S. (2014) *How to Critique Journal Articles in the Social Sciences*. Thousand Oaks, CA: Sage.
Holosko, M. (2006) *Primer for Critiquing Social Research: A Student Guide*. Belmont, CA: Wadsworth Publishing Co, Inc.
Shon, P. (2012) *How to Read Journal Articles in the Social Sciences: A Very Practical Guide for Students*. London: Sage.
Wallace, M. and Wray, A. (2011) *Critical Reading and Writing for Postgraduates*, 2nd edition. London: Sage.

Activity 21

Activity · · · · · · · · · ➔ 22

Taking notes effectively

The activity

Introduce the idea of a tip exchange to your students. You can do this in class or online. Explain that the resource is available for all students to exchange tips about how to take notes effectively and that it will be available throughout their course, if required. Set up a suitable digital platform on which students can post and read tips, ensuring that all students have access to this platform. Begin the tip exchange with a few of your own tips to get the resource started (see below). Encourage students to post and read tips as their course progresses, sending them a reminder from time to time. Monitor the posts to ensure that information is correct, constructive and useful.

An alternative way to run this activity is to ask students to produce a vlog or blog that provides advice and guidance to their peers about how to take notes effectively. Again, use a suitable digital platform and ensure that all students have access. Provide a deadline by which time vlogs and blogs must be posted. You can ask students to undertake this activity in small groups or individually, depending on your student cohort.

Key issues

Students post a wide variety of tips about taking notes effectively. This activity takes place throughout the course and, therefore, provides a useful indication of how students are learning and developing: tips at the beginning tend to be practical and straightforward, but then become more complex as courses progress (highlighting the need for critical note-taking and addressing epistemological assumptions, for example). Summaries of tips that have been posted are given below. They relate to note-taking from academic texts and note-taking in class (some of these can be used to get the resource started, if you feel it will be of benefit to your students).

- Develop a system of symbols and abbreviations that will help you to take notes more quickly. However, ensure that you know what the symbols and abbreviations mean when you review or revise your notes (produce and keep a symbols key, for example).
- Make notes that will aid your understanding and help you to review and revise what you have read.
- Don't copy chunks of text from a book or journal. Read the relevant sections, think about what you have read and make a few brief notes written in your own words. This will help you to understand what you are reading and will help you to avoid plagiarism (see Activity 56).
- If you come across a useful quotation, copy it exactly, word-for-word. Check that you have copied it correctly if you intend to use it in an assignment. In your notes, write 'quotation' in the margin, or use quotation marks so that you are clear that it is a quotation (see Activity 29). Take note of all the required bibliographical details.
- Organise your notes as soon as you start taking them (see Activity 23).
- When you have read a relevant text, take careful bibliographical details of what you have read. This will help you to find the source again, if you need to, and will enable you to include all the relevant information in the reference section and bibliography of your essays, assignments, projects and dissertations (see Activity 30). Apps and software are available for this task (students post links and reviews of the most useful tools).

- Use the correct referencing procedure as soon as your course begins so that you can develop good habits from the start (see Activity 30).
- Use online note-taking apps or software (students tend to provide links to these, along with comments about their usefulness and user-friendliness).
- Don't try to write down everything you read. Instead, stay alert for the main points and make sure that these are included in your notes. However, in maths and science subjects you might need to copy everything verbatim, as every symbol means something specific.
- Be selective about when you decide to write so that you don't miss any salient points.
- Use diagrams, if appropriate, to aid understanding.
- Leave wide margins on either side of your notes if using A4 paper so that you can add extra information when you review or revise your notes.
- Use question marks to query any information that you don't understand and to which you may need to return at a later date.
- If you read actively questions will form in your mind (see Activity 16). Jot down these questions: you can search for answers and clarification from a different source, if required.
- Take notes critically: think about what is written and provide a critique in your notes.
- Think about what you are reading: question assumptions and be a partner in knowledge construction when you take notes. Use these notes to develop further knowledge and test epistemological assumptions.

→ Related activities

Activity 23: Editing and organising notes

Activity 29: Paraphrasing, quoting and summarising

Activity 30: Citing, referencing and producing a bibliography

Activity 55: Organising, managing and storing information

Activity 56: Referencing, copyright and plagiarism

→ Preparatory reading

A useful summary of relevant journal papers about note-taking is in Oxford Bibliographies: http://www.oxfordbiblio graphies.com/view/document/obo-9780199756810/obo-9780199756810-0110.xml. These papers provide interesting preparatory reading for tutors [accessed 5 September 2017].

'The Conversation' is an 'independent source of news and views, sourced from the academic and research community and delivered direct to the public'. This site contains some interesting material on taking notes, which provides useful preparatory reading for this activity: http://theconversation.com/whats-the-best-most-effective-way-to-take-notes-41961 [accessed 5 September 2017].

→ Further reading

The following books provide comprehensive information about taking notes and can be recommended to students who need further help and advice (or they can be posted on the tip exchange).

Godfrey, J. (2014) *Reading and Making Notes*, 2nd edition. Basingstoke: Palgrave Macmillan.
Williams, K. (2017) *Referencing and Understanding Plagiarism*, 2nd edition. Basingstoke: Palgrave Macmillan.

Activity 22

Activity · · · · · · · · · · 23

Editing and organising notes

The activity

Ask your students to imagine that they are a writer for their student newspaper. They will be assigned a particular method that can be used for editing and organising notes (software, app or paper method: examples are given below). They must produce a review of this method for their student newspaper. Therefore, the review must be interesting and useful for other students, containing detailed information that will help their peers to assess the usefulness and user-friendliness of the method. Explain that all the reviews will be compiled into one resource, which will be sent to all students as a PDF. This will enable them to read each review and decide, for themselves, which method(s) would be useful to help them to edit and organise notes as their course progresses. You can ask students to undertake this activity on an individual basis or in small groups, depending on your student cohort. Provide a deadline by which time all reviews should be received.

The following list provides examples of software, apps and paper methods that you can assign to students. You can add to, delete and alter this list as appropriate (when new software or apps come on the market, for example). If you have a large number of individual students (or groups) you can assign methods more than once: reviews usually highlight different aspects of the method, so repetition tends to be avoided. The following list is produced in alphabetical order and contains a variety of different editing and organising methods.

A4 paper, dividers and ring binders	OneNote (www.onenote.com)
A5 shorthand notepads	Paper (www.fiftythree.com/paper)
Bear (www.bear-writer.com)	Paperwork (http://paperwork.rocks)
Box Notes (www.box.com/en-gb/notes)	Penultimate (https://evernote.com/products/penultimate)
Bullet Journal (http://bulletjournal.com)	Quip (https://quip.com)
Dropbox Paper (www.dropbox.com/paper)	Simplenote (https://simplenote.com)
Evernote (https://evernote.com)	SomNote (https://somcloud.com)
Ghostnote (http://www.ghostnoteapp.com)	Squid (http://squidnotes.com)
Google Keep (www.google.com/keep)	TiddlyWikki (http://tiddlywiki.com)
Letterspace (https://programmerbird.com/letterspace)	Workflowy (https://workflowy.com)
Notability (http://gingerlabs.com)	Zoho Notebook (https://zapier.com)

An alternative way to run this activity is to ask students to produce their review as a vlog or blog, which can be posted on a suitable digital platform for their peers to access. Again, this can be done on an individual or group basis, depending on your student cohort. Provide a deadline by which time all vlogs and blogs should be received. Monitor posts from time to time to ensure that information is correct, useful and constructive.

This activity covers similar ground to that presented in Activity 55, so choose the activity that is best suited to your students.

Key issues

This activity results in a number of comprehensive, useful and practical reviews about the different methods that students can use to edit and organise their notes. Reviews tend to cover some or all of the following issues (if you think students need further guidance in producing their reviews turn this list into a Student Handout):

- price (or free to access);
- contact details of supplier or links to websites;
- ease of use;
- scope;
- features;
- functionality;
- interface;
- sharing, collaboration and team communication;
- relevance to university-level study;
- usefulness for university-level study;
- compatibility with other software/devices;
- synchronisation (to the cloud, for example);
- strengths and weakness (or good and bad points);
- personal comments and preferences;
- availability of basic and premium versions, with associated costs and features.

→ **Cautionary note**

When you allocate the methods to your students, give the paper versions to some of the more tech-savvy students. At first they may be surprised or disappointed by this assignment. However, although they may perceive these methods to be old-fashioned, they tend to work hard on the review, sometimes applying technological features to the paper method (file management systems, tagging and synchronisation, for example). There is a danger that, if you assign the paper methods to students who are less tech-savvy, their reviews are perceived to be old-fashioned, less important or irrelevant in a modern world.

··

→ **Related activities**

Activity 22: Taking notes effectively

Activity 29: Paraphrasing, quoting and summarising

Activity 23

Activity 30: Citing, referencing and producing a bibliography

Activity 55: Organising, managing and storing information

....

➜ Preparatory reading

If you are unfamiliar with any of the software, apps or paper methods listed, you may find it useful preparatory work to visit the relevant websites to find out more about the methods. It is also useful to visit some product review sites for software and apps so that you can check that students do not merely copy existing reviews, vlogs or blogs.

....

➜ Further reading

Godfrey, J. (2014) *Reading and Making Notes*, 2nd edition. Basingstoke: Palgrave Macmillan. Parts 5, 6 and 7 provide useful information for students who want to follow up the issues raised in this activity.

Greetham, B. (2008) *How to Write Better Essays*, 2nd edition. Basingstoke: Palgrave Macmillan. Stage 2 of this book covers relevant issues and can be recommended to students who need more help on this topic.

Activity 23

Section 4 Writing

Activity • • • • • • • • • • ➜ 24

Developing academic writing skills

TUTOR NOTES

Purpose: This activity helps students to develop their academic writing skills through a structured support group. The group is 'structured' because it works through the following set tasks: discuss requirements, worries and concerns; practise writing and receive peer feedback; discuss writing experiences and develop a plan of action for further development.

Type: Structured support group.

Alternative type(s): One-to-one support session.

Level: Elementary, intermediate and advanced. Students at all levels of study might need help with their academic writing so these support sessions can run with students from the same level, or it is possible to combine students from all levels into one group.

Duration: Up to two hours of contact time (two sessions of 50 minutes to one hour) and several hours of work during independent study (the amount depends on student needs).

Equipment/materials: None required.

Learning outcome: By the end of this activity students will have practised and developed their academic writing skills, with peer support and encouragement, and will feel more confident about their ability to produce written work at the required level as their studies progress.

The activity

Invite together a group of students who feel that they need help to develop their academic writing skills (try to ensure that those who could benefit most from the group are invited to attend). The students that join the group could be from one course and one level or from a range of courses and levels. The group should not be too large: ten to 14 participants is ideal (even numbers are desirable so that students can be paired together). Explain the purpose and format of the structured support session. First, you will meet in a 50 minute to one hour session to discuss what is meant by academic writing, what is required and talk about worries and concerns that students may have about producing written work at the required level.

At the end of this session you will pair students together so that they can provide help, support and encouragement for their partner in the second stage of this activity. This stage requires students to practise writing by completing an assignment, project or other written coursework. When they have produced a draft copy of their work they should swap with their partner for constructive feedback, support and encouragement, before producing their final version. The duration of this stage depends on assignment/project timetables (these differ considerably, depending on level of study: if you have a group of students from different levels you may need to set a piece of written work that they can all work on over the same period of time). Students can also meet other group members on an informal basis at this stage, if they feel that support and encouragement from other group members would be of use.

The final stage of this activity requires the group to reconvene for another 50 minutes to one hour session to discuss their writing experiences and talk about any other worries and concerns they may have. They then go on to build a plan of action that will help them to develop their academic writing skills further and enable them to feel confident that they can produce written work at the required level as their studies progress.

It is possible to run this activity as a one-to-one support session with individual students, if you have time available and it better suits your students. You will need to be available to offer support throughout the activity if this option is chosen.

Key issues

The first session can address the following questions:

1. What is meant by the term 'academic writing'? What level, standard and content of work is required?
2. Do students have any worries and concerns about their ability to produce academic writing? If so, what are their worries and concerns and what strategies can be adopted to overcome these concerns? Issues raised include:

   a. not knowing the level and standard of work required;
   b. fearing that they will fail or that their work is not good enough;
   c. thinking that everyone can write better than them;
   d. negative feelings from poor performance at school;
   e. writer's block (see Activity 32);
   f. not knowing where to start;
   g. difficulty reading texts (see Activity 16) and knowing how to take notes (see Activity 22);
   h. wanting to know more about how to read and write critically and produce an argument that is more than mere opinion (see Activity 28);
   i. wanting to know how to cite and reference correctly (see Activity 30);
   j. difficulties with punctuation, spelling and grammar (see Activity 31);
   k. producing work at the required intellectual level (this is often mentioned by postgraduate students who have returned to education after a period of time away in employment).

3. How can students overcome negative feelings about writing? What positive feelings do they have about writing and how can they use these positive feelings to help them produce good written work?
4. What is involved in the writing process? This discussion can focus on both the practicalities, such as how to structure an assignment and produce an argument (see Activity 28), but also on attitudes and attributes required, such as discipline, persistence, collaboration, diligence, concentration and attention to detail.
5. How to provide constructive and supportive peer feedback for the second part of this activity (see Baker 2016 for an interesting paper on student peer review).

The second session can be used to evaluate students' experiences of their first writing assignment. This session should discuss how they felt about producing the assignment, possible problems encountered, how these were overcome and the usefulness of receiving peer feedback, support and encouragement. It should go on to look at what action students can take to develop their writing skills and increase their confidence. This can include:

- reading books such as those listed below;
- writing as much as possible;
- attending relevant workshops or enrolling on relevant courses;
- listening to and acting on tutor feedback (see Activity 48);
- offering and receiving peer support and encouragement;
- developing support networks or writing circles (see Activity 25).

➜ Related activities

Activity 16: Reading academic texts effectively

Activity 26: Structuring written work

Activity 28: Producing an effective argument

Activity 30: Citing, referencing and producing a bibliography

Activity 31: Engaging with spelling, punctuation and grammar

Activity 32: Overcoming difficulties with writing

....

Activity 24

➜ Preparatory reading

Baker, K. (2016) 'Peer review as a strategy for improving students' writing process', *Active Learning in Higher Education*, 17 (3): 179-92, first published 30 June 2016, http://doi.org/10.1177/1469787416654794. This paper reports on a study that looks at the peer review process. The section on peer feedback is of particular relevance and provides useful preparatory reading for tutors for this activity.

➜ Further reading

The following books can be recommended to students studying at various levels who feel they need more help with their academic writing.

Day, T. (2013) *Success in Academic Writing*. Basingstoke: Palgrave Macmillan.
Greetham, B. (2013) *How to Write Better Essays*, 3rd edition. Basingstoke: Palgrave Macmillan.
Osmond, A. (2016) *Academic Writing and Grammar for Students*, 2nd edition. London: Sage.
Redman, P. and Maples, W. (2017) *Good Essay Writing*, 5th edition. London: Sage.
Wallace, M and Wray, A. (2016) *Critical Reading and Writing for Postgraduates*, 3rd edition. London: Sage.

Activity 24

Activity · · · · · · · · · → 25

Establishing academic writing circles

The activity

Invite together students who feel that they could benefit from becoming a member of a writing circle. This could be because they wish to improve their writing, they need support and encouragement from their peers, they want feedback on their work, they wish to share ideas or purely for interest and enjoyment, for example. Lead a discussion on expectations, code of conduct, goals and outcomes and discuss their preferred structure (see below). Set a date, time and venue for their first meeting and discuss whether or not preparation is required (see below). Once you have done this, the group can be left to its own devices, although you may find it prudent to make contact a few weeks later to check that the circle is running smoothly and that all students are happy with the structure and format.

Key issues

There are different structures and formats for writing circles, so it is important that you discuss preferences with students before the group convenes for the first time. In some cases you may need to set up several groups to suit different tastes and levels of study, or you might need more than one group if a large number of students have expressed an interest (five to seven students is a good number for a productive writing circle). The following list provides examples of different types of writing circle and students should be encouraged to discuss the format that works best for them.

- Structured workshops at the same time each week, in the same location, with the same members. There is an expectation that all members will attend, if possible. The group is led by an experienced facilitator who helps members to improve their writing and feel more confident about completing written work.

- Informal gatherings where members come together to discuss a piece of writing they are in the process of completing (an assignment, project or thesis chapter, for example). They share ideas, offer support and give feedback on what has already been written. The date and time for the next meeting is discussed at the end of each session, and depends on study commitments and assignment deadlines. Refreshments can be taken during the meeting. Members can attend when they feel the need and new members can join at any time.
- Email groups that respond to short literacy challenges, contribute to group discussions and cooperate in group

writing projects. The expectation is that all members will contribute when required.

- Monthly meetings with specific timetables that include invited guest speakers, exercises to improve writing and stimulate ideas, group discussions and the completion of specific writing tasks.
- Online communities that post examples of their writing, offer and receive peer feedback and join online discussions to share ideas, tips and writing experiences.
- Weekly or fortnightly meetings in which participants write for a set period of time. This can be for an assignment, dissertation or thesis chapter, for example. Writing is conducted in silence, but time can be set aside at the end for discussion, if required.

When establishing a writing circle it is important to ensure that:

- all group members are clear about the purpose;
- all group members know how to behave;
- every member of the group has a chance to speak, read out their work or comment on another's work, depending on the format of the circle;
- writing and literary tasks are manageable and aimed at the right level;
- there is a competent person available to lead, coordinate, facilitate or manage the group (this depends on student preferences for structure and format);

- all group members are clear about time and dates;
- meetings are arranged when everyone can attend;
- the meeting space is appropriate for the type of group and free from disturbances and distractions;
- all group members feel that attendance is of personal benefit and that the writing circle meets their needs and expectations.

➜ Related activities

Activity 8: Becoming part of a learning community

Activity 24: Developing academic writing skills

Activity 26: Structuring written work

Activity 65: Getting the most out of group work

Activity 71: Understanding group dynamics and avoiding conflict

➜ Preparatory reading

Plakhotnik, M. and Rocco, T. (2012) 'Implementing writing support circles with adult learners in a nonformal education setting', *Adult Learning*, 23 (2): 76–81, first published 1 May 2012, http://doi.org/10.1177/1045159512443507. This paper discusses Writing Support Circles that were set up for a small group of Latina students at a large South Eastern public research university in the US and provides interesting preparatory reading for tutors.

➜ Further reading

Aitchison, C. and Guerin, C. (eds) (2014) *Writing Groups for Doctoral Education and Beyond: Innovations in Practice and Theory*. Abingdon, Oxon: Routledge. This collection of papers provides an interesting and relevant read for tutors and advanced-level students.

Martin, K. and Ko, L. (2011) 'Thoughts on being productive during a graduate program: the process and benefits of a peer working group', *Health Promotion Practice*, 12 (1): 12–17. This paper provides some interesting material on the advantages of peer support groups for doctorate students, and provides useful reading for tutors.

Pasternak, D., Longwell-Grice, H., Shea, K. and Hanson, L. (2009) 'Alien environments or supportive writing communities? Pursuing writing groups in academe', *Arts and Humanities in Higher Education*, 8 (3): 355–67, first published 23 September 2009. This paper presents an interesting dialogue about joining and becoming a member of a writer's group.

Activity 25

Activity · · · · · · · · · · ➔ 26

Structuring written work

Student handout page 304

TUTOR NOTES

Purpose: This activity is aimed at students who are new to writing assignments at university level. It requires students, in small groups, to read, discuss and critique the structure of two written assignments (a well-structured assignment and a badly structured assignment). Groups then go on to produce a checklist that will help them to structure assignments as their course progresses. The group exercise is followed by a tutor-led discussion on the issues raised.

Type: Group exercise followed by tutor-led discussion.

Alternative type(s): Self-guided individual exercise followed by tutor-led discussion.

Level: Elementary.

Duration: Students require a few hours during independent study to work on the exercise with their group members, followed by up to 50 minutes of contact time for the tutor-led discussion. A similar amount of time is required if the self-guided individual exercise option is chosen. Tutors need to spend a few hours writing, preparing or finding suitable assignment examples when this activity is run for the first time.

Equipment/materials: Two sample assignments.

Learning outcome: By the end of this activity students will have a greater understanding of how to produce a well-structured assignment, which will help them to feel more confident and knowledgeable about producing assignments as their course progresses.

The activity

Divide your students into small groups and give them a copy of the Student Handout along with your examples of a well-structured and a badly structured assignment (both assignments should address the same question). Students are to read through the assignments and discuss and critique them with their group members during independent study. They must then develop a checklist that will help them to produce well-structured assignments as their course progresses. Explain that you will discuss the issues raised by this exercise when you next meet, so students should think about questions that they might like to ask during the session. If contact time is limited you can hold, instead, an online discussion using a suitable digital platform. It is possible to ask students to undertake this activity on an individual basis, rather than in groups, if it better suits your student cohort (the Student Handout will need to be amended accordingly).

Key issues

This activity needs two assignments: one well-structured and the other badly structured. They must reflect the type of assignment that students will face on your course. If you choose to produce the assignments yourself you can ensure that they are relevant in terms of topic, content and length. You can also ensure that all the pertinent points listed below are included for students to discover (some should be obvious and others more subtle). It takes time to produce these assignments, but they only need to be produced once and can be reused with subsequent cohorts. It is an interesting process that helps tutors to reconnect with students. However, if you do not have the time available, find examples of previous assignments that you can prepare for the exercise, ensuring anonymity and paying close attention to any other ethical issues that reuse may entail. Some universities provide model papers for the use of students and tutors (see, for example, papers at Yale Center for Teaching and Learning: http://ctl.yale.edu/writing/undergraduate-writing/model-papers-disciplines).

Issues that can be incorporated into your two assignments are listed below. These issues can be used as a basis for discussion when you next meet. Ensure that you also take time to answer student questions and discuss the criteria that will be used to evaluate or assess student assignments (see Activity 88).

A well-structured assignment should have a clear and distinct introduction, discussion and conclusion:

- The introduction articulates the question to be addressed, suggesting why the question is of interest and stating clearly the writer's position on the topic.
- The discussion consists of a series of paragraphs, each of which focuses on one point towards proving the argument (or answering the question). Each paragraph forms a chain of reasoning that provides a logical and/or convincing argument, backed up by relevant evidence. Topic sentences introduce each paragraph and transition sentences, phrases or words are used to move to the next point. Facts and evidence are analysed and discussed. Quotations, summaries, data and references are used, where required. Relevance of evidence is demonstrated and generalisations are avoided. Each paragraph is concluded before moving to the next (with bridges and transitions used to move the argument forward).
- The conclusion re-establishes the main claim or position that was presented in the introduction. It illustrates the importance and relevance of the argument or shows the overall significance of what has been covered. In some cases it can also point to the limitations of the argument and the possibility for further research.

A badly structured assignment does not have a clear and distinct introduction, discussion and conclusion. In particular:

- The introduction is missing. The student begins to answer the question immediately with no introductory paragraph about what the assignment sets out to achieve.
- Too many ideas are contained within one paragraph and there are no topic sentences or concluding sentences to move the argument forward.
- Arguments are muddled and do not follow a logical or convincing order (see Activity 28).
- Paraphrases and summaries ramble on and miss the point of the argument (see Activity 29).
- Opinions are disguised as arguments and statements are not backed up by evidence (see Activity 28).
- References and quotations are missing, irrelevant, in the wrong place or written incorrectly (see Activities 29 and 30).
- Visual data are presented in the wrong place or not referred to in the text.
- Too many bullet points are used (there are not enough well-written paragraphs and sentences).
- New ideas are introduced into the conclusion.
- There is no conclusion or the conclusion is a mere sentence that restates that given in the introduction.

➜ Related activities

Activity 24: Developing academic writing skills

Activity 25: Establishing academic writing circles

Activity 28: Producing an effective argument

Activity 88: Knowing about the different methods of assessment

....

➜ Preparatory reading

It is useful to prepare for this activity by finding out about assignment information and guidelines available on your institution's website, intranet or VLE so that you know what is available and can make suitable recommendations for students. It is also useful to find out what is available in terms of workshops or short courses, if students need more help with structuring and writing assignments.

....

Activity 26

➜ Further reading

The following books provide comprehensive information about structuring written work and can be recommended to students who wish to follow up any of the issues raised by this activity.

Day, T. (2013) *Success in Academic Writing*. Basingstoke: Palgrave Macmillan.
Godwin, J. (2014) *Planning your Essay*, 2nd edition. Basingstoke: Palgrave Macmillan.
Greetham, B. (2013) *How to Write Better Essays*, 3rd edition. Basingstoke: Palgrave Macmillan.

Activity 26

Activity • • • • • • • • • • ➔ 27
Editing and proofreading

Student
handout
page 305

TUTOR NOTES

Purpose: This activity is an entertaining game that enables students to think more about what is required when editing and proofreading their written work. It requires students, in small groups, to produce a piece of written work that deliberately contains a number of mistakes and errors that need to be corrected through editing and proofreading. This is done by other groups, with the most successful group deemed to be the winner.

Type: Game.

Alternative type(s): None.

Level: Elementary and advanced (this is useful for students studying at postgraduate level who have had some time away from education, before returning to their studies: the level of study is reflected in the written work that is produced).

Duration: Students need to spend a few hours in their groups during independent study producing their piece of written work. Up to two hours of contact time is required to play the game (the actual time spent on this depends on the number of student groups and the length of written work produced: see below).

Equipment/materials: None required.

Learning outcome: By the end of this activity students will have a greater understanding of what to look for when editing and proofreading their work and will feel more confident in carrying out these tasks as their course progresses.

The activity

Divide your students into groups (three or four groups is usually a good number for this activity). Give each group a copy of the Student Handout. This explains how to play the game and what is required of them (a piece of written work of a specific length containing deliberate errors for others to spot). Run the game when you next meet. If you only have three or four groups it is possible to complete this game in an hour: if you have more groups you may need up to two hours (you can reduce the contact time required if you reduce the length of written work produced by groups).

During the game element of this activity students must edit and proofread the written work that has been produced by other groups, making a list of all the errors and mistakes they have found. When the game has concluded (groups need to spend around 20 minutes on each piece of written work) spend a little time discussing the issues raised. This can include, for example:

- The difference between editing (how ideas and information are presented) and proofreading (errors in spelling, grammar, syntax, punctuation and formatting, for example). Were all these included in the written work and did students spot them?

- Editing is an essential part of forming a good argument and can, therefore, occur at several stages during the writing process, rather than just at the end (ask whether students edited the written piece of work they produced for this activity: some will not have realised that they were doing this as the written work was produced).

- What to edit (content, overall structure, paragraph structure, clarity, style, citations, argument and evidence, for example).
- Proofreading tips:

  o don't rely on spelling and grammar checking software;

  o leave time between finishing writing and proofreading;

  o read slowly and read every word, out loud if it works for you;

  o choose a medium that works for you (paper or electronic);

  o swap with a friend and proofread each other's work.

At the end of the game and discussion ask students to count the total errors and mistakes they have spotted and award a small prize to the winning group, if you feel this is appropriate. On occasions you will notice that groups find an unintentional error (one that their peers did not place deliberately within their text), which raises an interesting discussion in itself (did groups edit and proofread their own piece of written work before passing it on, for example?).

Key issues

This activity works well because students, in their groups, must think about what editing and proofreading entails, the tasks that are involved and the type of errors and mistakes that need to be spotted and corrected when editing and proofreading. It raises issues such as citing, referencing, quoting and paraphrasing (see Activities 29 and 30); producing arguments (see Activity 28); spelling, punctuation and grammar (see Activity 31); and the use, abuse and misuse of statistics (see Activity 36). Students are able to learn from each other in their groups, bounce ideas off each other and offer advice and guidance to those with less experience. Also, because this activity is a game (with a competition element if you think this is suitable for your students) it makes what can sometimes be seen as a mundane and monotonous task more interesting, entertaining and memorable.

➜ Cautionary note

There are various editing and proofreading digital tools available and often it is too easy for students to rely on these tools. This activity is best conducted as a paper exercise: when it was tried as a digital exercise, students tended to use the digital tools and little benefit was gained from the activity. If you have time available it is important to stress that students should not rely on these tools when completing their own work. The tools should only be used to complement and enhance personal, diligent editing and proofreading.

··

➜ Related activities

Activity 24: Developing academic writing skills

Activity 28: Producing an effective argument

Activity 30: Citing, referencing and producing a bibliography

Activity 31: Engaging with spelling, punctuation and grammar

Activity 36: The use, abuse and misuse of statistics

··

➜ Preparatory reading

Schrier, K. (2016) *Knowledge Games: How Playing Games can Solve Problems, Create Insight, and Make Change*. Baltimore, MD: Johns Hopkins University Press. This book provides useful preparatory reading for tutors who are interested in using games in their teaching.

··

➜ Further reading

Students and tutors in the UK can refer to the *New Oxford Style Manual* (2016), *New Oxford Spelling Dictionary* (2014) and the *New Hart's Rules* (2014), all produced by Oxford University Press.

Students and tutors in the US can refer to the Chicago Manual of Style online: www.chicagomanualofstyle.org/help-tools/resources.html. The *Chicago Manual of Style* is now in its seventeenth edition (2017) and provides the 'definitive guide for anyone who works with words'.

Activity 27

Activity • • • • • • • • • → 28

Producing an effective argument

Student handout page 306

TUTOR NOTES

Purpose: This activity encourages students to think about how to produce an effective argument by requiring them, in small groups, to produce a poster presentation on this topic that is presented to their peers in a dedicated session.

Type: Group exercise followed by poster presentation.

Alternative type(s): Tip exchange.

Level: Elementary, intermediate and advanced.

Duration: Students need to spend a few hours working with their group members to hold discussions, carry out research and produce their poster presentations. One to two hours of contact time is required for students to present their posters and discuss with their peers (the actual time taken depends on the number and content of poster presentations).

Equipment/materials: Students need access to poster presentation software. A suitable venue in which posters can be displayed and discussed is required.

Learning outcome: By the end of this activity students will have a greater understanding of how to produce an effective argument and will feel more confident and knowledgeable about producing such arguments as their course progresses.

The activity

Divide your students into small groups and ask them to research, prepare and create a poster presentation on how to produce an effective argument. They must do this during independent study. Give a date, time and venue when the posters are to be presented so that each group can work to the given deadline (if you choose a time that is outside your usual class hours, ensure that all students are able to attend the session). Give details of the venue so that groups know what equipment and space is available for their poster presentation.

Decide how you wish to run the poster presentation session. You can keep it free-flowing and informal, enabling students to wander between posters and discuss them with the presenters, or you can ask each group to present their poster in turn to their peers, allowing enough time for questions and discussion after each presentation. Some students may be unfamiliar with the poster presentation technique. If this is the case, give them a copy of the Student Handout as this gives advice and information about producing a poster presentation.

It is possible to run this activity as a tip exchange if you do not have the contact time available for poster presentations. Ask your students to think about useful tips that will help their peers to produce an effective argument and post them on a suitable digital platform. Begin the tip exchange with a few of your own tips to get the resource started. Decide whether to make it compulsory for students to add tips (provide a deadline if this option is chosen) or whether to make it a voluntary resource. Monitor the posts from time to time to ensure that information is correct, constructive and useful.

Key issues

Students must produce a clear and concise poster presentation for this activity. To do this they must first of all get to grips with the topic and think carefully about how to produce an effective argument. This activity helps them to focus their thoughts, think about the pertinent points and work out how best to communicate these to their peers.

No two poster presentations are the same. Some students focus on one particular issue, such as how to back up an argument with evidence or how to construct an argument, whereas others cover a series of stages including choosing a topic, predicting opposing arguments, considering audience, deciding on points to argue (or refute), finding and analysing evidence, drafting, revising, editing and proofreading. Others provide examples of how argumentation can be conflated with opinion, with advice offered about how to avoid this. One group of advanced-level students chose to highlight 'the flawed logical thinking' of argumentation that works on the assumption that facts and certainties are there to be discovered, reported and analysed. Another group chose to critique the way that argumentation is taught in school (interpretation of a text from a personal viewpoint), rather than finding, critiquing, analysing and interpreting other viewpoints, in addition to one's own.

This activity is flexible enough to enable students to choose an issue that is of interest and relevance and it encourages a wide coverage of the topic. This helps to motivate and inspire students so that they can learn from each other, and it enables them to remember information because it is presented in a visually engaging way.

➜ Related activities

Activity 24: Developing academic writing skills

Activity 26: Structuring written work

Activity 27: Editing and proofreading

Activity 29: Paraphrasing, quoting and summarising

Activity 63: Analysing and critiquing

➜ Preparatory reading

Swatridge, C. (2014) *Oxford Guide to Effective Argument and Critical Thinking*. Oxford: Oxford University Press. This book provides comprehensive information about arguing and critical thinking and is useful for tutors who would like to prepare for this activity. It can also be recommended as further reading to students who are studying at intermediate and advanced level.

➜ Further reading

The following books can be recommended to students who wish to follow up the issues raised in this activity.

Birkenstein, C. and Graff, G. (2018) *They Say/I Say: the Moves that Matter in Academic Writing*, 4th edition. New York: W.W. Norton and Co., Inc.
Bonnett, A. (2011) *How to Argue*, 3rd edition. Harlow: Pearson Education Ltd.
Cooper, H. and Shoolbred, M. (2016) *Where's Your Argument?* London: Palgrave.
Weston, A. (2009) *Rulebook for Arguments*, 4th edition. Indianapolis, IN: Hackett Publishing Co., Inc.

Activity 28

Activity • • • • • • • • • • ➔ 29

Paraphrasing, quoting and summarising

Student
handout
page 307

> **TUTOR NOTES**
>
> **Purpose:** This activity is a worksheet that enables students to understand what is meant by paraphrasing, quoting and summarising, and work out how, when and why these techniques should be used in their written work.
>
> **Type:** Student worksheet.
>
> **Alternative type(s):** Tutor-led class discussion followed by individual exercise.
>
> **Level:** Elementary.
>
> **Duration:** Students will spend one or two hours working on the questions during independent study. If the tutor-led class discussion option is chosen you need 50 minutes to one hour of contact time and one or two hours during independent study for students to work on the individual exercise.
>
> **Equipment/materials:** None required for the worksheet. If the tutor-led class discussion option is chosen, you need to provide a suitable piece of written work for the individual exercise component of the activity.
>
> **Learning outcome:** By the end of this activity students will understand what is meant by paraphrasing, quoting and summarising and will know how, when and why to use these techniques in their written work.

The activity

Give the Student Handout to your students. This is a worksheet that helps students to understand what is meant by paraphrasing, quoting and summarising, and encourages them to think about how, when and why these techniques are used in written assignments. Students should complete the worksheet during independent study. Decide whether you would like students to hand their work in for assessment and feedback and, if so, give a deadline by which time the work should be submitted.

It is possible to run this activity as a tutor-led class discussion followed by an individual exercise. Use the questions given in the Student Handout as a basis for the class discussion. Once this has been completed, give your students a suitable piece of written work and ask that they practise paraphrasing, quoting and summarising during independent study. Again, decide whether you would like the work to be handed in for assessment and feedback.

Key issues

This activity is a quick and simple way to introduce the topics of paraphrasing, quoting and summarising without taking up contact time. It is useful to ask students to complete this worksheet early in their course so that you can check that they have understood and can use the techniques when you assess their first assignment. Further reading and free courses are listed below if you feel that they need more help and guidance after having assessed their first assignment.

➜ Cautionary note

There are a variety of paraphrasing and summarising tools (software, apps and free online converters) available. It is important to stress to students that these tools are no substitute for personal, critical reading and analysis. Cutting and pasting into these tools is not acceptable and it is easily spotted when students do this (you may find it useful to try out some of these tools so that you become familiar with the way that they paraphrase and summarise text and can recognise their use in the work of students, if you have not already done so). An interesting discussion about the use of paraphrasing software can be found in the following paper:

Rogerson, A. and McCarthy, G. (2017) 'Using internet based paraphrasing tools: original work, patchwriting or facilitated plagiarism?', *International Journal for Educational Integrity*, 13 (2), http://doi.org/10.1007/s40979-016-0013-y.

➜ Related activities

Activity 28: Producing an effective argument

Activity 30: Citing, referencing and producing a bibliography

Activity 51: Using primary and secondary sources

Activity 56: Referencing, copyright and plagiarism

Activity 63: Analysing and critiquing

➜ Preparatory reading

Preparatory reading is not required for this activity (students will read around the subject when they complete the worksheet and tutors will be familiar with the topic).

Further reading

McMillan, K. and Weyers, J. (2013) *How to Cite, Reference and Avoid Plagiarism at University*. Harlow: Pearson. Chapters 7, 8 and 9 of this book provide information about, and practical examples of, paraphrasing, quoting and summarising and can be recommended to students who wish to follow up issues raised by this activity.

Godfrey, J. (2016) *Writing for University*, 2nd edition. London: Palgrave. 'Essential element 2' of this book covers quoting, paraphrasing and summarising and is a simple guide that can be recommended to students.

The Open University in the UK has two free courses available called 'Paraphrasing text' and 'Summarising text' (http://www.open.edu/openlearn). These courses are aimed at university students and provide the opportunity to practise paraphrasing and summarising. They can be recommended to students who need further help with these tasks (perhaps when problems become apparent after their first assignment has been assessed, for example).

Activity 29

Activity · · · · · · · · · · ➔ 30

Citing, referencing and producing a bibliography

Student
handout
page 308

TUTOR NOTES

Purpose: This activity helps students to understand how to cite, reference and produce a bibliography by asking them, in their groups, to teach these topics to their peers. To do this effectively they must first understand how to carry out these tasks themselves.

Type: Peer teaching.

Alternative type(s): Video/podcast production (in groups during independent study).

Level: Elementary, intermediate and advanced (this activity can act as a refresher for students studying at intermediate and advanced levels).

Duration: Students need to spend a few hours during independent study preparing their teaching session with their group members. One to two hours of contact time is required for students to teach their peers (this depends on the number of groups). If the video/podcast option is chosen students need to spend a few hours preparing, producing and uploading their video/podcast, and up to an hour viewing and commenting on the videos/podcasts of their peers. Tutors need to spend a little time reviewing and checking the videos and posts.

Equipment/materials: Students can use any presentation/teaching equipment, materials and props that they deem appropriate and these should be made available for their use.

Learning outcome: By the end of this activity students will understand how to cite, reference and produce a bibliography and will be able to apply this understanding during their course when producing assignments, projects and dissertations.

The activity

Divide your students into groups and give them a copy of the Student Handout. This asks them to teach about citing, referencing and producing a bibliography to their peers in the next contact session. They must prepare and practise their teaching session during independent study. When you next meet, allocate 20 minutes for each teaching session, with a small amount of time at the end to discuss issues raised. You can also ask students to evaluate each other's teaching sessions, perhaps deciding on the most useful, effective, memorable and interesting session.

If contact time is not available you can ask that students turn their teaching session into a video/podcast that can be uploaded, viewed and discussed on a suitable digital platform (the Student Handout will need to be adapted accordingly). If you choose this option, give a deadline by which time all videos must be uploaded. Encourage students to view and discuss each other's videos and monitor videos and posts to ensure that information is correct, supportive and encouraging.

Key issues

This activity has produced some interesting teaching sessions. Some groups concentrate on the minutiae of the topic, producing concise slides and/or handouts that explain, in detail, how to cite, reference and produce a bibliography. Others consider the overall topic, illustrating why it is important to undertake these tasks correctly (avoiding plagiarism, copyright infringement and highlighting 'best practice', for example). Some groups teach about software and apps that are available, explaining how they can be used, highlighting potential problems and suggesting solutions to overcome these problems. One group produced an exercise where they had removed references from a paper and asked their peers to work through the paper, pointing out where work had been cited and where references were missing.

➜ Cautionary note

This activity tends to produce a variety of teaching sessions in which most aspects of citing, referencing and producing a bibliography are covered. However, some teaching sessions are more useful and informative than others. You may find it useful, therefore, to produce a handout containing specific information about following correct procedures at your institution that can be given to students at the end of the session, if this information is not given by any of the student groups. Alternatively, you can ensure that your students know where to obtain this information from your institution's website/VLE. If you choose the video/podcast option, this information can be uploaded onto the digital resource.

➜ Related activities

Activity 22: Taking notes effectively

Activity 23: Editing and organising notes

Activity 29: Paraphrasing, quoting and summarising

Activity 51: Using primary and secondary sources

Activity 55: Organising, managing and storing information

Activity 56: Referencing, copyright and plagiarism

➜ Preparatory reading

Most universities produce information about citing, referencing and producing a bibliography on their website, intranet or VLE. This includes information about their referencing policy. Also, your institution may run workshops or tutorials on topics such as using reference managing software and tools, annotated bibliographies, citing quotations and referencing. It is useful to find out what is available so that these can be recommended to students who wish to follow up any of the issues raised by this activity.

➜ Further reading

The following books can be recommended to students who need more information (the references can be posted on your digital resource if the video/podcast option is chosen).

Godfrey, J. (2013) *How to Use Your Reading in Your Essays*, 2nd edition. Basingstoke: Palgrave Macmillan.
Neville, C. (2016) *The Complete Guide to Referencing and Avoiding Plagiarism*, 3rd edition. London: Open University Press.
Pears, R. and Shields, G. (2016) *Cite Them Right: the Essential Referencing Guide*, 10th edition. London: Palgrave.
Williams, K. and Carroll, J. (2009) *Referencing and Understanding Plagiarism*. Basingstoke: Palgrave Macmillan.

Activity 30

Activity • • • • • • • • • • → 31

Engaging with spelling, punctuation and grammar

TUTOR NOTES

Purpose: This activity helps students to engage with spelling, punctuation and grammar through the establishment of a tutor-led information and support network that provides information, guidance, encouragement, support and mentoring at the beginning and throughout their course. It is of particular use for students who have entered higher education through non-traditional routes who may feel unconfident about engaging with spelling, punctuation and grammar.

Type: Tutor-led information and support network (face-to-face and online).

Alternative type(s): None.

Level: Elementary (this activity should be started at elementary level, but can continue right through an undergraduate course: students who need help at the beginning of their course often return in their third year to offer support to new students).

Duration: Fifty minutes to one hour for an informal introductory session. Additional tutor time depends on student requirements (see below). The amount of time students spend on this activity depends on personal requirements.

Equipment/materials: It is useful to have an informal meeting space, away from the classroom. You also need a suitable digital platform on which to build the digital resource.

Learning outcome: By the end of this activity students will feel more engaged with spelling, punctuation and grammar, which will help them to feel more confident when producing written work for their studies and beyond.

The activity

This activity is aimed at students who do not feel engaged with spelling, punctuation and grammar, perhaps because they have had a long time away from education, have experienced problems in the past or generally feel unconfident about their ability to produce written work at the required level for university study. Invite these students to attend a special session, in a comfortable environment away from the classroom, where you can introduce the information and support network. Try to ensure that those students who could benefit most are invited. Use this session to discuss issues such as worries and concerns, previous educational experiences and hopes and aspirations for the future. Find out what students hope to gain from being part of this information and support network (the structure, style and content of support network depend on your student cohort: see key issues).

This activity should be introduced early in the course, for students studying at elementary level. However, the network can be available for the duration of a three-year course so that students can access information and support when required, throughout their studies. Students that have been involved with the network and received support and encouragement from their peers often return to mentor new students. They provide invaluable help and support because they have had similar experiences and can empathise with their peers.

Key issues

The structure, style and content of the information and support network can vary, depending on your student cohort. The following list provides examples of what can be included:

- A digital resource that includes:

  o details of relevant courses and workshops, including times and dates;
  o links to relevant learner development or study skills advice from your institution (if available);
  o information about learner development units/study skills staff who are available to offer one-to-one support and guidance;
  o times of tutor availability to offer support for students who are struggling with an assignment;
  o a tip exchange for students to offer tips such as rhymes to help remember rules, examples of good and bad punctuation, links to useful websites and details of relevant apps, for example;
  o useful references (see further reading);
  o a discussion forum or question and answer section for students to seek advice about specific issues they encounter when producing written work.
- A peer mentoring programme so that third-year students can offer support, advice and encouragement to first-year students (see Activity 12 for more information on voluntary peer mentoring).
- Informal social gatherings for students to meet and discuss relevant issues in a supportive and non-competitive environment.
- A student partner programme that pairs students together to proofread each other's work to help them gain skills and confidence.
- Presentations and talks given by third-year students who have been able to overcome issues with engagement.

→ Related activities

Activity 12: Completing coursework and meeting deadlines

Activity 24: Developing academic writing skills

Activity 25: Establishing academic writing circles

Activity 26: Structuring written work

Activity 27: Editing and proofreading

....

→ Preparatory reading

The BBC website in the UK provides useful and straightforward information and advice on literacy skills for adults (www.bbc.co.uk/skillswise/english). The website contains videos, games and factsheets on reading, writing, spelling and grammar at Entry levels 1, 2 and 3, and at Level 1. A link to this site can be added to your digital resource if you think it would be of benefit to your students.

....

→ Further reading

The following books are useful for students and can be added to your digital resource.

Butterfield, J. (2013) Oxford A-Z of English Usage, 2nd edition. Oxford: Oxford University Press.
Buxton, C. (2013) Oxford A-Z of Better Spelling, revised 2nd edition. Oxford: Oxford University Press.
Seely, J. (2013) Oxford A-Z of Grammar and Punctuation, revised 2nd edition. Oxford: Oxford University Press.
Thornton, R. (2006) Adult Learners' Writing Guide: Improve Your Writing Skills, Edinburgh: Chambers Harrap Publishers Ltd.

Activity 31

Activity • • • • • • • • • • ➔ 32

Overcoming difficulties with writing

TUTOR NOTES

Purpose: This activity enables students to exchange tips about how to overcome difficulties with writing. It builds a useful resource that can be accessed by students when required over the duration of their course.

Type: Tip exchange (student-centred digital resource).

Alternative type(s): Vlogs and blogs.

Level: Elementary, intermediate and advanced (the level is reflected in the tips offered).

Duration: A few minutes of tutor time is required to set up the tip exchange and a few minutes to monitor the resource. Students will spend a few minutes posting and reading tips, when required.

Equipment/materials: A suitable digital platform and access for all students.

Learning outcome: By the end of this activity students will have built a useful resource that enables them to exchange tips about how to overcome difficulties with writing, which will help them to address problems and complete written work as their course progresses.

The activity

Introduce the tip exchange to your students, in class or online. Explain that the resource is available for all students to exchange tips about how to overcome difficulties with writing and that it will be available throughout their course. Set up a suitable digital platform on which students can post and read tips and ensure that all students have access to this platform. Begin the tip exchange with a few of your own tips to get the resource started (see below). Decide whether to make it compulsory for students to add tips (provide a deadline if this option is chosen) or whether to make it a voluntary resource. Monitor the posts from time to time to ensure that information is correct, constructive and useful.

An alternative way to run this activity is to ask students to produce a vlog or blog that provides advice and guidance to their peers about how to overcome difficulties with writing. Again, use a suitable digital platform and ensure that all students have access. Provide a deadline by which time vlogs and blogs must be posted. You can ask students to undertake this activity in small groups or individually, depending on the needs and abilities of your students.

Key issues

Students post a wide variety of tips about overcoming difficulties with writing. Summaries are given below. Use some of these to get the resource started, if you feel it would be of benefit to your students.

- Create a space for writing. Make sure that your space is comfortable and is at the correct temperature with good lighting. Ensure there will be no distractions or disturbances.

- Get into a routine for writing. Make sure that everyone knows that you are not to be disturbed when you are writing.

- Enjoy your writing. Choose a topic that is of interest, if possible. It will help you to stay motivated and remain enthusiastic.
- Read around your subject for ideas and inspiration.
- Brainstorm ideas. Write down everything you can think of without judgement. Do this when you are relaxed and not rushing to get something done. Return to your list to sort out the most important issues or topics.
- Write down a list of bullet points with all the things you want to include in your assignment. It is easier to write bullet points than complete sentences and paragraphs and it may help you to get started. You can write up each bullet point later when you feel it is easier to write.
- Use a thesaurus (paper or online) when struggling for the right word.
- Keep a notebook (or mobile device) with you at all times so that you can record ideas as soon as they pop into your head. Ideas can come at very strange times: make sure that you take notes so that you don't forget.
- If you are finding it hard to start an essay or dissertation, don't start at the beginning. Write the middle part, your analysis or the conclusion first. Sometimes the introduction can be the hardest part to write.

- Read *Writing Essays by Pictures: a Workbook* by Alke Gröppel-Wegener. It provides a fresh perspective that works.
- Don't put yourself under pressure because it can be harder to write when you've got a deadline looming. Start early so that you have plenty of time to complete your work without feeling stressed.
- Don't try to be perfect all the time. It can stifle the writing process and stop you writing. Write something down, even if you are not completely happy. Have a break and then change what you have written to make it better, if you need to.
- Don't worry about your work not being good enough. Get a draft together and go through it with your supervisor for feedback, advice and support.
- Build a network with fellow students. Help each other through the writing process. Join a writing circle if you think it would help (see Activity 25).
- Stop trying. Go out and enjoy yourself. Start again tomorrow refreshed and invigorated.
- Control your social media, texting and gaming habits.
- If you are struggling with academic writing, write something else for a while. Maybe a poem, blog or short story. Be creative and imaginative as it can help you when you go back to your academic writing.

➜ Related activities

Activity 24: Developing academic writing skills

Activity 26: Structuring written work

Activity 28: Producing an effective argument

Activity 33: Engaging in reflective writing

Activity 85: Producing a dissertation

➜ Preparatory reading

Huerta, M., Goodson, P., Beigi, M. and Chlup, D. (2017) 'Graduate students as academic writers: writing anxiety, self-efficacy and emotional intelligence', *Higher Education Research and Development*, 36 (4): 716-29, first published online 4 October 2016, http://doi.org/10.1080/07294360.2016.1238881. This paper provides interesting and relevant preparatory reading for tutors and advanced-level students.

Search 'overcoming writer's block' on YouTube and search blogs by writers, academics or PhD students for more information and advice. Links to the best of these can be posted on your tip exchange (students tend to do this when offering tips; however, you can post your own if they are not forthcoming from students).

➜ Further reading

The following books provide information and advice for students about writing at university and can be posted on the tip exchange (depending on level of study).

Day, T. (2013) *Success in Academic Writing*. Basingstoke: Palgrave Macmillan.
Greetham, B. (2013) *How to Write Better Essays*, 3rd edition. Basingstoke: Palgrave Macmillan.
Greetham, B. (2014) *How to Write Your Undergraduate Dissertation*, 2nd edition. Basingstoke: Palgrave Macmillan.
Gröppel-Wegener, A. (2016) *Writing Essays by Pictures: a Workbook*. Tallinn, Estonia: Innovative Librairies.
Levin, P. (2009) *Writing Great Essays*, 2nd edition. Maidenhead: Open University Press.
Oliver, P. (2014) *Writing Your Thesis*, 3rd edition. London: Sage.
Page, M. (2009) *Writing Essays for Dummies*, Chichester: John Wiley & Sons, Ltd.

Activity 32

Activity • • • • • • • • • • → 33

Engaging in reflective writing

Student
handout
page 309

TUTOR NOTES

Purpose: This activity asks students to choose or design a tool or medium that will enable them to engage in reflective writing as their course progresses. They are required, at the start of their course, to describe their chosen method and illustrate how it will be used, with a follow-up session midway to discuss progress and a session at the end of their course to evaluate their reflective writing and the tool/medium used.

Type: Self-guided individual exercise with progress and evaluation sessions.

Alternative type(s): Self-guided individual exercise.

Level: Elementary, intermediate and advanced (the level will be reflected in the writing produced).

Duration: Students should work on this activity throughout their course: the actual time spent depends on individual motivation. You need 50 minutes to one hour of contact time at three stages during your course: at the beginning, midway and at the end to introduce, review and evaluate reflective writing and the tool/medium used.

Equipment/materials: Students can choose or design the tool/medium that they wish to use and these should be made available, where appropriate.

Learning outcome: By the end of this activity students will have chosen, used and evaluated a tool or medium that has helped them to engage in reflective writing over the duration of their course, which will help to raise awareness of the value of reflective writing during their studies and beyond.

The activity

Give your students a copy of the Student Handout at the beginning of your course. This asks them to choose or design a tool or medium that will help them to engage in reflective writing (examples are given in the Student Handout: delete this information if you feel that students should work this out for themselves). Meet early in the course so that each student can give a brief description of their chosen method and illustrate how it will be used to help them to engage in reflective writing. This session should also be used to explain more about reflective writing and illustrate how it can be of benefit to their studies and life in general. Also, it is important to stress that students can change tools/medium as their course progresses if, through their reflective writing, they decide that another method would be more appropriate.

Meet again midway through the course to discuss progress and to find out whether or not their chosen method is helping them to engage in reflective writing. This session should also be used to help students gain a deeper understanding of what is meant by reflective writing and to help them move beyond purely descriptive writing, based on what they have already produced (see below).

Run a final session at the end of the course to evaluate chosen tools, consider how reflective writing has improved and assess the usefulness and relevance of reflective writing to their studies and life in general. Provide references for those students who wish to follow up the issues raised in more depth.

It is possible to run this activity as a self-guided individual exercise without meeting with students at three points during the course. This option can be chosen if contact time is limited and/or if you feel that your students can complete this activity without meeting to discuss progress.

Key issues

This activity provides a practical way for students to engage in reflective writing. It involves personal choice and preference for a particular method: this tends to encourage students to become more engaged in a topic that, for some, can appear irrelevant, of little value or a waste of their time. Encourage some of the more reluctant students to become involved in the activity by stressing that there will be follow-up sessions in which students need to discuss and demonstrate their progress in reflective writing.

➜ Cautionary note

Some students find it very difficult to move beyond the descriptive phrase of writing. If this is the case you should be able to pick up on this when you meet midway through the course. You can discuss these issues in the session, perhaps by providing examples of reflective writing that have moved beyond description, into the interpretative, critical and analytical stages, for example. In some cases you may need to meet with individual students to discuss their progress and work through any concerns or problems they are experiencing. Alternatively, you can pair students together to help and support each other, offering advice and feedback on each other's reflective writing. If you choose this option find out first whether students are happy to share their reflections with another person.

➜ Related activities

Activity 2: Becoming a reflective learner

Activity 4: Developing metacognition

Activity 46: Learning through storytelling

Activity 57: Developing thoughts and imagination

Activity 58: Reflecting, thinking and making connections

➜ Preparatory reading

Ayres, D. (2015) *Reflective Writing Exercises*, http://danieljayres.blogspot.co.uk [accessed 19 September 2017]. This blog is produced by Daniel Ayres, senior lecturer in education at the University of East London. It contains a list of inventive and useful exercises that can be used to encourage reflective writing. This blog can be recommended to students who may struggle with deciding on a suitable tool or medium for reflective writing and it provides useful preparatory reading for tutors who would like to know more about the different methods that can be used to encourage reflective writing.

➜ Further reading

Bolton, G. (2014) *Reflective Practice: Writing and Professional Development*, 4th edition. London: Sage. This book is useful for tutors who are interested in finding out more about reflective practice in their teaching and writing.

Williams, K., Woolliams, M. and Spiro, J. (2012) *Reflective Writing*. Basingstoke: Palgrave Macmillan. This book can be recommended to students who wish to follow up the issues raised in this activity.

Wright, J. and Bolton, G. (2012) *Reflective Writing in Counselling and Psychotherapy*. London: Sage. This is a useful book for both tutors and students who want to know more about how to engage in reflective writing.

Activity 33

Section 5

Numeracy, statistics and mathematics

Activity · · · · · · · · · · → 34

Building confidence with maths

The activity

Invite together a group of students who feel unconfident with maths. These can be students from one course and one level or students across a range of courses and levels. The group should not be too large: seven to ten participants is ideal. Explain the purpose and format of the structured support session: first, you will meet in a 50 minute or one hour session to discuss worries and concerns about maths; second, students will work on an action plan that will help them to overcome these worries and concerns; third, students will implement their action plan over the next few weeks (the time-scale depends on your timetable and that of your students: four or five weeks is usually a good length of time); fourth, the group will reconvene for another 50 minutes or one hour session to evaluate the action that has been taken and to set long-term goals based on the outcome of the structured support group.

It is possible to run this activity as a one-to-one support session with individual students, if you have the time available and it better suits your students. You will need to be available to offer support throughout the activity if this option is chosen.

Key issues

Students discuss a wide variety of worries and concerns they have about maths, including 'being scared' of numbers; not understanding numbers; memories of bad experiences at school; a fear of being 'shown up'; concerns about being 'left behind'; 'maths phobia' or a predisposition toward a fear of maths and personal, 'illogical anxiety'. They find it useful to discuss these worries and concerns with others who may be feeling the same: this enables them to bounce ideas off each other and discuss practical and effective solutions to the problems they are experiencing.

Action that can be taken includes:

- Take a course aimed at helping adults to get to grips with maths. These can be at your institution or online courses. Some students make a commitment to take this type of course so that it can be evaluated when you next meet (and recommended to others if it is considered useful).
- Take advantage of any help that is available at your college or university. Students identify seminars, support sessions, study skills units, learning development units and any other sources that are available. If students attend any of these sessions they can be evaluated (and perhaps recommended) when you next meet.
- Set a small maths task for each week day (have a break at weekends). Some students decide to meet informally to set tasks and work through them together. Books are available to help (see further reading).
- Practise taking tests. This can be done individually or in groups: again, some students decide to meet to support each other through the tests, before they try to take them individually. Books are available to help (see further reading).
- Read around the subject. Students find and share resources that they find interesting and useful, either by meeting in an informal group or by setting up a chat group or using another social media platform.
- Talk to others about maths. Try to demystify it to overcome anxieties. Parents, spouses, peers and children can all help maths to become more familiar and less daunting.
- Take responsibility. Students tend to discuss the reasons why they are worried about asking questions in class and, realising the importance of seeking further information, help or clarification, they decide to make this part of their action plan. Again, they can then evaluate this action and show how it has helped them to not only feel more confident about maths, but also helped them to feel more confident about their studies in general.

➜ Related activities

Activity 35: Introducing statistics

Activity 37: Understanding graphs, charts and visual representations

Activity 47: Engaging with lecturers and tutors

....

➜ Preparatory reading

Cheng, E. (2015) *Cakes, Custard and Category Theory: Easy Recipes for Understanding Complex Maths*. London: Profile Books Ltd. This book provides useful preparatory reading for tutors as it provides an excellent way to help students think differently about maths. It can also be recommended to students who wouldn't be put off by some of the more complex maths discussed in the book.

....

➜ Further reading

There are two 'Teach Yourself' books that students may find useful if they are happy to work through this type of resource, either on their own or with their support group.

Graham, T. (2013) *Mathematics: a Basic Introduction: Teach Yourself*. London: Hodder & Stoughton Ltd.
Neill, H. (2013) *Mathematics: a Complete Introduction: Teach Yourself*. London: Hodder & Stoughton Ltd.

The 'For Dummies' series of books has three titles that may be of use to students during this activity, especially if they want to practise taking tests (you can let students discover these books for themselves due to the inappropriate 'For Dummies' title, which sends completely the wrong message for this activity).

Beveridge, C. (2011) *Basic Maths for Dummies*. Chichester: John Wiley & Sons, Ltd.
Beveridge, C. (2012) *Numeracy Tests for Dummies*. Chichester: John Wiley & Sons, Ltd.
Beveridge, C. (2012) *Basic Maths Practice Problems for Dummies*. Chichester: John Wiley & Sons, Ltd.

Activity 34

Activity • • • • • • • • • • ➔ 35

Introducing statistics

Student handout page 310

TUTOR NOTES

Purpose: This activity is a group exercise and tutor-led discussion that enables students to find out what is meant by the term 'statistics', what they are, how they are used (and abused) in the real world and how to assess reliability. It does not cover statistical procedures.

Type: Group exercise followed by tutor-led discussion.

Alternative type(s): Self-guided individual exercise; workshop.

Level: Elementary.

Duration: Fifty minutes to one hour for the group exercise and discussion (and the workshop option). If the self-guided individual exercise option is chosen students need to spend one or two hours on the tasks during independent study.

Equipment/materials: None required.

Learning outcome: By the end of this activity students will have a greater awareness of statistics, understand how they can be used and abused in the real world and know how to evaluate the reliability of statistics that are presented.

The activity

Divide your students into small groups and ask that they undertake the tasks contained in the Student Handout. They will need to spend five to ten minutes on each task. Once this has been done lead a class discussion on the issues raised (for clarification and to answer potential questions). The tasks cover defining the terms 'statistics', discussing descriptive and inferential statistics, highlighting cases where statistics are unreliable, abused or misused and producing a checklist that will help students to work out whether statistics are reliable or not. If contact time is not available, and if it better suits your student cohort, you can ask that students work through the tasks as a self-guided individual exercise during independent study. Alternatively, you can run this exercise as a workshop on a voluntary basis for students who are interested in this topic.

This activity does not cover statistical procedures. It is useful, therefore, to find out about courses, videos and publications that cover statistical procedures so that these can be recommended to students who are interested in the subject (see below).

Key issues

Examples of the type of discussion that can take place between group members for each task are given below. It is useful to walk among groups as they work through the tasks, offering prompts where required. If students wish to gain a deeper understanding of the issues raised by Tasks 3 and 4 you can ask them to take part in Activity 36, which requires them to build a student-centred digital resource on the use, abuse and misuse of statistics.

Task 1

There are four ways that the term 'statistics' is used:

1. a subject or discipline and the work carried out within that discipline;
2. the methods that are used to collect and process quantitative data;
3. the collections of data that are produced from the methods used to collect and process the data;
4. specifically calculated figures (such as the mean, mode and median) that are used to characterise the quantitative data that have been collected.

Task 2

'Descriptive statistics' are used to describe the population that is under study. They include measures of central tendencies (such as averages) and measures of the variability about the average. This can include 'range' (a measure of the spread of the data between the largest and smallest values) and 'standard deviation' (the variation from the average). These statistics are only used to describe; they are not used to generalise.

'Inferential statistics' are used by researchers to analyse samples and draw conclusions. They help deductions to be made from the data collected and enable the researcher to test hypotheses and relate findings to the sample or population. 'Tests of significance' (determining whether the null hypothesis is rejected in favour of the alternative hypothesis) are used to address issues of generalisability.

Task 3

Answers depend on recent news coverage, your student cohort and their subject of study. They may discuss examples such as politicians using statistics to fit their argument without providing evidence or sources for figures; advertisers using questionable statistics to sell a product; statistics that are influenced by prejudices, beliefs or bias; a lack of statistical knowledge and misunderstanding, for example.

Task 4

Questions that can be asked include the following, depending on your student cohort:

- What are the credentials and motivation of the person producing or quoting the statistics?
- Are statistics relevant to the argument?
- Have unfavourable statistics been disregarded?
- Have statistics been manipulated to fit the argument? Have they been influenced by personal prejudice, bias or beliefs of the person quoting or producing the statistics?
- Are all sources and/or evidence clearly laid out? Is the origin of statistics quoted clearly and is it possible to check on the information provided?
- Are statistical methods and procedures clearly laid out/ explained?
- Have incorrect procedures been used?
- Is correlation confused with causation?
- Has causality been interpreted deterministically when the evidence is statistical?
- Are there errors in the sampling (is it possible to determine and analyse the sampling methods and procedures)?
- Has certainty been suggested when this is not possible?

➜ **Related activities**

Activity 34: Building confidence with maths

Activity 36: The use, abuse and misuse of statistics

Activity 38: Introducing data mining

Activity 39: Finding and using datasets

....

Activity 35

➜ Preparatory reading

Stowell, J. and Addison, W. (eds) (2017) *Activities for Teaching Statistics and Research Methods: A Guide for Psychology Instructors*. Washington, DC: American Psychological Association. This book provides useful preparatory reading for tutors who would like inspiration for further activities that can be used to teach statistics (and research methods).

The Open University (www.open.edu/openlearn/free-courses) in the UK has a wide selection of mathematics and statistics short courses that are freely available online and can be recommended to students who need further help on these topics. It is useful preparatory work to find out what is available before this activity takes place.

Visit YouTube (www.youtube.com) for some useful and interesting videos on topics such as choosing a statistical procedure, types of data, important statistical concepts, variation and sampling error and hypothesis testing. Some of the better videos can be recommended to students who wish to follow up the issues raised in this activity.

➜ Further reading

The following books can be recommended to students who want to find out more about statistical procedures.

Graham, A. (2013) *Statistics: a Complete Introduction*, reprint edition. London: Hodder & Stoughton.
Hand, D. (2008) *Statistics: a Very Short Introduction*. Oxford: Oxford University Press.
Rowntree, D. (2000) *Statistics without Tears: an Introduction for Non-Mathematicians*. London: Penguin Books Ltd.

Activity 35

Activity • • • • • • • • • → 36

The use, abuse and misuse of statistics

The activity

Choose a suitable digital platform on which you can build this resource. Ensure that all students have access to this platform and that it is available throughout their course. Call it 'The Use, Abuse and Misuse of Statistics' and provide a few initial entries to get the resource started. Ask students to contribute to the resource whenever they find suitable examples that they would like to share with their peers. These could be examples where statistics have been used well and can be considered reliable or examples where statistics are abused in public life for personal gain, for example. Students should post their examples (with links, if appropriate) and comment on the reliability and trustworthiness of the information. Their peers should be encouraged to discuss the posts and add further comments, where appropriate. Decide whether to make this a voluntary or compulsory exercise (if the latter is chosen give a deadline by which time all posts should be made: you can then ask that students continue the resource on a voluntary basis). The intention is to provide a practical, creative, useful and instructive resource for students that can be accessed at any time.

This activity can be used for students studying at all levels as the type and standard of information posted will reflect the level of study. Explain that the resource will be available for everyone throughout their course so that they can access it when appropriate. You may need to remind students to post information and you may also find it useful to post some of your own examples to keep the resource going. You will also need to monitor posts to ensure that the information provided by students is correct: sometimes students can post misleading or wrong information, especially where statistical techniques and formulas are concerned, for example. You will also need to ensure that any problematic posts and comments are taken down or modified (see below).

It is possible to run this activity as a vlogs and blogs exercise. If you choose this option ask your students to produce a vlog or blog about the use, abuse and misuse of statistics that can be uploaded for peer review and discussion. Students can discuss one particular example in depth, or they could choose to cover a variety of examples. Give a deadline by which time all vlogs and blogs should be uploaded and encourage students to provide constructive feedback on the work of their peers.

Key issues

This activity tends to generate a wide variety of creative and sometimes unbelievable posts about the use, abuse and misuse of statistics. These can be from academic journals (providing examples of the correct use of statistics), from politicians (providing some unbelievable examples of misuse) and from advertisers (providing examples of both obvious and subtle abuse). It is an entertaining way to highlight the issues and builds a useful resource that students can access throughout their course. However, there are potential problems that can be encountered, and these are discussed below.

➜ Cautionary note

When you set up the digital platform for this resource, ensure that it is internal. This activity could, potentially, generate posts that could be considered libellous, disparaging or derogatory. This is why it is important for you to monitor the posts on a regular basis to ensure that any problematic posts are taken down or modified quickly. You can help to reduce this problem by talking to your students about the nature and type of posts that are acceptable:

- comments should demonstrate critical thought and analysis;
- examples given and comments made should be instructional and informative;
- examples, comments and discussion must remain on topic;
- examples can be entertaining, creative, fun or jaw-dropping;
- all comments and discussion should remain courteous and polite;
- ensuing posts and discussion should add to, or aid, understanding and knowledge of the original post;
- anything considered to be libellous, slanderous or in breach of copyright will be taken down.

➜ Related activities

Activity 52: Evaluating sources

Activity 53: Finding truth and fact in mass information

Activity 54: Recognising statistics, facts, arguments and opinions

➜ Preparatory reading

Bad Science (www.badscience.net) is a website containing blogs and articles about bad science, written by Dr Ben Goldacre. The articles were written for the Bad Science column in the *Guardian* newspaper in the UK and highlight the misuse of science and statistics by journalists, politicians and drug companies, for example. Students can be directed to this site for interesting reading on this topic.

The Radical Statistics Group (www.radstats.org.uk) is a group of researchers and statisticians who are concerned about the way that 'official statistics reflect governmental rather than social purposes'. The organisation produces an interesting blog and journal that can be accessed on their website, covering a wide variety of topics on statistics, government figures, abuse and misuse.

More or Less is a radio programme that is broadcast on BBC Radio 4 in the UK and produced in association with the Open University. The programme discusses the use and misuse of statistics in everyday life. Podcasts and downloads are available from the BBC website (www.bbc.co.uk/programmes) and are useful as preparatory work for both tutors and students.

Smaldino, P. and McElreath, R. (2016) 'The natural selection of bad science', *Royal Society Open Science*, published 21 September 2016, http://doi.org/10.1098/rsos.160384. This paper and associated comments provide interesting and relevant reading for tutors and advanced-level students, illustrating how bad science is passed on in the lab.

Activity 36

➜ Further reading

The following references can be recommended to students who want to follow up the issues raised in this activity.

Bakker, M. and Wicherts, J. (2011) 'The (mis)reporting of statistical results in psychology journals', *Behavior Research Methods*, 43 (3): 66-78 [electronic].

Huff, D. (1991) *How to Lie with Statistics*. London: Penguin. This book has been published since 1954 is and still very relevant and useful today.

O'Neil, C. (2017) *Weapons of Math Destruction: How Big Data Increases Inequality and Threatens Democracy*. London: Penguin.

Vigen, T. (2015) *Spurious Correlations*, New York: Hachette Books. The website associated with this amusing book may be of interest to students: http://tylervigen.com/spurious-correlations [accessed 20 September 2017].

Activity 36

Activity · · · · · · · · · ➔ 37

Understanding graphs, charts and visual representations

Student handout page 311

TUTOR NOTES

Purpose: This activity helps to improve understanding of graphs, charts and visual representations by asking students, in their groups, to teach this topic to their peers. To do this effectively they must increase their own understanding through research and group discussion. It is aimed at students who have little experience of using graphs, charts and visual representations, or those who feel unconfident when approaching this type of material.

Type: Peer teaching.

Alternative type(s): Video/podcast production (in groups during independent study).

Level: Elementary.

Duration: Students need to spend a few hours during independent study researching and preparing their teaching session with their group members. One to two hours of contact time is required for students to teach their peers (this depends on the number of groups). If the video/podcast option is chosen students need to spend a few hours preparing, producing and uploading their video/podcast, and up to an hour viewing and commenting on the videos/ podcasts of their peers. Tutors need to spend a little time reviewing and checking the videos and posts.

Equipment/materials: Students can use any presentation/teaching equipment, materials and props that they deem appropriate and these should be made available for their use.

Learning outcome: By the end of this activity students will have a deeper understanding of graphs, charts and visual representations and will feel more confident when approaching and using this type of material during their studies and beyond.

The activity

Divide your students into groups and give them a copy of the Student Handout. This asks them to teach about understanding graphs, charts and visual representations to their peers in the next contact session. They must research, prepare and practise their teaching session during independent study. When you next meet, allocate 20 minutes for each teaching session, with a small amount of time at the end to discuss issues raised. You can also ask students to evaluate each other's teaching sessions, perhaps deciding on the most useful, effective, memorable and interesting session, if appropriate.

If contact time is not available ask students to turn their teaching session into a video/podcast that can be uploaded, viewed and discussed on a suitable digital platform (the Student Handout will need to be adapted accordingly). If you choose this option, give a deadline by which time all videos must be uploaded. Encourage students to view and discuss each other's videos and monitor videos and posts to ensure that information is correct, supportive and encouraging.

Key issues

This activity has produced some interesting teaching sessions. For example, some groups concentrate on one particular graph, chart or visual representation explaining, in detail, how to approach and understand the information they have provided. Others present a wide variety of different representations, comparing, contrasting and discussing issues relevant to each. Others prepare a session in which they ask their peers to look at a visual representation and discuss any problems and concerns they may have. Some students take a different approach, teaching their peers how to produce or draw graphs, charts or visual representations using the relevant software. On one occasion a group of students chose a number of poorly constructed and confusing visual representations so that they could discuss, and work out how to overcome, problems identified by their peers. The title of this activity is deliberately vague so that it produces a wide variety of teaching sessions. This enables students to learn more about a topic that, for some, can appear daunting and confusing.

Examples of specific tips and advice that can be given in teaching sessions include the following:

- Look first at the main headings to ascertain whether they give an idea of what the table, chart or graph is about.
- Look at the headings in each column or the titles on the axis for clarity and understanding.
- Scan the table or graph for interesting figures or anomalies.
- Look for particular trends. Try to work out what they mean.
- Look at the high and low points or the largest or smallest figures and try to work out what they mean.
- Scan for blips or unusual figures and work out what they show. Think about why they are unusual.
- Pick a figure inserted into one part of the table or on the graph. Try to work out what the figure is telling you.

- Summarise the main conclusions.
- If you are struggling to understand a visual representation, write down any ideas you have as it helps you to move your thinking from abstract numbers to written material, which can aid understanding. Think about the stories told by the numbers.
- If interpretation is difficult, try reading off some values and thinking about what they mean.
- Critique and analyse what you see: don't presume that all visual representations, graphs and tables are correct. Think about why they have been produced, by whom and for what purpose. Think about how they can be improved.

→ Related activities

Activity 34: Building confidence with maths

Activity 35: Introducing statistics

Activity 36: The use, abuse and misuse of statistics

Activity 39: Finding and using datasets

Activity 77: Using data visualisation tools and software

....

→ Preparatory reading

Few, F. (2012) *Show Me the Numbers: Designing Tables and Graphs to Enlighten*, 2nd edition. Burlingame, CA: Analytics Press. This book provides excellent preparatory reading for this activity for both tutors and students, covering issues such as simple statistics, fundamental variations of tables and graphs, visual perception and design for communication.

....

→ Further reading

Evergreen, S. (2016) *Effective Data Visualization: the Right Chart for the Right Data*. Thousand Oaks, CA: Sage. This book covers a wide range of topics on data visualisation and contains useful exercises for students to undertake.

The Open University in the UK has a free online course called 'Diagrams, charts and graphs' (http://www.open.edu/openlearn/science-maths-technology/mathematics-and-statistics/mathematics-education/diagrams-charts-and-graphs/content-section--learningoutcomes). This course is at introductory Level 1 and can be recommended to students who need more help with this topic.

Activity 37

Activity · · · · · · · · · ➔ 38

Introducing data mining

Student handout page 312

TUTOR NOTES

Purpose: This activity introduces students to data mining by asking them to imagine that they work as a data scientist. In this role they must produce a document that explains data mining to the organisation's directors who know little about the subject. All documents are uploaded to build a useful student-centred digital resource. This is an entertaining way to introduce data mining to students who are new to this topic.

Type: Self-guided individual exercise with student-centred digital resource.

Alternative type(s): Self-guided individual exercise followed by student presentations.

Level: Elementary, intermediate and advanced (this activity can be used at all levels for students who are new to data mining).

Duration: Students need to spend a few hours during independent study researching, producing and uploading their documents. They also need to spend some time reading, reviewing and voting on the documents produced by their peers. Tutors need to spend one or two hours setting up the digital resource and reading uploaded documents. If the student presentation option is chosen you will need one to two hours of contact time, depending on the number of student presentations.

Equipment/materials: A suitable digital platform and access for all students. If the presentation option is chosen students can use any presentation equipment they deem appropriate and this should be made available for their use.

Learning outcome: By the end of this activity students will understand what is meant by data mining, know about the processes involved and understand the potential benefits and problems associated with data mining in the 'real world'.

The activity

Give a copy of the Student Handout to your students. This asks them to imagine that they have obtained a job as a data scientist. As their first task they must produce a document that explains data mining to their organisation's directors who know little about data mining, what it entails and how it can be of benefit to their organisation. The documents are to be uploaded onto a relevant digital platform. Give a deadline by which time all documents should be uploaded. Students should read and review the documents produced by their peers and vote on the best, if appropriate. This document will explain data mining in a clear, succinct and user-friendly way. It should also be imaginative, creative and hold the interest of their peers.

If contact time is available and if you think it would better suit your students, you can ask them, instead, to make a short presentation on data mining to their peers when you next meet (the Student Handout will need to be adapted slightly if this option is chosen). Again, students can vote on the best presentation, if appropriate.

Key issues

'Data mining' is the term that has been coined to describe the processes involved in analysing data to identify patterns and relationships. These processes involve searching, collecting, examining, visualising, identifying, summarising, concluding and predicting. It can also involve the development of recommendations and the creation of solutions. Companies and organisations use data mining techniques for a variety of reasons, for example to:

- better understand the needs and behaviours of clients or customers;
- evaluate new products or treatments;
- overcome problems and develop solutions;
- identify best practices;
- increase revenue;
- improve branding;
- break into new markets;
- develop new marketing strategies.

Data mining techniques, and opportunities within the field of data mining, are expanding rapidly with increasing technology and the availability of big data. Opportunities are growing in various fields, including banking, retail, financial markets, healthcare, charities and telecommunications. However, organisations need to be aware of problems that could occur, usually in terms of privacy, security and the misuse or abuse of data.

Most students have heard of data mining and the opportunities available, but may not understand what it is and what it entails. This activity positions data mining in the 'real world' and asks them to think about the issues involved in practical, employment-related terms. This approach enables students to understand practical applications while getting to grips with a topic that, for those with a non-scientific background, can appear daunting and confusing. They learn from researching and producing their own documents and then reinforce this learning by reading the documents produced by their peers.

An important part of data mining is the ability to produce, use and present effective data visualisations to better understand the data, see patterns and recognise trends. If this is a topic that is of interest to your students you can expand the digital resource by combining this activity with Activity 77. This asks students to identify, test, review and critique a visualisation tool or type of software and post the information on the relevant digital platform (including links or uploaded visualisations, where appropriate). Through combining these two activities your students will create a comprehensive and useful digital resource that can be accessed throughout their course, when required.

→ Related activities

Activity 35: Introducing statistics

Activity 37: Understanding graphs, charts and visual representations

Activity 39: Finding and using datasets

Activity 77: Using data visualisation tools and software

....

→ Preparatory reading

Brown, M. (2014) *Data Mining for Dummies*. Hoboken, NJ: John Wiley & Sons, Inc. This book provides useful preparatory reading for this activity for those who are new to data mining.

....

→ Further reading

The following books provide comprehensive guides to data mining, including practical algorithms that can be applied to datasets. However, they are quite complex and can appear daunting to those who have no experience of data mining and statistical analysis, so they should be recommended with care.

Aggarwal, C. (2015) *Data Mining: the Textbook*. New York: Springer.
Hastie, T., Tibshirani, R. and Friedman, J. (2017) *The Elements of Statistical Learning: Data Mining, Inference, and Prediction*, 2nd edition. New York: Springer.

Activity 38

Leskovec, J., Rajaraman, A. and Ullman, D. (2014) *Mining of Massive Datasets*, 2nd edition. Cambridge: Cambridge University Press.

Witten, I., Frank, E., Hall, M. and Pal, C. (2017) *Data Mining: Practical Machine Learning Tools and Techniques,* 4th edition. Cambridge, MA: Morgan Kaufmann.

There are various MOOCs (massive open online courses) available covering data mining that can be recommended to students who wish to study this subject in more depth. Details of courses can be obtained from MOOC platforms. Examples of these include:

- FutureLearn (www.futurelearn.com)
- Coursera (www.coursera.org)
- edX (www.edx.org)
- open2study (www.open2study.com)

Activity 38

Activity • • • • • • • • • • • • • ➔ 39

Finding and using datasets

Student handout page 313

TUTOR NOTES

Purpose: This activity requires students to find, use, discuss and critique two datasets that are relevant to an assignment, project or dissertation. It is of particular use for students who have no experience of using datasets, for those who feel that datasets are not relevant to their studies, for those who need encouragement to move on with the background research for a project or dissertation and for those who need to use datasets to help explain emerging results, for example.

Type: Self-guided individual exercise followed by tutor-led discussion.

Alternative type(s): Self-guided individual exercise with student-centred digital resources.

Level: Elementary, intermediate and advanced (this activity works best if students are embarking on, or engaged in, personal research for a project, assignment or dissertation and this can be at any level of study).

Duration: Students need to spend a few hours during independent study finding, using and critiquing two datasets. Fifty minutes to one hour of contact time will be required to discuss the issues raised by the self-guided exercise. If the digital resource option is chosen tutors need to spend an hour or two setting up the resource and monitoring posts. Students need to spend a little time uploading posts and reviewing those of their peers.

Equipment/materials: Students need access to the relevant datasets and access to the digital platform, if this option is chosen.

Learning outcome: By the end of this activity students will understand how to find, use and critique datasets that are relevant to their assignments, projects and research.

The activity

Give a copy of the Student Handout to your students. This asks them to find and use two datasets that are relevant to a particular assignment, project or dissertation (the handout relates to student dissertations undertaken in the third year of an undergraduate degree course in the UK: you can adapt it depending on the level of study and type of assignment, project or research). As students undertake this task they should answer the questions posed in the Student Handout. These questions will form the basis of your tutor-led discussion when you next meet.

It is possible to ask students to use their findings to create a student-centred digital resource if contact time is limited or if you think this option better suits your students (you will need to adapt the Student Handout accordingly). If you choose this option give a deadline by which time links to their chosen datasets along with answers to the questions should be posted. Encourage your students to review the posts of their peers and to engage in digital discussion. Monitor posts from time to time to ensure that information posted is timely, constructive, informative and correct.

Key issues

Some students find this an interesting and simple activity to complete, whereas others struggle, both with finding suitable datasets and with using them (although they are able to provide useful information about the difficulty of using particular datasets). If you think that your students will struggle with this activity, provide further information on the Student Handout (such as that given below) or pair students together so that they can help and support each other with this activity.

Students can find suitable data by using the Google Public Data Explorer (www.google.com/publicdata/directory) or by visiting the following websites:

- The UK Government's open datasets can be found at www.data.gov.uk. This site brings together data from all central government departments and a number of other public sector bodies and local authorities.
- The Economic and Social Research Council (www.esrc.ac.uk) in the UK has published details of almost 1,000 datasets generated by ESRC-funded grants. The data are free to access and use.

- The US Government's open datasets can be found at www.data.gov. Data are provided by a wide variety of organisations, including Federal agencies, the US Geological Survey and the National Aeronautics and Space Administration (NASA).
- World Bank Open Data can be found at http://data.worldbank.org. This site provides free and open access to global development data.

➜ Related activities

Activity 35: Introducing statistics

Activity 37: Understanding graphs, charts and visual representations

Activity 38: Introducing data mining

Activity 77: Using data visualisation tools and software

➜ Preparatory reading

Yau (2011) presents an interesting discussion on using visual tools to work with large datasets and Kitchin (2014) provides an interesting critical analysis of the data revolution. Both of these provide useful preparatory reading for tutors. Anderson and Semmelroth (2015) provides useful preparatory reading for students.

➜ Further reading

The following books are useful for both tutors and students who wish to follow up the issues raised by this activity. The first book is useful for those who are new to this topic, whereas the other three are more complex and should be recommended to students who have a little more understanding and experience.

Anderson, A. and Semmelroth, D. (2015) *Statistics for Big Data for Dummies*. Hoboken, NJ: John Wiley & Sons, Inc.
Kitchin, R. (2014) *The Data Revolution: Big Data, Open Data, Data Infrastructures and Their Consequences*. London: Sage.
O'Neil, C. (2017) *Weapons of Math Destruction: How Big Data Increases Inequality and Threatens Democracy*. London: Penguin.
Yau, N. (2011) *Visualize This: the Flowing Data Guide to Design, Visualization, and Statistics*. Indianapolis, IN: Wiley Publishing, Inc.

Activity 39

Section 6

Speaking, listening and observing

Activity •••••••••• ➔ 40

Becoming an active listener

Student
handout
page 314

TUTOR NOTES

Purpose: This activity is a simple exercise that introduces students to the idea of active listening. It provides a brief description of what is meant by the term and then asks them to undertake a practical exercise that involves listening to a radio talk show or an audio podcast. This helps them to practise active listening and raises awareness of distractions that can have an influence on the way they listen. They are encouraged to continue practising and develop their active listening skills, with tips provided for guidance.

Type: Self-guided individual exercise.

Alternative type(s): None.

Level: Elementary.

Duration: One or two hours during independent study to listen to, and summarise, a suitable radio talk show or audio podcast. Students will practise and hone their active listening skills as their course progresses.

Equipment/materials: Students need to find, and have access to, a suitable radio talk show or audio podcast.

Learning outcome: By the end of this activity students will have an increased understanding and awareness of what is meant by active listening, which will help them to develop and use their skills as their course progresses and in life in general.

The activity

Give your students a copy of the Student Handout and ask them to work through the exercise during independent study. This gives a description of what is meant by active listening, before asking students to practise and develop these skills first by listening to a radio talk show or an audio podcast, and then during lectures, seminars, in group work and when communicating with tutors and peers. Tips for improving their active listening skills are provided in the Student Handout. However, if you feel that too much information is provided, and that students should work this out for themselves, you can modify or dispense with the handout.

Key issues

Feedback from this activity suggests that students are sometimes surprised to find that they do not listen well. Once their awareness has been raised they realise that they often only half-heartedly hear what is being said without taking note of, interpreting or understanding the ideas or arguments. However, when they begin to practise active listening they find that their understanding improves, they get more out of lectures and seminars, and they even report better relationships with spouses, partners, friends and peers.

This activity can be run quickly and easily at the start of your course so that students develop good active listening habits from the outset. If you want to gain a more complete coverage of this topic you can run this activity together with Activity 41, which asks students, in groups, to develop a game that will help their peers to improve their listening skills.

➔ Related activities

Activity 41: Improving listening skills

Activity 48: Getting the most from tutor feedback

Activity 65: Getting the most out of group work

Activity 81: Improving interview techniques

➔ Preparatory reading

McNaughton, D., Hamlin, D., McCarthy, J., Head-Reeves, D. and Schreiner, M. (2008) 'Learning to listen: teaching an active listening strategy to preservice education professionals', *Topics in Early Childhood Special Education*, February, 27 (4): 223-31. This paper provides interesting insight into active listening strategies and is useful tutor preparation for this activity.

➔ Further reading

Nichols, P. (2009) *The Lost Art of Listening: How Learning to Listen can Improve Relationships*. New York: Guilford Press. Although this book is aimed at those interested in family therapy, it has some useful and interesting advice about improving listening skills.

Rogers, C. and Farson, R. (2015) *Active Listening*, reprint edition. Mansfield Centre, CT: Martino Publishing. This is a reprint of the 1957 book in which the authors describe the development of 'active listening' as a therapeutic and communication technique.

Activity 40

Activity • • • • • • • • • • → 41

Improving listening skills

TUTOR NOTES

Purpose: This activity provides an entertaining and memorable way for students to think about how they can improve their listening skills by asking students, in groups, to invent a game that will help players to improve their listening skills. They must develop and test their game during independent study before trying it out on their peers in class.

Type: Game development in groups.

Alternative type(s): None.

Level: Elementary and intermediate.

Duration: Groups need a few hours during independent study to develop and test their games. You need one to two hours of contact time for groups to run their games (depending on the number of student groups).

Equipment/materials: Students can use any equipment or props they deem appropriate and these should be made available for their use.

Learning outcome: By the end of this activity students will understand how to improve their listening skills and will be able to apply this understanding to their studies, research and life in general.

The activity

Divide your students into groups and ask that they invent a game that will help players to improve their listening skills. The games should be entertaining, creative and memorable, and enable players to learn something new. Students should try to develop original games, although relevant adaptations of existing games are acceptable (see below). They are to research, develop and test their game during independent study and then try out their game on their peers when you next meet. The time allocated for each game depends on the number of student groups and the contact time you have available (groups can be quite large for this activity if you have limited contact time). Set a time limit on each game to ensure that all games are tried during your session.

Ask students to vote on the best game at the end of the session, if appropriate. When voting, students should consider issues such as creativity, inventiveness, effectiveness, entertainment value and ease of play (students should bear these issues in mind when developing their games). Conclude the session with a discussion on the issues raised by the activity (see below).

Key issues

A wide variety of games can be produced by this activity. Examples include:

- A guessing game in which a speaker is nominated and all other players must pick a card on which is printed a 'non-listening' activity (see list, below). The speaker must then speak (or read a text, if this is easier) for five minutes. Each player must display their non-listening activity while the speaker is speaking. After the end of the five minutes the players must try to guess all the non-listening activities that have been displayed.
- Players sit in a circle and one player is chosen to start the game. They must say 'I can improve my listening skills by ...' Once they have offered a tip the next player repeats the sentence and tip, before offering their own. The next player must repeat the sentence and the first two tips before adding a third. This continues around the circle with more tips added and repeated. Students must remember what has come before (and must, therefore, listen) and also think about their own tips for improving listening skills. Players are eliminated if they repeat a tip, are unable to provide tips in the correct order or cannot think of a tip. The last player remaining is the winner.

- Players are split into pairs and both are given a short phrase that they must incorporate into dialogue with another player. The two players then chat for five minutes, covering any topic they wish. However, the short phrase must be included in the dialogue. Both players must try to discover the phrase given by their partner and this involves careful listening throughout the dialogue.
- A list of statements relevant to the course of study is developed (in this case it was research methods). Some are quite complex whereas others are fairly simple. Statements are read out only once. Players must decide whether statements are true, false or unclear by giving a 'thumbs up', a 'thumps down' or a neutral palm. They must listen carefully to each statement to do this effectively.
- Players are split into pairs. This first player asks a series of pre-prepared questions, listening carefully to the answers. Once the answers have been given the questioner must try to repeat all the answers. Pairs swap roles and repeat the exercise with a different set of pre-prepared questions.

Issues that can be raised by this activity and discussed in the concluding part of the session include the following:

- Adopt active listening strategies (see Activity 40):

  o be prepared;
  o assume a positive attitude;
  o focus on the speaker;
  o listen willingly;
  o listen for useful, important and salient points;
  o hear what is being said rather than what you expect or want to hear;
  o concentrate on the message, not on the delivery;
  o avoid emotional involvement;
  o become aware of, and reduce, distractions (personal or external);
  o don't jump to conclusions;
  o defer judgement;
  o ask questions to clarify;
  o probe for further information;
  o summarise what has been said;
  o practise as much as possible.

- Clues that someone is not listening:

  o no eye contact;
  o fidgeting, fiddling and/or doodling;
  o not acknowledging what has been said with nods and smiles, for example;
  o interrupting what is being said;
  o speaking over the speaker;
  o finishing sentences;
  o turning away or becoming distracted;
  o responding to external stimuli, such as noises outside the room;
  o checking phones, laptops or tablets;
  o saying something that has no relevance to what the speaker has said;
  o asking a question that has already been answered;
  o repeating something that has already been said (unless this is done to clarify a point).

➜ Related activities

Activity 40: Becoming an active listener

Activity 46: Learning through storytelling

Activity 81: Improving interview techniques

....

Activity 41

➜ Preparatory reading

Short videos on improving listening skills can be found by using the search term 'listening skills' on YouTube (www.youtube.com). Videos produced by experts in the field provide interesting preparation for this activity for both tutors and students. You may also find it prudent to run a search on 'listening skills games' to ensure that students do not merely copy an existing game (adaptions of games are acceptable as they require students to get to grips with the issues surrounding listening skills, as you can see from the examples given above).

➜ Further reading

Nichols, P. (2009) *The Lost Art of Listening: How Learning to Listen Can Improve Relationships*. New York: Guilford Press. This book is aimed at those interested in family therapy but has some useful and interesting advice about improving listening skills.

Seidman, I. (2013) *Interviewing as Qualitative Research: a Guide for Researchers in Education and the Social Sciences*, 4th edition. New York: Teachers College Press. Chapters 6 and 7 of this book provide some insightful information about listening well and talking less, establishing rapport and exploring laughter for students who are interested in improving their listening skills when undertaking research interviews.

Activity 41

Activity ·········· → 42

Improving observation skills

The activity

This activity can be run in two ways: as a tutor-led exercise and class discussion with your usual cohort of students or as a workshop with new students from a variety of courses and levels of study (students who are interested in observation techniques for their research, for example). For both activities you need to prepare the exercise before you meet with your students. This involves composing a series of questions that will test their powers of observation. It is an entertaining way to encourage students to think about observation skills and techniques that they can develop and utilise as their course progresses.

Choose a venue for this activity. This can be your usual classroom or a new venue, if the workshop option is chosen. Walk to the venue, taking note of anything that can be developed into a question that will help to test your students' powers of observation. Try to develop at least 20 questions that test different ways to observe, including sight, sound, smell and touch. These will depend on your venue and location, but could include issues such as:

- The colour of paint in the corridor.
- The number of doors through which students pass to get to the venue.
- The number of trees outside.

- Sounds that may be present such as traffic, birds, running water, ticking clocks or humming lighting.
- Smells that may be present (if there are none you could introduce your own, such as an essential oil in the

classroom or sweet-smelling flowers). Ensure that the smell you take note of is present at the time you run your class: cleaning product smells fade, for example.
- The feel and texture of flooring that they walk over to get to the venue.
- The texture or coverings on walls, including pictures and signage.
- The amount and type of light, whether natural or artificial.

- The number of seats/desks/tables in the classroom (students should give an answer without taking time to count).
- The number of fellow students in the group (again, without time to count).
- The weather conditions outside and the temperature inside.

If you are using your usual venue you can also introduce changes in the room, asking students to list changes that they can observe since they were last in the room. This helps them to think about what they have observed previously, recall the information and observe possible differences. Changes that can be introduced include:

- Textbooks placed on desks, covering a completely different subject area.
- Chairs and tables rearranged in a slightly strange pattern (if possible) or cushions placed on a few chairs.
- A radio with the sound turned down very low, hidden from view.

- A loudly ticking clock placed near to students but out of view.
- Another student/researcher who is not normally part of the group, sitting in a chair and acting as if they have always been part of the group.
- Equipment moved to different locations in the room.

When you meet with your students ask them to work through the questions. This can be done as a tutor-led exercise (quick-fire questions) with your usual student cohort or, if in a workshop, you can ask students to do this in small groups. Once they have worked through the questions, lead a class discussion on the issues raised, relating the discussion to observation skills and techniques (see key issues). Conclude the session by asking students to develop a plan of action that will help them to improve their observation skills as their course progresses.

Key issues

Students tend to enjoy this activity, especially if you turn it into a game or quiz, perhaps by firing questions quickly at students and asking for a quick response. It raises awareness about observation, illustrating that we often do not observe as well as we think we do. It also helps to introduce the different ways that we observe, including sight, sound, smell and touch. These issues should be related to studies, projects and research activities during your discussion. The content and level of discussion will vary, depending on subject and level of study, but could include the following:

- Staying alert, thinking about how we observe and practising better observation.
- Recognising that observation can use all the senses (if you have someone within your group who is visually impaired or has hearing difficulties, this can lead to an interesting discussion about alternative ways to observe).
- Building awareness of how distractions can have an influence on observation (technology, people, unexpected events, preoccupation, for example).
- Relating observation techniques to research:
  o clear, structured and systematic observation for experimental research;
  o immersion, concentration and focus for participant observation;

  o setting aside expectations, prejudices and prejudgements when observing in social research and experimental research;
  o unobtrusive or covert observation and the ethical implications;
  o the effect of observing and how this can change behaviour;
  o observation from different theoretical and methodological perspectives (a realist perspective that suggests there is a real world to observe, experimental research that manipulates and contrives in a systematic way or naturalistic observations and narrative approaches that tell a story, for example).
- Understanding the importance of reflecting on what has been observed.

→ **Related activities**

Activity 41: Improving listening skills

Activity 81: Improving interview techniques

Activity 42

➜ Preparatory reading

Students do not need any preparatory reading for this activity (it seems to have more resonance if they approach the topic with a fresh mind).

....

➜ Further reading

The following books can be recommended to students who want to follow up specific issues raised in this activity, depending on level and subject of study.

Angrosino, M. (2007) *Doing Ethnographic and Observational Research*. London: Sage.

DeWalt, K. and DeWalt, B. (2011) *Participant Observation: a Guide for Fieldworkers*, 2nd edition. Lanham, MD: AltaMira Press.

Hingley-Jones, H., Parkinson, C. and Allain, L. (eds) (2017) *Observation in Health and Social Care*. London: Jessica Kingsley.

Smart, B., Peggs, K. and Burridge, J. (eds) (2013) *Observation Methods* (4-volume set). London: Sage.

Activity 42

Activity • • • • • • • • • • → 43

Making oral presentations

The activity

Divide your students into groups. The size of group depends on how many students you have and the amount of contact time you have available for groups to make their presentations. Ask each group to produce a ten-minute presentation on a topic related to your course. They should work together during independent study to design, produce and practise their presentation. The style and content are group choices. The only stipulation is that every group member should speak, at some point, during the presentation.

When you next meet each group should make their presentation. Allocate ten minutes for the presentation and up to ten minutes for peer feedback, which should be constructive and supportive. Finish the session with a discussion to sum up the issues raised. You will need one to two hours of contact time, depending on the number of student groups. You can extend this activity if you wish by asking students to develop a checklist that will help them to produce effective oral presentations as their course progresses.

Key issues

This activity enables students to practise producing and presenting oral presentations with the support and help of group members and with constructive feedback from their peers. It tends to make the process less daunting, in particular, for students who are nervous or unconfident about making oral presentations. Students all have to contribute, which tends to make them more supportive and less critical of others' presentations. However, you must play an active role in feedback sessions to ensure that all feedback given is supportive, encouraging and positive.

Issues that can be raised during the feedback session and discussion depend on subject and level of study and on the type of presentation given by students. Examples include:

- controlling nerves;
- maintaining and displaying confidence;
- delivering at the right pitch, tone and level;
- knowing what makes a good presentation;
- avoiding mistakes;
- managing non-verbal communication;
- understanding the audience;
- developing content;
- using visual aids effectively;
- choosing and using presentation software;
- working together as a group;
- practising presentations and receiving feedback;
- presenting seminar papers;
- presenting at conferences (preparing abstracts and writing conference papers for students studying at advanced level, for example);
- inviting questions and giving answers (when to take questions and how to respond);
- knowing how to give positive and supportive peer feedback.

➜ Related activities

Activity 44: Producing and presenting a seminar paper

Activity 45: Presenting in groups

....

➜ Preparatory reading

Students can prepare for this activity by reading the books listed below and by visiting YouTube (www.youtube.com) to view some of the videos from academics on 'making oral presentations'. No preparation is required for tutors who are familiar with oral presentation techniques.

....

➜ Further reading

The following books can be recommended to students who want to learn more about making presentations.

Becker, L. (2014) *Presenting Your Research*. London: Sage.
Chivers, B. and Shoolbred, M. (2007) *A Student's Guide to Presentations*. London: Sage.
Schwabish, J. (2017) *Better Presentations: a Guide for Scholars, Researchers, and Wonks*. New York: Columbia University Press.
Shephard, K. (2005) *Presenting at Conferences, Seminars and Meetings*. London: Sage.
Van Emden, J. and Becker, L. (2016) *Presentation Skills for Students*, 3rd edition. London: Palgrave.

Activity 43

Activity • • • • • • • • • • → 44

Producing and presenting
a seminar paper

TUTOR NOTES

Purpose: This activity is for students who are required to produce and present a seminar paper during their course. It provides advice and guidance about how to do this through the development of a student-centred digital resource, which students can access, and refer to, when they need to produce and present a seminar paper.

Type: Student-centred digital resource.

Alternative type(s): One-to-one support session.

Level: Elementary and intermediate.

Duration: A few minutes of tutor time is required to set up the digital resource. Fifteen minutes to half an hour of contact time is required to introduce the activity and explain requirements (the time spent on this depends on the level of study and the depth of information required: see below).

Equipment/materials: A suitable digital platform on which to build the resource and the required access details for all students.

Learning outcome: By the end of this activity students will have developed a useful digital resource that they can access when required to help them feel more confident and knowledgeable about producing and presenting a seminar paper.

The activity

Set up a digital resource called 'producing and presenting a seminar paper', using the relevant platform. Post some information to get the resource started (see key issues). Introduce the resource to your students, explaining what it is, why it has been set up and how it will help students to produce and present seminar papers. Ask students to build the resource by making their own contributions. This could include tips and advice on writing and producing seminar papers, possible worries and concerns about presenting a paper, or specific questions that need addressing through the help and advice of their peers, for example. Students can also post short abstracts of their paper as it is being developed to receive constructive and supportive peer feedback. Explain that this resource will be available throughout their course so that it can be accessed when required. Monitor the resource from time to time to ensure that information posted is correct, supportive, useful and encouraging.

Some students may need specific help and advice when producing a seminar paper. In this case it is possible to run this activity as a one-to-one support session. Meet with the student to discuss the issues involved and to address possible worries and concerns. Offer feedback on their written paper before it is presented, again offering support and encouragement and addressing worries and concerns.

Key issues

This activity builds a useful student-centred resource that can be accessed when students need to produce and present a seminar paper. Although it is a student-centred resource it is advisable to start to build the resource with a few of your own posts so that students can understand what is required and see the benefits to be gained. Posts depend on your level and subject of study, but can include the following:

- A code of conduct for using the resource:

  o ensuring posts are supportive, encouraging and positive;
  o ensuring that posts do not breach copyright;
  o avoiding plagiarism;

  o respecting confidentiality;
  o acting with integrity and respect for others.

- Examples of well-produced seminar papers.
- Links to videos, vlogs and blogs illustrating how to present a seminar paper.
- Useful references (see below).

Students should be encouraged to make their own posts, building and growing the resource so that it is useful and of benefit to peers. They can pose questions, seek answers from peers (or from you, if necessary), or discuss worries and concerns they may have about making a presentation.

Some students will not take part in this activity. They feel that they do not need additional help when producing and presenting a seminar paper and are happy to work independently with no input from others. For other students, however, this is an invaluable resource: they ask questions, give answers and post useful and interesting information for their peers. It is for these reasons that this activity should be voluntary and non-assessed.

➜ Related activities

Activity 43: Making oral presentations

Activity 45: Presenting in groups

....

➜ Preparatory reading

Students can prepare for this activity by reading the books listed below (these can be posted on the digital resource). You can also find out if your university provides relevant information on their website/intranet, or runs workshops on producing seminar papers. Information about these can be posted on the digital resource as preparatory work and to get the resource started.

....

➜ Further reading

The following books provide further information on producing and presenting seminar papers.

Becker, L. (2014) *Presenting Your Research*. London: Sage.
Chivers, B. and Shoolbred, M. (2007) *A Student's Guide to Presentations*. London: Sage.
Shephard, K. (2005) *Presenting at Conferences, Seminars and Meetings*. London: Sage.
Van Emden, J. and Becker, L. (2016) *Presentation Skills for Students*, 3rd edition. London: Palgrave.

Activity 44

Activity · · · · · · · · · · ➔ 45

Presenting in groups

TUTOR NOTES

Purpose: This activity helps students to learn more about presenting in groups by asking them to make a group presentation to their peers. The topic of the presentation is 'how to make effective group presentations'. This encourages students to explore the issues involved, gain a deeper understanding and reinforce their learning through practice, observation and peer feedback.

Type: Group exercise followed by group presentation.

Alternative type(s): Video/podcast production (in groups during independent study).

Level: Elementary.

Duration: Students need to spend a few hours designing, producing and practising their group presentation during independent study. One to two hours of contact time is required for groups to make their presentation and receive peer feedback (the actual time required depends on the number of student groups).

Equipment/materials: Groups can use any presentation equipment and software that they deem appropriate and this should be made available for their use.

Learning outcome: By the end of this activity students will have a greater understanding of how to present in groups and will feel more confident and knowledgeable about doing so, having researched, discussed, practised, observed and received feedback on group presentations.

The activity

Divide your students into groups. The number of groups depends on the size of your student cohort and the amount of contact time that you have available. Ask them to prepare a 15-minute group presentation on the topic of 'how to make effective group presentations'. The focus, content, structure and style of presentation, within this topic, are group choices. Explain that each group will make their presentation to their peers when you next meet. There will be five minutes for discussion and feedback after each presentation. Encourage your students to produce an interesting, informative and creative presentation that will help their peers to learn more about the topic. You can ask students to vote on the best presentation at the end of the session, if you feel this is appropriate.

It is possible to ask students to produce a video or podcast of their presentation, if contact time is not available for this activity. If this option is chosen, set up and provide access to a suitable digital platform on which videos/podcasts can be uploaded. Ask your students to view each presentation and provide constructive feedback where appropriate. Again, encourage your students to provide a creative, informative and interesting video that will help their peers to learn more about the topic.

Key issues

This activity provides an entertaining way to help students learn about presenting in groups. They must first understand the issues involved in making group presentations before working out how best to present this information to their peers, ensuring that they put into practice what they have learnt. They are able to reinforce this learning by observing, and commenting on, the presentations made by other groups.

Students produce a wide variety of entertaining, creative and informative presentations in this activity. This has included an interactive presentation where their peers have been invited to spot deliberate mistakes introduced into the presentation; creative use of software to explain and entertain; light-hearted role plays of students trying to present in a group (including various mishaps); serious and informative, carefully crafted speeches; and presentations with visually captivating images.

➜ Related activities

Activity 43: Making oral presentations

Activity 65: Getting the most out of group work

Activity 71: Understanding group dynamics and avoiding conflict

Preparatory reading

Students can prepare for this activity by reading some of the books listed below. No preparation is required for tutors who are familiar with presenting in groups.

➜ Further reading

The following books can be recommended to students who want to find out more about working in groups and making presentations.

Chivers, B. and Shoolbred, M. (2007) *A Student's Guide to Presentations*. London: Sage.

Levin, P. (2005) *Successful Teamwork! For Undergraduates and Taught Postgraduates Working on Group Projects*. Maidenhead: Open University Press.

Schwabish, J. (2017) *Better Presentations: a Guide for Scholars, Researchers, and Wonks*. New York: Columbia University Press.

Van Emden, J. and Becker, L. (2016) *Presentation Skills for Students*, 3rd edition. London: Palgrave.

Activity 45

Activity • • • • • • • • • ➜ 46

Learning through storytelling

Student handout page 315

TUTOR NOTES

Purpose: This activity introduces students to learning through storytelling, first, by asking them to reflect on how they have learnt from stories in the past and, second, by creating and telling a digital story related to their course.

Type: Digital storytelling.

Alternative type(s): Storytelling in class.

Level: Elementary, intermediate and advanced (the level will be reflected in the type and complexity of story and related discussion).

Duration: Fifty minutes to one hour to introduce and discuss the idea of learning through storytelling. Students need several hours during independent study to create, design, complete and upload their stories. If the in-class option is chosen you need another 50 minutes to one hour of contact time for students to tell their stories.

Equipment/materials: The digital storytelling option will require a suitable digital platform for uploading students' stories. Students may need access to presentation equipment if the storytelling-in-class option is chosen.

Learning outcome: By the end of this activity students will recognise the potential for learning through storytelling, having reflected on stories from their past and having produced, presented and received feedback on their own story related to their course.

The activity

Introduce the idea of learning through storytelling to your class. This can be done in various ways, depending on the time you have available and your student cohort:

- Hold a class discussion asking students to think about how they have learnt from stories in the past. Ask them to provide examples of these stories and discuss how and why the stories provide an effective (or ineffective) way to learn.
- Tell a story, if you are happy to do so. Discuss the story with your students, obtain feedback and find out whether they believe storytelling is an effective way to learn.

- Brainstorm the question 'How can we learn through storytelling?'
- Divide your class into small groups and give them a copy of Part 1 of the Student Handout. If contact time is limited you can ask that they work on this during independent study. This works best as a group exercise, but it is possible to adapt the handout so that the activity can be run as a self-guided individual exercise during independent study, if this better suits your students.

Once you have introduced the idea of learning through storytelling, divide your students into small groups and ask them to create a digital story that will help their peers to learn something related to your course. Part 2 of the Student Handout provides guidance. You can be quite specific, providing a relevant topic for each group, or you can leave the decision to your students. They can use any methods or media that will help to tell their story (photographs, data visualisations, audio and text content, for example). Stories should be uploaded on to the relevant digital platform (internal or external, depending on what is available at your institution).

This activity produces an interesting, creative and useful digital resource that can be used in further classes to discuss and illustrate how storytelling can aid learning, if contact time is available. Alternatively, you can ask that students read all the stories and post feedback and comments, where appropriate. You will need to monitor the posts to ensure that comments are positive, constructive and correct.

If you choose, instead, to ask students to tell their stories in class, ensure that presentation equipment and software are available for their use. Give a time for each story and ask that students adhere to this time so that all stories can be completed in the session. Stories will need careful management: try to ensure that they do not veer off-track or are not too long-winded. If possible, reserve a little time at the end to discuss the issues raised by the activity.

Key issues

This activity has, over the years, been adapted to take advantage of rapid technological advances and to make the most of the technological knowledge and experiences of students. In this activity students produce interesting and creative stories: they can be nonlinear, interactive and meaningful stories, using a wide variety of features such as photography, music, text, graphics, narration, title screens and sound effects.

Points that are raised during the discussion and feedback depend on your subject and the level of study. They can include:

- Storytelling can be entertaining, memorable, relaxing and have significant impact on learning.
- Students learn more from stories to which they can relate or with which they identify.
- Stories can make complex material easier to understand.
- Storytelling encourages students to share experiences, ideas and learning.
- Stories capture attention.
- Students can react intellectually and emotionally to stories.
- It is possible for students to interpret a story in different ways, depending on their connection with the story, the emotional impact and previous experiences.
- There are different types of story, including reflective accounts, anecdotes, case studies, fiction, myth, life histories, scenarios and personal examples from experience.
- Stories can contain characters, plots, languages and settings.
- Producing a story in a group can aid collaborative learning, help students to understand others, help group cohesion and enhance learning among group members.
- Stories may not work for some subjects and certain subjects generate more interesting stories than others.
- Some people are better at telling stories than others: working in groups helps to pool strengths and enables those who do not wish to narrate the story to adopt a different role within the group.

→ Cautionary note

Some students can get caught up in the technological aspects of digital storytelling and neglect the purpose of this activity, which is learning through storytelling. It is useful to emphasise this point in your introduction: ask that students remain mindful of the fact that they should be teaching their fellow students something related to their course with their story. The questions asked on the Student Handout should help them to do this.

→ Related activities

Activity 40: Becoming an active listener

Activity 45: Presenting in groups

Activity 57: Developing thoughts and imagination

Activity 46

➜ **Preparatory reading**

The Higher Education Academy in the UK has a useful section on 'Learning through Storytelling': www.heacademy.ac.uk/enhancement/starter-tools/learning-through-storytelling. Here you can find information about the history of storytelling, how it can be used and how to get started, all of which provide useful preparatory work for this activity.

➜ **Further reading**

Alterio, M. and McDrury, J. (2003) *Learning through Storytelling in Higher Education: Using Reflection and Experience to Improve Learning*. London: Routledge. This is a useful book for tutors who are interested in using storytelling in the classroom as it outlines the different models of storytelling and explains how techniques can be used.

Hertz, S. (2016) *Write Choices: Elements of Nonfiction Storytelling*. Thousand Oaks, CA: CQ Press. This book is useful for anyone who wishes to write nonfiction stories and can be recommended to students who are interested in this topic.

Ohler, J. (2013) *Digital Storytelling in the Classroom: New Media Pathways to Literacy, Learning, and Creativity*, 2nd edition. Thousand Oaks, CA: Corwin. This book provides useful further reading for tutors who are interested in the different types of digital storytelling methods that can be used in the classroom.

Activity 46

Activity • • • • • • • • • • ➔ 47

Engaging with lecturers and tutors

Student
handout
page 316

TUTOR NOTES

Purpose: This activity is an entertaining way to help students engage with lecturers and tutors. It is based on the board game 'Scruples', which presents players with a number of dilemmas, along with possible solutions. They must discuss each dilemma and reach a consensus on the solution(s). The dilemmas are based on real cases and help students to think about how to deal with issues that could arise when engaging with lecturers and tutors. It can be used at the start of your course as a type of ice-breaker or introductory session.

Type: Game.

Alternative type(s): Student worksheet.

Level: Elementary.

Duration: Fifty minutes to one hour of contact time. If you choose the worksheet option students will spend one or two hours during independent study on this activity.

Equipment/materials: Card on which to print the dilemmas.

Learning outcome: By the end of this activity students will feel more engaged with lecturers and tutors, which will help them to feel more confident about developing a good working relationship as their course progresses.

The activity

Print each of the dilemmas and associated solutions presented in the Student Handout onto separate pieces of card (about the size of a playing card to give the impression of this being a 'game'). Produce several identical packs of these cards. You can adapt, delete or add to the dilemmas, depending on what you feel to be appropriate and on your student cohort (the dilemma concerning alcohol and making a pass at a tutor might not be appropriate for some students, for example). You will also need to adapt some questions to better suit your country and type of institution. This game is based on the board game 'Scruples': some older tutors and students may remember the game, but younger ones will not understand the reference, which will need to be explained.

When you meet give a brief explanation of the game and its purpose (see key issues). Divide your students into groups and give each group a pack of the dilemma cards. Ask groups to work through the dilemmas and discuss and agree on a given solution(s). Some dilemmas are straightforward and students find it easy to reach consensus, whereas others are more complex and require in-depth discussion before consensus can be reached. In some cases students might decide that more than one solution is appropriate and in others they might decide that none of the given solutions are appropriate (or they may develop their own solution). Allocate up to 40 minutes for this activity, before bringing the groups together for a class discussion on the issues raised. Conclude by asking students whether they have any additional questions about how to engage with lecturers and tutors.

It is possible to adapt the dilemmas presented in the Student Handout into a worksheet that students can work on during independent study. If you choose this option try to find a little time in one of your teaching sessions to discuss students' responses to the dilemmas.

Key issues

This activity should take place at the beginning of your course as it helps students to think early on about how to engage with lecturers and tutors. It also helps to act as an ice-breaker or introductory session. It is informal, entertaining, useful and informative, and helps students to get to know others in their group. All the dilemmas are based on real cases that should help students to think more deeply about the issues presented. Some solutions are ironic or amusing, which helps to keep students entertained.

An important part of the activity is that students have the chance to discuss issues, negotiate, compromise and reach consensus, in addition to understanding more about how to engage with lecturers and tutors as their course progresses. It enables students to empathise with members of teaching staff and understand more about their work, role and expectations. It also encourages students to see that engagement is a two-way, and shared, process: some of the dilemmas are posed from a student's point of view, some are posed from a tutor's point of view and some solutions are from both points of view, for example.

➔ Cautionary note

On occasions you may find that some groups are unable to reach consensus and, on rare occasions, the discussion can develop into an argument, in particular, if you have two students with strong, opposing views. It is important that you walk among the groups listening to discussions so that you can diffuse any problems that may arise and before they escalate. If groups cannot reach consensus you may need to emphasise that there are no right or wrong answers and that, in some cases, it is possible to reach consensus on more than one solution or provide an alternative solution. Specific, correct answers are not the goal of this activity: instead it is the ability to discuss, negotiate, compromise, display compassion and understand engagement that are important.

➔ Related activities

Activity 40: Becoming an active listener

Activity 41: Improving listening skills

Activity 48: Getting the most from tutor feedback

Activity 86: Working with supervisors and personal tutors

Activity 98: Collaborating and cooperative ethically

➔ Preparatory reading

Winstone, N. and Nash, R. (2016) *The Developing Engagement with Feedback Toolkit* (DEFT). This toolkit provides useful, interesting and practical information for tutors who are interested in improving the way that students use tutor feedback. It provides useful preparatory work for this activity and can be accessed on the Higher Education Academy website: https://www.heacademy.ac.uk/resource/developing-engagement-feedback-toolkit-deft.

Schrier, K. (2016) *Knowledge Games: How Playing Games can Solve Problems, Create Insight, and Make Change*. Baltimore, MD: Johns Hopkins University Press. This book provides useful preparatory reading for tutors who are interested in using games in their teaching.

Activity 47

→ Further reading

Blair, A. (2017) 'Understanding first-year students' transition to university: a pilot study with implications for student engagement, assessment, and feedback', *Politics*, 37 (2): 215-28, published online before print 17 May 2016, http://doi.org/10.1177/0263395716633904. This paper provides deeper insight into how students and tutors use and give feedback.

Havemann, L. and Sherman, S. (eds) (2017) *Assessment, Feedback and Technology: Contexts and Case Studies in Bloomsbury*. London: Bloomsbury Learning Environment (www.ble.ac.uk/ebook.html). This is a free e-book that contains interesting chapters covering issues of assessment, feedback and technology. It provides useful reading for tutors who are interested in these issues.

Activity 47

Activity · · · · · · · · · · · ➔ 48

Getting the most from tutor feedback

TUTOR NOTES

Purpose: This activity helps students to get the most from tutor feedback by asking them to brainstorm ideas, learn from each other and develop an individual feedback action plan that they can use, and refer back to, throughout their course.

Type: Brainstorm followed by tutor-led discussion and individual exercise.

Alternative type(s): Group exercise followed by poster presentation.

Level: Elementary.

Duration: Fifty minutes to one hour of contact time (up to 20 minutes for the brainstorm, up to 20 minutes for the tutor-led discussion and up to 20 minutes for the individual student exercise). If you choose to run this activity as a group exercise with a poster presentation, students need to spend a few hours during independent study producing their presentations, and one hour of contact time to make their presentations.

Equipment/materials: Interactive whiteboard, flipchart or chalkboard. Poster presentation materials, if this option is chosen.

Learning outcome: By the end of this activity students will know how to get the most out of tutor feedback, and will benefit from this understanding throughout their course.

The activity

Brainstorm with your students the question 'how do I get the most out of tutor feedback?' Write their answers on your board/flipchart without judgement, analysis or reflection. Don't be afraid of silences: students can, on occasions, take a few minutes to think about this topic before becoming more spontaneous with their suggestions. If students are unfamiliar with the brainstorming technique ask them to give any answer they can think of in relation to the question. They are not going to be judged and they should not judge or critique the answers given by other students (even if they do not agree with another's contribution). Each answer they give will be written on your board: the goal is to pool ideas and come up with a comprehensive list of tips, advice and techniques that will help students to get the most out of tutor feedback.

Once the brainstorm is complete (this usually takes about 20 minutes) discuss the issues raised with your students, combining, expanding on and improving ideas. Do this for a further 20 minutes until you feel that the discussion has run its course. During this discussion, make it clear that students should not be passive recipients of feedback, but should play an active role through seeking, finding, generating, engaging with and acting on feedback. Once the discussion is complete, ask your students to work on a personal action plan that will help them to get the most out of tutor feedback as their course progresses, based on the issues raised in the brainstorm and discussion.

It is possible to run this activity as a group exercise followed by a poster presentation. Introduce the topic to your students, asking that they work in groups to discuss and produce a poster on how they can get the most out of tutor feedback. Ask students to present their posters when you next meet, leaving enough time for discussion and questions after each presentation. If students are unfamiliar with the poster presentation technique, give them a copy of the Student Handout from Activity 28 (this gives information about producing a poster presentation).

Key issues

The following issues can be raised and discussed during the brainstorming session and discussion.

- Read and/or listen to all feedback carefully, taking note of everything that has been said.
- Take feedback for what it is: constructive criticism on what can be done better to improve your work.
- Think of your tutor as a partner in the learning process, helping you to utilise your experience and draw out your knowledge.
- Understand that feedback helps students to become independent learners and improves self-awareness and self-regulation. Realise that feedback is for your personal benefit.
- Try to get used to the 'styles' of different tutors (some are more abrupt and straightforward than others and some are better than others at providing positive and constructive feedback, for example).
- See feedback as a two-way process where responsibilities are shared. Students should not be passive recipients of feedback, but should play an active role by seeking out feedback, generating ideas and engaging in feedback.
- Recognise and utilise the wide variety of feedback opportunities that are available. Understand that feedback can come from various sources such as tutors, peers, learning supporters and self-assessment.
- Put yourself in the shoes of the tutor and think about how you would offer feedback.
- If you are unhappy with the type and standard of feedback, tell your tutor, but do this in a constructive, non-confrontational way.
- If you don't understand what has been written or said, ask for clarification.
- Be aware of how you react to criticism (think about behavioural and psychological reactions). Try to turn negative reactions into positive reactions.
- Don't take comments out of context and read more into them than was ever intended.
- Keep your emotions away from what you are being told.
- Don't take criticism personally.
- Be open and enthusiastic about change.
- Cultivate a desire to learn.
- Understand how the assessment process works (see Activities 87 and 88).
- Act on tutor advice.

→ Related activities

Activity 7: Fostering collaborative learning and interaction

Activity 40: Becoming an active listener

Activity 41: Improving listening skills

Activity 86: Working with supervisors and personal tutors

Activity 98: Collaborating and cooperating ethically

→ Preparatory reading

Winstone, N. and Nash, R. (2016) *The Developing Engagement with Feedback Toolkit* (DEFT). This toolkit provides useful, interesting and practical information for tutors who are interested in improving the way that students use tutor feedback. It can be accessed on the Higher Education Academy website: https://www.heacademy.ac.uk/resource/developing-engagement-feedback-toolkit-deft.

Song, G., Hoon, L. and Alvin, L. (2017) 'Students' response to feedback: an exploratory study', *RELC Journal*, 48 (3): 357–72, first published 25 April 2017, https://doi.org/10.1177/0033688217691445. This paper provides interesting information about how students respond to feedback (paying attention to clarity and logical development of ideas, for example).

Activity 48

→ Further reading

These two papers provide deeper insight into how students and tutors use and give feedback.

Blair, A. (2017) 'Understanding first-year students' transition to university: a pilot study with implications for student engagement, assessment, and feedback', *Politics*, 37 (2): 215-28, published online before print 17 May 2016, http://doi.org/10.1177/0263395716633904.

Winstone, N., Nash, R., Parker, M. and Rowntree, J. (2017) 'Supporting learners' agentic engagement with feedback: a systematic review and a taxonomy of recipience processes', *Educational Psychologist*, 52 (1): 17-37, http://doi.org/10.1080/00461520.2016.1207538.

Activity 48

Section 7

Finding and using information

Activity · · · · · · · · · · · → 49

Getting the most from the library

The activity

Contact your subject liaison librarian/subject librarian to organise a session called 'getting the most from the library'. Most will run a session lasting 50 minutes to one hour in the library/LRC to demonstrate the equipment, materials, software, facilities and services that are available and to offer advice and guidance on how to improve search techniques. If such a person is not available, lead a tour and talk yourself. Some key issues and discussion points are provided below as a guide.

This activity can be used for students at all levels of study: when you brief the librarian make sure that he or she is aware of the level of study and pitches their session accordingly. It is of particular use to students who are new to your institution and to those students who have demonstrated a certain level of reluctance to use the facilities available, perhaps because they are seen to be irrelevant in this digital age (see Walton and Matthews, 2016, for discussions about how libraries are changing due to technological advances). This activity is also of use to students studying at advanced level who need to search for information at a deeper level when conducting their research.

Key issues

This activity can raise the following issues, depending on the subject and level of study of your students, the preference of your subject liaison librarian and the equipment, facilities and services that are available in your library/LRC.

Equipment and materials

- Books and journals (printed and electronic): relevant literature will be highlighted and discussed (perhaps with a physical and/or virtual tour) and search techniques for library and e-resources will be explained. Information about borrowing books and access to the relevant journal databases will be provided (free to access, university subscription or CD-ROM, for example).
- Theses, dissertations and research papers: information about accessing and using university repositories will be provided, along with information about accessing electronic and/or printed theses and dissertations. Information about printing, binding and depositing an individual thesis or dissertation will be provided for students studying at advanced level.
- Archives: the librarian will discuss issues such as access, opening hours, reading rooms and copying material held in the archives (special collections, music, maps, catalogues and guides, for example).

- Exam papers: the librarian will show students how to access previous exam papers for specific courses.
- Audio-visual equipment, such as microform readers/printers, DVD/video playback equipment and data projectors: the relevance and use of this equipment will be demonstrated (where operated by debiting printing credit accounts, for example). The librarian will also explain how to search for multi-media materials and data, and discuss borrowing limits.
- IT facilities and software: equipment will be demonstrated and explained, where relevant and if time is available. This can include information about how to print and photocopy (including issues of copyright), netbooks and laptops available for loan, PCs available to book, connecting to the Wi-Fi network, bibliographic software, statistical software and data mining software, for example. Alternatively, Activity 73 can cover these issues.

Services and facilities

- Help-desk service: librarians will introduce this service and give details of opening hours. Some libraries offer a 'book a librarian' service for one-to-one help and advice.
- Inter-library loan services: these are available for students to access materials that are not available in their library. The librarian will explain how to use this service and discuss the costs involved.
- Workshops, training sessions and seminars: these may be available, covering topics such as reading and writing, revision and exam skills, citing publications, avoiding plagiarism, undertaking a literature search and

using databases and datasets. Information about dates, times and how to book will be provided.
- Social spaces, casual seating and group areas: libraries are, increasingly, creating this type of space for students. The librarian will provide a tour of these spaces and explain about rules (concerning food and drink, courtesy and respect, for example).
- Facilities for students with disabilities: these can include accessible rooms, one-to-one specialist help and reduced costs for printing and photocopying. Facilities will be discussed and demonstrated, where relevant. Alternatively, Activity 76 can cover these issues.

Search techniques

There are a wide variety of search techniques that can be used by students, and the librarian will discuss and demonstrate the most relevant. Examples of these include:

- Search operators (also known as Boolean operators) enabling the use of multiple words and concepts in the search (e.g. AND, OR, NOT).
- Search statements that combine search words using search operators such as those described above.
- Phrase searching for more specific searches.

- Proximity searching for more specific searching and the exclusion of irrelevant records.
- Advanced searching for field-specific searching (such as author, title and date) and index searching (alphabetical lists of authors or subjects, for example).

➜ **Related activities**

Activity 50: Conducting online research

Activity 51: Using primary and secondary sources

Activity 52: Evaluating sources

Activity 55: Organising, managing and storing information

Activity 49

➜ Preparatory reading

All university library websites contain useful information, tutorials and/or videos about using their facilities and services, and offer detailed advice about finding sources of data. They also provide printed or digital guidance leaflets, which are useful preparatory reading for tutors who intend to run this activity themselves.

Chapter 3 of Ridley (2012) provides a useful guide to finding sources of information and conducting searches.

Jantti, M. and Heath, J. (2016) 'What role for libraries in learning analytics?', *Performance Measurement and Metrics*, 17 (2): 203–10, http://doi.org/10.1108/PMM-04-2016-0020. This paper contains some interesting information about the link between time spent in the library and degree classification (useful for convincing your students it is a good idea to use the library frequently).

➜ Further reading

The first two books can be recommended to students who would like more information about the issues raised in this activity. The third book provides an interesting read for tutors who want to know about transformations taking place in libraries.

Fink, A. (2014) *Conducting Research Literature Reviews: From the Internet to Paper*, 4th edition. Thousand Oaks, CA: Sage.

Ridley, D. (2012) *The Literature Review: a Step-by-Step Guide for Students*, 2nd edition. London: Sage.

Walton, G. and Matthews, G. (eds) (2016) *University Libraries and Space in the Digital World*. Abingdon, Oxon: Routledge.

Activity 49

Activity • • • • • • • • • ➜ 50

Conducting online research

TUTOR NOTES

Purpose: This activity is a simple way to help students think more about how to conduct online research. It is a voluntary exercise that does not take up contact time. Students are asked to consider the dos and don'ts of conducting online research and build a useful tip exchange that can be developed and accessed throughout their course.

Type: Tip exchange (student-centred digital resource).

Alternative type(s): Brainstorm with tutor-led discussion and individual exercise.

Level: Elementary, intermediate and advanced (the level of study will be reflected in the tips offered).

Duration: Tutors need to spend a few minutes setting up a suitable digital platform for the tip exchange and a few minutes over the duration of the course to monitor posts. If the brainstorm option is chosen you need 50 minutes to one hour of contact time.

Equipment/materials: A suitable digital platform and the required access for all students. If the brainstorm option is chosen you need a flipchart, interactive whiteboard or chalkboard.

Learning outcome: By the end of this activity students will have built a useful digital resource about the dos and don'ts of conducting online research, which will help to build their confidence, increase their knowledge and enable them to avoid problems and pitfalls when conducting online research throughout their course.

The activity

Introduce the idea of a tip exchange to your students. You can do this in class or online. The tip exchange is to be called 'dos and don'ts of conducting online research'. Explain that the resource is available for all students to exchange tips about how to conduct online research. Tips can cover the following topics:

- searching for information for assignments and research projects (useful search techniques and useful sources of information, for example);
- evaluating sources (checking facts, verifying statistics and avoiding 'fake news', for example);
- using, quoting, citing and referencing information found online;

- using online research methods to gather data (this will be of relevance to students studying at intermediate and advanced level who are undertaking a research project, and can include online questionnaires, focus groups, observations, data analytics and social media analytics, for example).

Set up a suitable digital platform on which students can post and read tips and ensure that all students have access to this platform. Begin the tip exchange with a few of your own tips to get the resource started (see key issues). Explain that the tip exchange is a voluntary, non-assessed activity, but that the resource will be available throughout the course so that students can add posts when a useful tip occurs to them. They can also access the tip exchange on a regular basis as it will help to improve their online research techniques and enable them to avoid problems and pitfalls. Monitor the posts from time to time to ensure that information is correct, constructive and useful.

It is possible to run this activity as a brainstorm followed by a tutor-led discussion and individual exercise if you have the contact time available and if it better suits your student cohort. Brainstorm with your students the topic of 'dos and don'ts of conducting online research'. Draw two columns on your flipchart, interactive whiteboard or chalkboard and slot students' responses into either column, without judgement, analysis or reflection. Don't be afraid of silences: students can, on occasions, take a few minutes to think about this topic before becoming more spontaneous with their suggestions.

Once the brainstorm is complete (this usually takes about 20 minutes) discuss the issues raised with your students, combining, expanding on and improving ideas. Do this for a further 20 minutes until you feel that the discussion has run its course. Once the discussion is complete ask your students to work on an individual basis to develop a personal action plan that will help them to conduct online research, based on the issues that have been raised during the brainstorm and discussion. Students can refer back to their action plans as their course progresses, enabling them to conduct effective and efficient online research.

Key issues

Summaries of tips that have been posted on the tip exchange include the following.

Do

- Evaluate, analyse and critique all sources carefully, even if you believe them to be valid and reliable.
- Determine the authority of the author (or originator) in terms of credentials, education, experience and bias.
- Determine the validity, quality and reliability of the information that is being presented.
- Check all sources for accuracy and cross-check, where possible.
- Recognise that figures can be misleading, incorrect (whether deliberate or by mistake) and open to misinterpretation.
- Use reliable sources (this listing will depend on country, subject and level of study, but could include):

  o the Directory of Open Access Journals (www.doaj.org);
  o the Social Sciences Research Network (www.ssrn.com);
  o the UK Data Service (http://ukdataservice.ac.uk);
  o the Library of Congress (www.loc.gov);
  o the National Library of Australia (www.nla.gov.au).

- Recognise that some people do not have access to the internet and some are much more active in their participation than others. Usage can be segregated by demographics such as age, gender, nationality and socio-economic group, for example. This must be taken into account when thinking about samples and selection for personal research projects involving online research methods.

Don't

- Believe everything you read online.
- Be influenced by your own personal bias when finding and evaluating sources online.
- Assume that primary sources found online are always the most reliable and valid (primary sources such as diaries and blogs can be full of personal bias, whereas an academic critique of such material can be accurate and unbiased, for example).
- Assume that all freely available data are available for research purposes. Check whether permission is required to use data.
- Assume that data are equally accessible (users can set their own privacy controls on social networking sites; search engines prioritise data based on complex algorithms; publishers of data may have complex reasons for making sure that some data are in the public domain, while limiting access to other data, for example).
- Administer an online questionnaire or interview without piloting (testing) to iron out all ambiguities and to ensure that the method will generate the type of information you require to address your research question.
- Begin a research project using online methods until you are certain the technology is available for your use and that you know how to use it (distribution methods and data analysis methods, for example).

➜ **Related activities**

Activity 21: Reading, critiquing and questioning

Activity 30: Citing, referencing and producing a bibliography

Activity 50

Activity 36: The use, abuse and misuse of statistics

Activity 51: Using primary and secondary sources

Activity 53: Finding truth and fact in mass information

Activity 54: Recognising statistics, facts, arguments and opinions

··

→ Preparatory reading

The books listed below provide useful preparatory and follow-up reading for students. These can be posted on the tip exchange.

··

→ Further reading

Ford, N. (2012) *The Essential Guide to Using the Web for Research.* London: Sage.

Halfpenny, P. and Proctor, R. (eds) (2015) *Innovations in Digital Research Methods*. London: Sage.

Harris, R. (2017) *Using Sources Effectively: Strengthening Your Writing and Avoiding Plagiarism*, 5th edition. Glendale, CA: Pyrczak Publishing.

Hooley, T., Marriott, J. and Wellens, J. (2012) *What is Online Research? Using the Internet for Social Science Research.* London: Bloomsbury Academic.

Ó Dochartaigh, N. (2012) *Internet Research Skills*, 3rd edition. London: Sage.

Stebbins, L. (2015) *Finding Reliable Information Online: Adventures of an Information Sleuth*. Lanham, MD: Rowman & Littlefield.

Activity 50

Activity • • • • • • • • • • • • ➔ 51

Using primary and secondary sources

Student
handout
page 318

TUTOR NOTES

Purpose: This activity helps students to understand how to recognise and use primary and secondary sources. It is aimed at students who have had little experience of using these sources. First, students are asked to undertake a group exercise that enables them to understand what is meant by primary and secondary sources. Second, a tutor-led discussion helps students to understand more about finding, choosing, using, citing, referencing and managing sources.

Type: Group exercise followed by tutor-led discussion.

Alternative type(s): None.

Level: Elementary.

Duration: Fifty minutes to one hour of contact time.

Equipment/materials: None required.

Learning outcome: By the end of this activity students will know what is meant by primary and secondary sources and will have a greater understanding of how to find, choose, use, cite, reference and manage both primary and secondary sources in their academic work.

The activity

Divide your students into groups and give each group a copy of the Student Handout. This provides a definition of 'primary source' and 'secondary source' and asks groups to compile a list of examples of both types of source (see key issues). Allocate around 20 minutes for this group exercise. When complete, lead a class discussion to expand on the issues raised. This can include:

- clarifying ambiguities (a journal paper, for example, could be a primary source if it is purely a report on an original piece of research by the author or a secondary source if it is an analysis of data that have been collected in a different research project);
- knowing how to find the most useful and accessible primary and secondary sources for their subject, and considering sources they may not otherwise have considered (see Activity 49);
- analysing possible problems with accessing primary and secondary sources and working out strategies to overcome these problems;
- understanding what information needs to be gathered to critique, analyse and evaluate primary and secondary sources (see Activity 52);
- working out what information needs to be gathered for correct referencing and citing (see Activity 30);
- knowing how to store and record the information gathered (see Activity 55).

Key issues

Examples of the types of source that are listed in this activity are given below.

Primary sources

- Historical records, texts and original manuscripts;
- eyewitness accounts;
- government records (if they have not been processed, interpreted or analysed);
- company/organisation records (if they have not been processed, interpreted or analysed);
- personal documents (diaries, journals, letters and memoirs, for example);
- recorded or transcribed speeches or interviews;
- raw statistical data (if they have not been processed, interpreted or analysed by others);
- works of literature;
- works of art;
- theatrical works;
- film/video;
- published results of laboratory experiments;
- published results of clinical trials;
- published results of research studies;
- conference and seminar proceedings that report up-to-date, original and ongoing research;
- patents;
- artefacts;
- buildings;
- technical reports.

Secondary sources

- Scientific debates;
- analyses of clinical trials;
- analyses/interpretations/critiques of previous research;
- datasets and databases that have been processed, analysed or interpreted by others;
- texts and books that use a variety of primary sources as evidence to back up arguments and/or conclusions;
- book and article reviews;
- biographies;
- critiques of literary works;
- critiques of art;
- television documentaries or science programmes;
- analyses of historical events.

→ **Related activities**

Activity 21: Reading, critiquing and questioning

Activity 30: Citing, referencing and producing a bibliography

Activity 49: Getting the most from the library

Activity 52: Evaluating sources

Activity 55: Organising, managing and storing information

··

→ **Preparatory reading**

Chapter 2 of Harris (2017) provides useful preparatory reading for students.

··

→ **Further reading**

Brundage, A. (2013) *Going to the Sources: a Guide to Historical Research and Writing*, 5th edition. Chichester: John Wiley & Sons Ltd. This book is aimed at history students, but has some interesting material about finding and engaging with sources that is relevant for students studying other social science and humanities subjects.

Harris, R. (2017) *Using Sources Effectively: Strengthening Your Writing and Avoiding Plagiarism*, 5th edition. Glendale, CA: Pyrczak Publishing. Chapter 2 of this book provides information about finding, choosing and evaluating sources and discusses the use of primary and secondary sources.

Ridley, D. (2012) *The Literature Review: a Step-by-Step Guide for Students*, 2nd edition. London: Sage. Chapter 3 covers finding and using sources of information and chapter 5 looks at recording, storing and managing information from different sources.

Activity 51

Activity • • • • • • • • • • ➔ 52

Evaluating sources

The activity

Print the sources listed below onto card. Make sure that the font is large enough to be read at a distance. You can add to the list, change entries or delete entries, depending on what is suitable for your student cohort (the number of students and relevance to their subject and country of study, for example).

When you begin your session allocate one card to each student (if you have a large number of students, and/or you have students with mobility difficulties, you can ask that they observe the exercise and make comments at the end). Ask your students to line themselves up in order, with the most reliable, accurate and trustworthy sources on the left and the least reliable, accurate and trustworthy sources on the right. Students should discuss their position and rank as they try to establish some kind of order. In some cases you may find that students are unable to make a decision between two sources, believing that they should be ranked the same. If this is the case they can stand one in front of the other.

This part of the activity tends to take ten to 15 minutes. Once this has been done and all students are happy with the rankings, introduce the changes listed below. Ask students to change ranks accordingly, again discussing their reasoning as they do so. This section of the exercise usually takes around ten minutes. Once this is complete, ask students to return to their seats and lead a class discussion on the issues raised (see key issues). You can also ask the observers (if you have any) to make comments about what they have observed. If you have students who are blind or partially sighted, ask students to call out the sources on their card at the beginning of the exercise, when their rankings have been formed and when the rankings change.

It is possible to run this activity as a group exercise followed by tutor-led discussion if you feel it is not appropriate to ask students to move around the room or you do not have the space available. Divide your students into groups and ask each group to rank the sources, with the most reliable, accurate and trustworthy at the top of the list and the least accurate, reliable and trustworthy at the bottom. Encourage students to discuss their reasoning as they form their ranking. Check to see whether all groups have the same list and, if not, discuss differences. Introduce the changes and ask them to re-rank, discussing their reasoning as they go. Once this is complete, lead a class discussion on the issues raised.

Sources

(One source per card to be introduced at the start of the game.)

Widely cited academic monograph

Peer-reviewed journal paper

Paper in a university repository

Paper in an open access
repository

University website

Academic's blog

Academic's YouTube video

Wikipedia article

Channel 4 TV documentary (or an equivalent TV channel in your country)

BBC Radio 1 news programme (or an equivalent radio station in your country)

Newspaper article

Sky News broadcast

Political party manifesto

Activist's website

Drug company website

Advertiser's direct email

Changes

(Write these onto cards, ready to swap later in the game.)

The Sun newspaper article (or an equivalent tabloid newspaper in your country)

Academic activist's website

Channel 5 TV documentary (or an equivalent TV channel in your country)

Medical school website

Non-peer-reviewed journal paper

Popular, mainstream blog

Refuted academic monograph

Russia Today news broadcast

Swap the cards in the following way (one at a time, with the students realigning themselves each time, if deemed necessary)

Newspaper article → The Sun newspaper article

Activist's website → Academic activist's website

Channel 4 TV documentary → Channel 5 TV documentary

Sky News broadcast → Russia Today news broadcast

Drug company website → Medical school website

Peer-reviewed journal paper → Non-peer-reviewed journal paper

Widely cited academic monograph → Refuted academic monograph

Academic's blog → Popular, mainstream blog

Key issues

Students tend to enjoy this activity, finding it an entertaining way to help them to think about how to evaluate sources effectively. It helps them to remain alert and motivated and they report that it is easy to remember what they have learnt and apply it to their studies. At times this activity can be a little chaotic, but students are able to work through the chaos and come up with a ranking with which everyone is happy. Questions that can be raised during the tutor-led discussion include:

1. Were students able to reach consensus on their ranking? If not, why not?

2. Were some sources more difficult to rank than other sources? If so, why was this?

Activity 52

3. Were students influenced by any form of bias when ranking the sources? If so, what types of bias? What can students do to reduce this bias when evaluating sources?

4. Were there any disagreements? If so, what were they? How were disagreements resolved?

5. Why were the three sources on the far left placed there (why were they deemed to be the most reliable, accurate and trustworthy)?

6. Why were the three sources on the far right placed there (why were they deemed to be the least reliable, accurate and trustworthy)?

7. Are there any sources in the ranking that should not be used in academic work? If so, why not? How do students know if a source is suitable for academic work?

8. Which sources in the rankings are primary sources and which are secondary sources (see Activity 51)? How do students go about evaluating primary and secondary sources? Is there a difference between the two?

9. When evaluating sources, what should students look out for to be able to evaluate the reliability and trustworthiness of sources?

➜ Related activities

Activity 21: Reading, critiquing and questioning

Activity 36: The use, abuse and misuse of statistics

Activity 51: Using primary and secondary sources

Activity 53: Finding truth and fact in mass information

Activity 54: Recognising statistics, facts, arguments and opinions

➜ Preparatory reading

AllSides (www.allsides.com) is a website that offers information and guidance to readers about the potential political bias of articles and news providers. It also illustrates how controversial topics and news items are viewed by those with different political perspectives. It provides useful preparatory reading for tutors and can be recommended to students after this activity has taken place.

➜ Further reading

Brundage, A. (2013) *Going to the Sources: a Guide to Historical Research and Writing*, 5th edition. Chichester: John Wiley & Sons Ltd. This book is aimed at history students, but has some interesting material about finding and engaging with sources that is relevant for students studying other social science and humanities subjects.

Hammersley, M. (2013) *Media Bias in Reporting Social Research? The Case of Reviewing Ethnic Inequalities in Education*. Abingdon, Oxon: Routledge. This book provides an interesting discussion on how social science is reported by the media and can be recommended to students who are interested in this topic.

Harris, R. (2017) *Using Sources Effectively: Strengthening Your Writing and Avoiding Plagiarism*, 5th edition. Glendale, CA: Pyrczak Publishing. Chapter 2 of this book provides information about finding, choosing and evaluating sources.

Activity 52

Activity · · · · · · · · · · · · ➔ 53

Finding truth and fact in mass information

Student handout page 319

TUTOR NOTES

Purpose: This activity is an individual exercise and tutor-led role play that helps students to identify facts and assertions that have been made in written text. It asks them to imagine that they are applying for job as a 'fact checker' within a national organisation. As part of the selection process they must choose a piece of text, identify facts and assertions that have been made and produce a plan of action for checking each of the facts/assertions they have identified. The tutor plays the role of potential employer and uses their analyses and plans as a basis for discussion and potential 'hiring' of candidates.

Type: Self-guided individual exercise followed by role play.

Alternative type(s): Student-centred digital resource.

Level: Elementary and intermediate.

Duration: Students need to spend a few hours choosing and checking a piece of text and producing their plan of action. Fifty minutes to one hour of contact time will be required for the tutor-led role play. If you choose the digital resource option you will need to spend a few minutes setting up the resource and monitoring the posts.

Equipment/materials: You need a suitable digital platform and the required access for students, if the digital resource option is chosen.

Learning outcome: By the end of this activity students will understand how to identify facts and assertions that have been made in written text and will know how to check facts and assertions to verify, confirm, disprove or refute what has been written.

The activity

Give the Student Handout to your students. This asks them to imagine that they are applying for a job as a 'fact checker' for a national organisation. During independent study they are to choose a piece of written text that they must work through to identify facts and assertions that have been made. They must then produce a plan of action that describes how they would go about checking each of the facts/assertions they have identified. Explain that when you next meet they will be playing the role of potential employees and you will be playing the role of potential employer. Your decision about whether or not to 'hire' them will depend on the thoroughness of their work and their contribution to the ensuing discussion.

Once they have completed the task ask them to hand in their work (including a copy of their chosen text) for you to read and digest before you next meet. Their work will be used as a basis for the tutor-led role play. In the next session introduce your role as potential employer and their roles as potential employee. Ask questions, in your role, that cover issues such as the attributes required for a fact checker, the ways that facts and assertions can be identified and methods that can be used to check facts (see key issues). Relate this discussion to the texts and action plans that have been handed in to you, pointing out where students have excelled, where suggestions may be problematic and where facts and assertions have been missed, for example. You can decide who to hire at the end of the session if this type of competition suits your students (several candidates or the whole class can be 'hired' if they have produced a thorough piece of work). Sum up the role play with a brief discussion on how this activity relates to academic study.

It is possible to ask students to post their text, analysis and plan of action on the relevant digital platform if you do not have the contact time available to meet with your students and run the role play. This builds a useful resource that students can access when relevant. Monitor posts from time to time to ensure that information is timely, correct, supportive and encouraging.

Key issues

The following issues can be raised and discussed during the role play.

- Fact checkers need good research skills (online, by telephone and face-to-face) along with knowledge and use of primary and secondary sources. They need to be methodical, accurate, diligent, analytical and pay attention to detail. All work must be carried out thoroughly within stated deadlines.
- Fact checkers need to be able to recognise facts and assertions when they are made in written text. To do this they need to understand differences between opinions, arguments, beliefs, claims and prejudice. They also need to be aware of the different kinds of bias that can influence written text (and their own biases that can influence their reading of the text).
- Fact checkers need to understand when a fact or assertion can be confirmed (or disproved). Several sources have to be used (a simple internet search, in most cases, is not enough). The reliability and validity of information presented, and sources used, must be checked and cross-checked. They need to ensure that all facts and assertions made are based on evidence.
- A variety of methods can be used to check facts, depending on the text that has been chosen by students. These can include:

  ○ contacting employers or institutions to check the credentials of authors or assertions made by them;
  ○ speaking face-to-face or by telephone with people who have been quoted in the text;
  ○ finding and checking the original source of statistics such as datasets, journal articles or books;
  ○ following up assertions through a detailed internet search with various cross-checks;
  ○ seeking advice from impartial experts and nonpartisan government agencies;
  ○ contacting a reputable fact checking organisation to find out whether specific facts and assertions have already been checked.

➔ **Related activities**

Activity 50: Conducting online research

Activity 51: Using primary and secondary sources

Activity 52: Evaluating sources

Activity 54: Recognising statistics, facts, arguments and opinions

Activity 97: Detecting and addressing bias

....

➔ **Preparatory reading**

Full Fact is a UK independent fact-checking charity (https://fullfact.org). It is useful to visit this site, or similar sites, in preparation for this activity as it provides a good example of the work carried out by fact checkers and illustrates how misinformation and misleading information is spotted and corrected (this organisation only fact-checks claims, not people).

....

Activity 53

➜ Further reading

Borel, B. (2016) *The Chicago Guide to Fact-Checking*. Chicago, IL: University Chicago Press. This is a comprehensive guide to fact checking and can be recommended to students who wish to follow up the issues raised in this activity. It also provides useful preparatory reading for tutors.

Tagg, C., Seargeant, P. and Brown, A. (2017) *Taking Offence on Social Media: Conviviality and Communication on Facebook*. Basingstoke: Palgrave Macmillan. This book provides an interesting read for tutors and students who are interested in 'fake news' and media manipulation.

The AllSides Dictionary (www.allsides.com/dictionary) has been established to provide a balanced definition of terms that can be considered controversial. It is a useful site to recommend to students as it illustrates how terms are perceived differently by people with different political and ideological perspectives, and offers further insight into issues of truth and fact.

Activity 53

Activity · · · · · · · · · · ➜ 54

Recognising statistics, facts, arguments and opinions

Student handout page 320

TUTOR NOTES

Purpose: This activity is a simple worksheet that helps students to recognise the difference between statistics, facts, arguments and opinions, understand how and when they are misused and think about how they can be used correctly in their own projects, reports and dissertations.

Type: Student worksheet.

Alterative type(s): Workshop.

Level: Elementary and intermediate (the level of study will be reflected in student answers).

Duration: Two or three hours during independent study. Fifty minutes to one hour if the workshop option is chosen.

Equipment/materials: None required.

Learning outcome: By the end of this activity students will be able to recognise the difference between statistics, facts, arguments and opinions, understand how and when they are misused and know how to use them correctly in their academic work.

The activity

Give the Student Handout to your students and ask them to work through the tasks and questions during independent study (the handout can be adapted to suit your student cohort and subject of study). Use this activity as a preparatory exercise for a session covering this topic, or ask that students complete this exercise before embarking on a project or dissertation. Decide whether you wish students to hand their answers to you for personal feedback or whether to hold a general discussion about the issues raised. If you prefer, ask that students post their answers onto a suitable digital platform so that they can share and discuss the issues raised.

This activity can also be run in a workshop setting if it better suits your students and you have time available. Divide your students into small groups and ask that they work through the questions with their group members. Conclude the workshop with a discussion on the issues raised.

Key issues

Issues raised by tasks 1–4 on the Student Handout

- 'Statistics' is a numerical discipline that involves collecting, organising, analysing, interpreting and presenting data. The data that are presented are also referred to as 'statistics'.

- Statistics are only as good as the methods used to create them and the skill of the statistician/researcher who collects the data.
- Figures can be misleading, incorrect and open to misinterpretation (a lack of statistical knowledge is displayed; correlation is confused with causation; incorrect statistical rules have been applied; the output of statistical programmes has been misread or misinterpreted; the statistics presented do not support the conclusions made, for example).
- It is important to analyse carefully all statistics presented in the media and in academic publications, and use statistics correctly in academic work.
- Students should ensure that they are well-trained, understand what they are doing and follow correct procedures.

Issues raised by tasks 5–7

- 'Facts' are things that can be investigated, checked or observed and are found to be true (they can be proved, confirmed or validated). They tend to be exact and specific.
- Not everything presented as a 'fact' is correct and true. Everything should be questioned.
- A careful analysis needs to take place to ensure that information presented as fact is valid and reliable. The evidence that is presented needs to be checked for validity (referring to the accuracy of the measurement, asking whether the tests that have been used by the researcher are measuring what they are supposed to measure) and reliability (referring to the way that the research instrument is able to yield the same results in repeated trials).
- If students use facts they must be checked and backed up with reliable and valid evidence.

Issues raised by tasks 8–10 (and 13–15)

- 'Arguments' are reasons or explanations given to support or reject a view. They are used to prove something through reason and supporting evidence, which can be facts, statistics and the arguments of experts in the field (these must be acknowledged so that plagiarism is avoided: see Activity 94).
- Researchers, reporters and students must demonstrate that the arguments they are using can be backed up by evidence (see Activity 28).
- Weak arguments are those that are not backed up adequately or those that focus only on supporting evidence.
- Students must present arguments in the best way that they can, paying attention to order, sequence and sentence construction, for example.

Issues raised by tasks 11–15

- 'Opinions' are personal thoughts, beliefs or judgements that are not based on proof or certainty. They are used in a wide variety of everyday situations.
- Problems arise when opinions are disguised as facts or arguments, in particular, when they are expressed with confidence.
- Students must be wary of opinions disguised as arguments in the work of others. They should look for personal beliefs or personal bias (an inclination or preference that influences judgement, often in a subtle way that is difficult to detect).
- Students must ensure that they do not mistake opinions for arguments in their work. They must pay attention to personal bias: raised awareness helps to eliminate or acknowledge bias, depending on standpoint (researchers approaching their work from an objective standpoint follow set rules and procedures to eliminate bias whereas researchers approaching from a subjective standpoint recognise, define, discuss and acknowledge bias, for example).

➜ **Related activities**

Activity 28: Producing an effective argument

Activity 30: Citing, referencing and producing a bibliography

Activity 52: Evaluating sources

Activity 53: Finding truth and fact in mass information

Activity 54

→ **Preparatory reading**

Bad Science (www.badscience.net) is a website containing blogs and articles about bad science, written by Dr Ben Goldacre. The articles were written for the Bad Science column in the *Guardian* newspaper in the UK and highlight the misuse of science and statistics by journalists, politicians and drug companies. Students can be directed to this site for preparatory reading.

More or Less is a radio programme that is broadcast on BBC Radio 4 in the UK and produced in association with the Open University. The programme discusses the use and misuse of statistics in everyday life. Podcasts and downloads are available from the BBC website (www.bbc.co.uk/programmes) and are useful for both tutors and students.

AllSides (www.allsides.com) is a website that offers information and guidance to readers about the potential political bias of articles and news providers. It also illustrates how controversial topics and news items are viewed by those with different political perspectives.

→ **Further reading**

The following books can be recommended to students who want to follow up this topic in more depth.

Brink-Budgen, R. van den (2010) *Critical Thinking for Students: Learn the Skills of Analysing, Evaluating and Producing Arguments*, 4th edition. Oxford: How to Books.

Goldacre, B. (2014) *I Think You'll Find it's a Bit More Complicated than That*. London: Harper Collins Publishers.

Huff, D. (1991) *How to Lie with Statistics*. London: Penguin. This book has been published since 1954 is and still very relevant and useful today.

Swatridge, C. (2014) *Oxford Guide to Effective Argument and Critical Thinking*. Oxford: Oxford University Press.

Activity 54

Activity · · · · · · · · · · → 55

Organising, managing and storing information

Student handout page 321

TUTOR NOTES

Purpose: This activity asks students to choose, test and evaluate a tool that will help them to organise, manage and store information collected for coursework and assignments. They must make a short presentation to their peers about their chosen tool. They can modify or change tools after having evaluated their tool and considered other options presented by their peers.

Type: Self-guided individual exercise followed by student presentations.

Alternative type(s): Video/podcast production with tutor-led viewing and discussion.

Level: Elementary.

Duration: Students need to spend several hours during independent study choosing, testing and evaluating a tool and preparing their presentation. One to two hours of contact time is required for presentations, depending on the number of students.

Equipment/materials: Students can choose any presentation equipment they deem appropriate and this should be made available for use. If the video/podcast option is chosen, this equipment should also be made available for use.

Learning outcome: By the end of this activity students will have chosen, tested and evaluated a tool that will help them to organise, manage and store information collected for coursework and assignments.

The activity

Give your students a copy of the Student Handout and ask them to undertake the activity in preparation for when you next meet. This asks them to choose, test and evaluate a tool that will help them to organise, manage and store information collected for their coursework and assignments. They must make a five-minute presentation to their peers about their chosen tool when you next meet. Once they have considered and evaluated the tools presented by their peers, they can adapt, modify or change their tool, as appropriate.

An alternative way to run this activity is to ask students to produce a short video/podcast to present their chosen tools to their peers. This can be done in groups or on an individual basis, depending on which method is better for your student cohort (you will need to adapt the Student Handout accordingly). You can view and discuss the videos/podcasts when you next meet or, if contact time is limited, you can ask students to upload them onto a suitable digital platform for peer viewing and comment.

This activity covers similar ground to that presented in Activity 23, so choose the activity that is best suited to your students.

Key issues

This activity encourages students to think more about how they are going to organise, manage and store information that they collect for their coursework and assignments (quotations, evidence for arguments, statistics, visual images, lecture notes and references, for example). It is of particular use for students who have not thought about how to organise and manage their work and for those who are unclear about tools that are available. The activity should be run fairly early in the course so that students can develop good organisation and information management skills from the start. There are a wide variety of tools from which to choose, or students can adapt, modify or design their own tool, depending on specific needs.

Students must test and evaluate their tool and then make a presentation to their peers, discussing issues such as advantages, disadvantages, strengths and weaknesses. This enables them to ascertain whether they have found an appropriate and helpful tool, and encourages them to consider alternatives, based on peer presentations.

➜ Related activities

Activity 23: Editing and organising notes

Activity 30: Citing, referencing and producing a bibliography

Activity 49: Getting the most from the library

Activity 50: Conducting online research

Activity 73: Making the most of IT facilities and support

➜ Preparatory reading

Tutors and students might find it useful preparatory work to find out what tools are available to help organise, manage and store information. Activity 23 lists a wide variety of tools (with websites) that help students to edit and organise notes. Tools to help with citing, referencing and producing a bibliography include BibMe (www.bibme.org), Cite This For Me (www.citethisforme.com), RefWorks (www.refworks.com) and EndNote (http://endnote.com). There are plenty more available, including useful apps for mobile devices, so students should be encouraged to hunt around for the tool that best suits their needs or to design their own tool (some students decide to produce their own spreadsheet using Excel or produce their own database using Access, for example). A wide variety of tools that can be used are listed in Activity 74.

➜ Further reading

No further reading is required for this activity, although students may decide to undertake further self-directed, online reading about their chosen tool.

Activity 55

Activity · · · · · · · · · · → 56

Referencing, copyright and plagiarism

Student handout page 322

TUTOR NOTES

Purpose: This activity introduces the topics of referencing, copyright and plagiarism by asking students, in small groups, to craft a story about these issues that they can tell to their peers. The story should be entertaining and informative, enabling their peers to learn and remember something new about the topic.

Type: Storytelling in class.

Alternative type(s): Digital storytelling.

Level: Elementary.

Duration: Students need to spend a few hours during independent study crafting their stories, with one to two hours of contact time to tell stories, depending on the number of student groups. If the digital storytelling option is chosen a few minutes of tutor time is required to develop a digital platform on which students can upload their stories, with an hour or two spent reading stories and monitoring posts. Students need to spend a few minutes uploading their stories and an hour or so reading and commenting on their peers' stories.

Equipment/materials: A suitable digital platform and the required access for students, if the digital option is chosen.

Learning outcome: By the end of this activity students will have a greater understanding of what is meant by referencing, copyright and plagiarism, having crafted, told, heard and discussed memorable stories on this topic.

The activity

Divide your students into small groups and give each group a copy of the Student Handout. This asks them to craft a story in their groups that will help their peers to understand more about referencing, copyright and plagiarism. They should make the story entertaining, informative and memorable. They will be required to tell their stories to their peers when you next meet and will be given up to 15 minutes for each story. Five minutes will be allocated after each story for discussion, with a few minutes at the end of the session to sum up the issues raised.

It is possible to ask students to upload their stories on the relevant digital platform if contact time is not available for this activity. You will need to adapt the Student Handout accordingly. Give a deadline by which time stories should be uploaded and ask students to spend some time reading, and commenting on, each group's story. You will need to read each story and monitor posts to ensure that information is correct, supportive and encouraging and to ensure that students are able to learn from the stories presented.

Key issues

Students tend to enjoy this activity, reporting that it is an entertaining and memorable way to learn about issues that can, on occasions, seem rather dull and too officious. Stories can cover various topics within the brief: one group told the story of a copyright theft trial, another told a fable of lost treasures (referencing details) and mythical creatures (plagiarism detectors). Some tell of the consequences of breaching rules and regulations, others tell of misunderstandings and misdemeanours.

In order to be able to tell an entertaining, informative and memorable story, students must first of all understand what is meant by referencing, copyright and plagiarism. They are then able to learn more about the topic as they listen to, and discuss, the stories told by their peers.

→ Related activities

Activity 30: Citing, referencing and producing a bibliography

Activity 49: Getting the most from the library

Activity 50: Conducting online research

Activity 55: Organising, managing and storing information

Activity 78: Copyright infringement and plagiarism of electronic materials

→ Preparatory reading

Alterio, M. and McDrury, J. (2003) *Learning through Storytelling in Higher Education: Using Reflection and Experience to Improve Learning.* London: Routledge. This is a useful book for tutors who are interested in using storytelling in the classroom as it outlines the different models of storytelling and explains how techniques can be used. It provides useful preparatory reading for storytelling activities.

The Higher Education Academy (HEA) in the UK has a useful section on 'Learning through Storytelling': www.heacademy. ac.uk/enhancement/starter-tools/learning-through-storytelling. Here you can find information about the history of story-telling, how it can be used and how to get started.

The HEA also provides useful information on academic integrity, including issues of student plagiarism: https://www. heacademy.ac.uk/knowledge-hub/supporting-academic-integrity-approaches-and-resources-higher-education.

→ Further reading

The following books can be recommended to students who wish to find out more about referencing, copyright and plagiarism.

Neville, C. (2016) *The Complete Guide to Referencing and Avoiding Plagiarism*, 3rd edition. London: Open University Press.
Pears, R. and Shields, G. (2016) *Cite Them Right: the Essential Referencing Guide*, 10th edition. London: Palgrave.
Williams, K. and Carroll, J. (2009) *Referencing and Understanding Plagiarism*. Basingstoke: Palgrave Macmillan.

Activity 56

Section 8

Critical and creative thinking

Activity • • • • • • • • • • → 57

Developing thoughts and imagination

Student
handout
page 323

TUTOR NOTES

Purpose: This activity helps students to develop their thoughts and imagination by asking them, in groups, to craft a story about 'Kim's determination to develop thoughts and imagination'. They must tell their story in class and listen to the stories of their peers, before discussing the issues raised.

Type: Storytelling in class.

Alternative type(s): Digital storytelling.

Level: Elementary, intermediate and advanced (the level of study will be reflected in the stories told).

Duration: Students need to spend a few hours in their groups during independent study crafting their stories. One to two hours of contact time will be required to tell their stories, depending on the number of student groups. If the digital storytelling option is chosen you will need to develop a digital platform on which students can upload their stories and spend an hour or two reading the stories and monitoring posts. Students will spend an hour or two uploading their stories and reading, and commenting on, the stories told by their peers.

Equipment/materials: A suitable digital platform and the required access for students, if the digital option is chosen.

Learning outcome: By the end of this activity students will have crafted, told and listened to stories about how to develop thoughts and imagination, which will provide a memorable way to help them to develop their own thoughts and imagination as their course continues.

The activity

Divide your students into small groups and give each group a copy of the Student Handout. This asks them to craft a story about 'Kim's determination to develop thoughts and imagination'. The age, gender, nationality and social situation of Kim and the context, content, style, structure and genre of story are group choices. Stories should be entertaining, informative and memorable. Groups will be required to tell their stories to their peers when you next meet and will be given up to 15 minutes for each story. Five minutes will be allocated after each story for discussion, with a few minutes at the end to conclude the session. Questions that can be posed after each story include:

1. What did you learn from the story?
2. What are the key points you have taken from the story?
3. How relevant is the story to the topic (developing thoughts and imagination)?
4. What are the strengths and weaknesses of the story?
5. Do you think the story is memorable? Will it help you to remember what you have learnt?

It is possible to ask students to upload their stories on to the relevant digital platform if contact time is limited (the Student Handout will need to be adapted accordingly). Give a deadline by which time stories should be uploaded and ask students to spend some time reading, and commenting on, each group's story. Monitor uploaded material to ensure that stories are suitable and posts are constructive, supportive and respectful.

Key issues

This activity provides an entertaining, informative and memorable way for students to think more about developing thoughts and imagination. For the groups to tell a good story, from which their peers can learn, they must first of all think about and discuss effective ways to develop thoughts and imagination. These are then crafted into creative, fascinating, humorous and/or poignant stories. The discussion after each story highlights pertinent issues and helps students to relate the story to their own learning.

   Stories that have been told in the past include:

- Kim living in a black and white world, striving to break into a world of colour;
- Kim as leader of a revolution in a society in which thoughts and imagination are supressed;
- Kim as experimenter or observer, following logical, linear or naturalistic approaches in the lab or in the field;
- dialogue between parent and Kim, the child;
- Kim as detective in a murder mystery;
- stories of personal Eureka moments with Kim as the narrator or observer.

➜ Related activities

Activity 1: Bringing learning to life

Activity 2: Becoming a reflective learner

Activity 46: Learning through storytelling

Activity 58: Reflecting, thinking and making connections

Activity 60: Solving problems

....

➜ Preparatory reading

Alterio, M. and McDrury, J. (2003) *Learning through Storytelling in Higher Education: Using Reflection and Experience to Improve Learning.* London: Routledge. This book provides useful preparatory reading for tutors who are interested in using storytelling in the classroom. It outlines the different models of storytelling and explains how techniques can be used.

The Higher Education Academy in the UK has a useful section on 'Learning through Storytelling': www.heacademy.ac.uk/ enhancement/starter-tools/learning-through-storytelling. Here you can find information about the history of storytelling, how it can be used in education and how to get started.

....

➜ Further reading

Madej, K., Judson, G. and Egan, K. (eds) (2015) *Engaging Imagination and Developing Creativity in Education.* Newcastle upon Tyne: Cambridge Scholars Publishing. This book is useful for tutors who want to read about recent ideas and debates concerning imagination and creativity in the classroom from a global perspective.

Ohler, J. (2013) *Digital Storytelling in the Classroom: New Media Pathways to Literacy, Learning, and Creativity,* 2nd edition. Thousand Oaks, CA: Corwin. This book provides useful further reading for tutors who are interested in the different types of digital storytelling methods that can be used in the classroom.

Activity 57

Activity • • • • • • • • • • → 58

Reflecting, thinking and making connections

Student
handout
page 324

TUTOR NOTES

Purpose: This activity is a simple, self-guided individual exercise that encourages students to reflect on, and think about, their learning, and make connections with learning and their personal and professional lives. It helps them to understand the benefits and relevance of learning. Students should work on this activity during independent study as their course progresses.

Type: Self-guided individual exercise.

Alternative type(s): One-to-one support session.

Level: Elementary and intermediate.

Duration: Students will spend one or two hours on this activity, with a little time to add to, and review, their notes as their course progresses.

Equipment/materials: None required.

Learning outcome: By the end of this activity students will have taken time to reflect on, think about and make connections between their learning and personal and professional lives, which will enable them to gain a deeper understanding of the benefits and relevance of learning.

The activity

Give a copy of the Student Handout to your students and ask that they work on the exercise individually during independent study. Explain that this is a personal exercise that will not be seen or assessed by the tutor (unless they wish to discuss the issues raised with their tutor on a personal basis). This exercise asks students to consider a number of questions that will help them to reflect on, think about and make connections between learning and their personal and professional lives. Students should be encouraged to continue with their thoughts and reflections as their course progresses so that they can see how they are developing on a personal level. This enables them to gain a deeper understanding of the benefits and relevance of learning.

It is possible to run this activity as a one-to-one support session if a student needs particular help and guidance. Use the Student Handout as a guide for your first session and meet again once the student has had time to think about, and reflect on, the issues raised in the first session.

Key issues

It is useful to run this activity midway through your course as students are able to consider the present and look both backward and forward, thinking about their past, present and future learning journey. This is a personal exercise and you will find that some students treat it much more seriously than others. Some, for example, find it extremely relevant and insightful, helping them to make connections with learning and life. Indeed, some get in touch after their course has finished, as their career progresses, to report connections that they had not noticed while they were studying. Others, however, find it 'rather irrelevant' and a little 'pointless' (these terms were used in course feedback). This is one reason why students should be left to their own devices in this activity. Also, some students write about very personal experiences that they do not want to share with others. Use your discretion with this activity: it tends to work best with adult returners who are able to make deep connections and who are excited about their learning journey and where it will take them.

➜ Related activities

Activity 1: Bringing learning to life

Activity 2: Becoming a reflective learner

Activity 3: Learning to learn

Activity 4: Developing metacognition

➜ Preparatory reading

Fook, J. and Gardner, F. (2007) *Practising Critical Reflection: a Resource Handbook*. Maidenhead: Open University Press. This book provides useful preparatory reading for tutors as it covers both theory and practical considerations for critical reflection.

The Open University in the UK has an interesting free course available called *Learning to Learn: Reflecting Backward, Reflecting Forward*. It can be found at http://www.open.edu/openlearn/education/learning-learn-reflecting-backward-reflecting-forward/content-section-0. This course can be recommended to students who wish to follow up the issues raised during this activity, or to those who might struggle with the idea of thinking about, and reflecting on, their learning.

➜ Further reading

Moon, J. (2004) *A Handbook of Reflective and Experiential Learning: Theory and Practice*. Abingdon, Oxon: Routledge Falmer. This is an informative book for tutors who are interested in reflective learning, containing both theory and practical tools and activities.

Schuller, T. (2004) *The Benefits of Learning: The Impact of Education on Health, Family Life and Social Capital*. London: Routledge. This is a good book to recommend to students who want to find out more about the benefits of learning.

Activity 58

Activity · · · · · · · · · · → 59

Learning how to question

Student
handout
page 325

TUTOR NOTES

Purpose: This activity helps students to learn how to question by asking them to take note of, and list, questions they hear in a week (from a variety of sources); think about the type, purpose and style of question; categorise the questions; think about how questions can be used in academic study; and develop a personal action plan that will help them to improve their ability to ask questions.

Type: Self-guided individual exercise.

Alternative type(s): If contact time is available, and if it better suits your student cohort, this activity can be run as a preparatory individual exercise followed by a class discussion.

Level: Elementary and intermediate.

Duration: Several hours of work for students during independent study. Fifty minutes to one hour of contact time, if this option is chosen.

Equipment/materials: None required.

Learning outcome: By the end of this activity students will have a raised awareness and understanding of the types of question that can be asked and will have developed a personal action plan that will help them to use questions effectively in their academic work.

The activity

This activity can be run in two ways: as a self-guided individual exercise during independent study or as a shorter preparatory exercise during independent study followed by a class discussion of up to one hour. If you choose the first option, use Student Handout 1. This asks students to take note of questions from a variety of sources that are asked during a week, build a list, analyse the list, think about how questions can be used in relation to their academic studies and develop a personal action plan to help them improve their ability to ask questions. This can be a personal endeavour that does not require tutor feedback, or you can ask that students hand in their action plan for you to review and offer feedback, if required.

If you choose the second option, use Student Handout 2. This asks students to build a list of questions that they hear over the week and bring this list to class when you next meet. Lead a class discussion on the issues involved. You can use the questions provided in Student Handout 1 as a guide for your class discussion. Allocate up to 30 minutes for the class discussion, 20 minutes for students to develop their personal action plan and 10 minutes to conclude the session.

Key issues

- Examples of good, useful questions include:

  - open questions that require more than one-word answers;
  - questions that make you think;
  - questions that stimulate reflection;
  - relevant and 'real' questions that have meaning;
  - questions that introduce a problem;
  - questions that help to solve a problem;
  - questions that help to demonstrate knowledge and comprehension;
  - questions that aid analysis;
  - questions that test existing assumptions;
  - questions to clarify or probe for more information;
  - questions related to a topic that encourage further exploration.
- Examples of bad or poor questions include:

  - trick questions;
  - sterile questions that constrain thought;
  - questions that are too simple, irrelevant or patronising;
  - questions for which the answer is readily available;
  - leading questions;
  - loaded questions;
  - ambiguous questions;
  - double-barrelled questions;
  - questions that confuse or confound;
  - closed questions that require only one-word answers (unless they are required on a structured question-naire, for example).
- Action plans can include:

  - continue to raise personal awareness (notice what, when, how and why a question is asked);
  - read around the subject;
  - take note of questions used by tutors;
  - practise asking questions (try both open and closed questions and note the different answers that are given);
  - develop a list of useful questions that can be asked when reading academic texts and practise asking and answering them;
  - ensure that questions have meaning, purpose and use (and are not wasted);
  - recognise how to ask the right questions;
  - take control of learning by asking questions;
  - learn how questions are used in questionnaires and interviews (read around the subject and enrol on relevant research methods courses or workshops).

➜ Related activities

Activity 21: Reading, critiquing and questioning

Activity 28: Producing an effective argument

Activity 52: Evaluating sources

Activity 60: Solving problems

Activity 63: Analysing and critiquing

....

➜ Preparatory reading

Chapter 1 of Browne and Keeley (2014) provides a useful introduction to this activity for tutors and students.

....

➜ Further reading

Berger, W. (2014) *A More Beautiful Question: the Power of Inquiry to Spark Breakthrough Ideas*. New York: Bloomsbury. This book is aimed at the mass market rather than academia but has some useful insight into asking questions for business and life.

Bradburn, N. (2004) *Asking Questions: The Definitive Guide to Questionnaire Design*. San Francisco, CA: John Wiley & Sons, Inc. Useful for students who are planning to use questionnaires in their research.

Browne, M. and Keeley, S. (2014) *Asking the Right Questions: a Guide to Critical Thinking*, 11th edition. Boston, MA: Pearson Education. This is a useful book to recommend to students.

Activity 59

Activity • • • • • • • • • • → 60

Solving problems

The activity

Divide your students into small groups and ask them to research, prepare and produce a poster presentation on how to solve problems. They must do this during independent study. Give a date, time and venue when the posters are to be presented so that each group can work to the given deadline (if you choose a time that is outside your usual class hours, ensure that all students are able to attend the session). Give details of the venue so that groups know what equipment and space is available for their poster presentation.

Decide how you wish to run the poster presentation session. You can keep it free-flowing and informal, enabling students to wander between posters and discuss them with the presenters, or you can ask each group to present their poster in turn to their peers, allowing enough time for questions and discussion after each presentation. Some students may be unfamiliar with the poster presentation technique. If this is the case, give them a copy of the Student Handout provided in Activity 28 as this gives advice and information about producing a poster presentation.

It is possible to run this activity as a tip exchange if you do not have the contact time available for poster presentations. Ask your students to think about useful tips that will help their peers to solve problems and post them on a suitable digital platform. Begin the tip exchange with a few of your own tips to get the resource started. Decide whether to make it compulsory for students to add tips (provide a deadline if this option is chosen) or whether to make it a voluntary resource. Monitor the posts from time to time to ensure that information is correct, constructive and useful.

Key issues

Students must produce a clear and concise poster presentation for this activity. To do this they must first of all get to grips with the topic and think carefully about how to solve problems. This activity helps them to focus their thoughts, think about the pertinent points and work out how best to communicate these to their peers. Different types, styles and structures of poster provide wide coverage of the topic, which enables students to learn from each other and remember the information because it is presented in a visually engaging way. Posters that have been produced by student groups in the past include:

- flowcharts illustrating different stages that can be worked through to solve a problem;
- columns containing lists of different approaches that can be used to solve problems, with descriptions or illustrations for each;
- stories (text or visual) that illustrate how to solve problems;
- illustrations of how problems can be broken down into smaller parts with irrelevant information omitted or discarded;
- diagrams illustrating the stages and benefits of collaborative or team problem solving;
- illustrations of a variety of critical problem-solving tools (mind-mapping, brainstorming, brain-writing and assumption reversal, for example);
- examples of role play or conversations that illustrate how problems can be approached and solved;
- questions that can be asked to help students to work through and solve problems, with specific examples offered;
- introduction to problem-solving software and apps and demonstrations of their use (these have been dynamic digital posters, rather than paper posters).

➜ Related activities

Activity 57: Developing thoughts and imagination

Activity 59: Learning how to question

Activity 63: Analysing and critiquing

....

➜ Preparatory reading

Students will carry out preparatory reading as part of their research for their poster presentation. They should be encouraged to find their own references, rather than rely on those suggested by their tutor. The articles listed below provide useful preparatory and further reading for tutors who are interested in different aspects of this topic.

....

➜ Further reading

Armoni, M., Gal-Ezer, J. and Tirosh, D. (2005) 'Solving problems reductively', *Journal of Educational Computing Research*, 32(2): 113-29, first published 1 March 2005, https://doi.org/10.2190/6PCM-447V-WF7B-QEUF. This paper provides interesting information for tutors in the sciences, illustrating how reductive thinking patterns can help to solve mathematical and scientific problems. It is based on a study carried out in ten Israeli high schools.

Guo, F., Yao, M., Wang, C., Yan, W. and Zong, X. (2015) 'The effects of service learning on student problem solving: the mediating role of classroom engagement', *Teaching of Psychology*, 43(1): 16-21, first published 3 December 2015, https://doi.org/10.1177/0098628315620064. This paper reports on a study carried out with students studying on a Psychology of Learning course at a university in China. It looks at the influence of service learning (community service) on students' problem-solving ability in the classroom.

Vernon, D., Hocking, I. and Tyler, T. (2016) 'An evidence-based review of creative problem solving tools: a practitioner's resource', *Human Resource Development Review*, 15(2): 230-59, first published 6 April 2016, https://doi.org/10.1177/1534484316641512. This paper provides a useful overview of various critical problem-solving tools and techniques.

Activity 60

Activity • • • • • • • • • • → 61

Hypothesising and theorising

Student
handout
page 327

TUTOR NOTES

Purpose: This activity helps students to get to grips with what is meant by hypothesising and theorising by asking them to produce a video/podcast that can be uploaded to build a useful digital resource for students. In the video/podcast students are asked to explain what is meant by hypothesising and theorising to an imaginary group of college students aged 16–18. This activity is aimed at students with little understanding or experience of working with hypotheses and theory.

Type: Video/podcast production.

Alternative type(s): Group exercise followed by group presentation.

Level: Elementary.

Duration: Students need to spend an hour or two in their groups during independent study researching, producing and uploading their video/podcast. They also need to spend a little time watching and commenting on the videos produced by their peers. Tutors need to spend an hour or two viewing and monitoring videos/podcasts.

Equipment/materials: Students need access to video/podcast production equipment and access to the digital platform.

Learning outcome: By the end of this activity students will have a clear understanding of what is meant by hypothesising and theorising, having researched and explained the terms to others and having built a useful bank of videos/podcasts that can be accessed throughout their course.

The activity

Divide your students into groups and give them a copy of the Student Handout. This asks them to imagine that they have been asked to produce a video/podcast for students at their local college on the topic of hypothesising and theorising. They are to upload their video/podcast onto the relevant digital platform and spend some time viewing, and commenting on, those produced by their peers. Give a deadline by which time all videos/podcasts should be posted and monitor all uploaded material, including comments, to ensure that information is correct, supportive and encouraging. Videos/podcasts can be assessed or you might prefer to run an informal competition, asking students to vote on the best.

It is possible to ask students to make a live presentation instead of a video when you next meet, if you have the contact time available. Allocate up to ten minutes for each presentation and five minutes for questions and answers after each group has made their presentation. Use the final few minutes of the session to summarise the issues raised.

Key issues

One of the most effective ways to encourage students to learn about, and understand, a topic that may appear daunting and complex is to ask them to explain it to others. In this activity they are asked to explain what is meant by hypothesising and theorising to students who are younger than themselves. This not only requires them to get to grips with the topic, but also requires them to explain it in a way that can be understood, and found interesting, by that particular age group. The generic nature of this activity enables students from a variety of disciplines to undertake the activity, as they are able to talk about hypothesising and theorising in a way that is relevant to their subject.

Students tend to be very creative in this exercise, talking about hypothesising and theorising using visual props, latest technology and software, role play and acting, audience participation, case studies, scenarios and practical examples. Students get to see alternative videos/podcasts that can raise additional issues and, therefore, enhance their learning. This produces a useful bank of videos that can be accessed by students throughout their course, when required.

➜ Related activities

Activity 60: Solving problems

Activity 62: Reasoning inductively and deductively

Activity 63: Analysing and critiquing

....

➜ Preparatory reading

More information about hypothesising in research can be found on the Research Methods Knowledge Base website (www. socialresearchmethods.net/kb/hypothes.php) and more information about hypothesising in psychology can be obtained from the AllPsych website (https://allpsych.com/researchmethods/developingthehypothesis).

....

➜ Further reading

Barnard, C., Gilbert, F. and McGregor, P. (2017) *Asking Questions in Biology: a Guide to Hypothesis Testing, Experimental Design and Presentation in Practical Work and Research Projects*, 5th edition. Harlow: Pearson Education Ltd. Although this book is aimed at biology students, it has some useful information about asking questions and hypothesis testing for students who are studying other sciences (chapter 2 contains information about forming hypotheses and can be recommended to students studying sciences).

Gimbel, S. (ed.) (2011) *Exploring the Scientific Method: Cases and Questions*, Chicago, IL: University of Chicago Press. This book contains interesting material on scientific reasoning and the structure of theories. It covers a variety of disciplines and can be recommended to students who wish to follow up some of the issues raised by this activity.

Activity 61

Activity · · · · · · · · · · → 62

Reasoning inductively and deductively

Student
handout
page 328

TUTOR NOTES

Purpose: This activity helps students get to grips with what is meant by inductive and deductive reasoning by asking them to find out what is meant by these terms before directing them to find two research reports, one that illustrates inductive reasoning and one that illustrates deductive reasoning. They must describe, analyse and critique the reasoning discussed in the reports, before taking part in a tutor-led class discussion on the topic.

Type: Self-guided individual exercise followed by tutor-led discussion.

Alternative type(s): Self-guided individual exercise with student-centred digital resource; self-guided individual exercise with assignment and assessment.

Level: Intermediate and advanced.

Duration: Students need to spend a few hours during independent study finding, analysing and critiquing two research reports. Fifty minutes to one hour of contact time will be required to discuss the issues raised. If you choose the digital resource option you need to spend a few minutes setting up and monitoring the resource. If the assignment and assessment option is chosen the usual time for marking and feedback will be required.

Equipment/materials: A suitable digital platform on which to upload work, if this option is chosen.

Learning outcome: By the end of this activity students will have a greater understanding of what is meant by inductive and deductive reasoning, and will know how to recognise, analyse and critique their use in different types of research.

The activity

Give your students a copy of the Student Handout. This asks them to find out what is meant by inductive and deductive reasoning. It goes on to ask students to find two research reports (journal papers, monographs or theses, for example), one that uses inductive reasoning and one that uses deductive reasoning. They can choose any research reports that they wish, as long as they are relevant in some way to their subject of study. Students are asked to describe how reasoning has been used in each research project and provide an analysis and critique of the reasoning methods and the way they have been reported. You will discuss their findings in class when you next meet.

It is possible to ask students to upload their findings on to a suitable digital platform for others to review and critique, if you do not have the contact time available. Or, if you prefer, you can ask students to produce a written piece of work that is handed in for assessment (the Student Handout will need to be altered for both these options).

Key issues

This activity encourages students to think more deeply about inductive and deductive reasoning and how these types of reasoning inform and influence research projects and methods. When you lead the class discussion you can also introduce abductive reasoning, if appropriate. Issues that can be raised during the discussion include:

- Inductive reasoning is open-ended and exploratory. It can generate new knowledge and is useful for making predictions and providing direction. However, it can be incomplete, uncertain, open to bias and lead to false conclusions.
- Deductive reasoning can provide certainty, is logically sound (providing the premise is true) and is seen to be objective. However, it is limited to exploring and testing the implications of what we already know or assume to be true and, therefore, does not enable us to learn anything new. It can also lead to false conclusions.
- When reasoning deductively, logical conclusions may seem to be right, because they appear to be logical. However, if they are based on generalisations that are wrong (or untrue) then the logical conclusion may also be untrue.
- Syllogisms are used to test deductive reasoning to make sure that the argument is valid. This is a form of deductive reasoning (or logical argument) that consists of

a major premise (or proposition), a minor premise (or proposition) and a conclusion. It is considered to be a useful way to test deductive reasoning and decide whether an argument is valid.
- Reasoning can be context-dependent (different operations and rules can be applied in different contexts).
- Reasoning (and flawed reasoning) can be historically, culturally and socially dependent.
- Researcher bias can influence reasoning and lead to invalid or untrue conclusions.
- It is possible to use inductive, deductive and abductive reasoning in the same research project. For example, some researchers may begin using one type of reasoning, but change as their research progresses, while other researchers use all three types of reasoning at different stages of the research process. It is possible that the three approaches, when used together, can give a more complete understanding of data.

This activity can be expanded or added to by asking students, in groups, to produce a scenario in which they deliberately incorporate some type of flawed reasoning, which must be detected by their peers. This activity is described in detail in Section 7 of Dawson (2016).

→ Related activities

Activity 60: Solving problems

Activity 61: Hypothesising and theorising

Activity 63: Analysing and critiquing

→ Preparatory reading

Dawson, C. (2016) *100 Activities for Teaching Research Methods*. London: Sage. This book contains three different activities about reasoning, which expand on the information presented in this activity. The activities are useful for students studying at advanced level who are embarking on their research project. The book also provides useful preparatory information for tutors who wish to cover this topic in depth with their students.

→ Further reading

The following books can be recommended to students who wish to follow up the issues raised in this activity.

Feeney, A. and Heit, E. (eds) (2007) *Inductive Reasoning: Experimental, Developmental, and Computational Approaches*. Cambridge: Cambridge University Press.

Holyoak, K. and Morrison, R. (2013) *The Oxford Handbook of Thinking and Reasoning*. New York: Oxford University Press.

Hughes, W., Lavery, J. and Doran, K. (2015) *Critical Thinking: an Introduction to the Basic Skills*, 5th edition. Peterborough, Ontario: Broadview Press.

Activity 62

Activity • • • • • • • • • → 63

Analysing and critiquing

Student
handout
page 329

TUTOR NOTES

Purpose: This activity helps students to build their understanding of analysing and critiquing by asking them, in pairs, to find a research paper from a journal that is relevant to their subject of study. They must read through the paper and answer a series of questions on an individual basis, before getting back together with their partner to discuss and compare their answers. This provides mutual encouragement and support for a task that some students find daunting and difficult.

Type: Self-guided exercise in pairs.

Alternative type(s): Self-guided individual exercise followed by tutor-led discussion.

Level: Elementary.

Duration: Students need to spend a few hours during independent study finding, reading, analysing and critiquing a research paper, and discussing this with their partner. If the self-guided individual exercise option is chosen students need to spend a few hours working on their own during independent study, followed by 50 minutes to one hour of contact time to discuss the issues raised.

Equipment/materials: Students need access to relevant academic journals.

Learning outcome: By the end of this activity students will have a greater understanding of how to analyse and critique academic papers and will feel more confident and knowledgeable about undertaking these tasks as their course progresses.

The activity

Divide your students into pairs and give them a copy of the Student Handout. This asks them to work in pairs to find a research paper in an academic journal that is relevant to their subject of study. They must read through the paper, on an individual basis, answering the questions given. Once they have done this they get together with their partner to discuss and compare their answers. If contact time is available you can follow this activity with a tutor-led discussion (see key issues).

It is possible to ask students to work on this activity on an individual basis, rather than in pairs, if this better suits your student cohort (they are happy and confident enough to work on this without the support of a peer, for example). If you choose this option ask them to work through the questions ready for your next contact session, when you will lead a class discussion on the issues raised (the Student Handout will need to be adapted accordingly).

This exercise takes a slightly different approach to that described in Activity 21, which asks students to read and critique a research paper that is chosen for them. They are to do this on an individual basis, before taking part in a tutor-led discussion on the issues raised. Two handouts are provided in Activity 21, covering similar questions to those listed below, although one of the handouts is aimed at students studying at advanced level. Therefore, choose the activity that is most suited to your student cohort and level of study.

Key issues

This activity asks students to work together to find a suitable paper: this gives them the confidence to find a paper that is relevant to their subject of study and suitable for this activity. If your students are not yet familiar with finding and reading academic papers, you may need to give some guidance on how to find relevant journals (see Activity 49) and how to assess the suitability of sources (see Activity 42). Students then read through the paper, answering the questions, before getting back together with their partner to discuss and compare their answers. This helps students to work through the exercise with the support and encouragement of their partner. It also provides a useful way to check that students understand what is required and are able to consider and discuss each question carefully.

The following issues can be discussed, if you choose to follow this activity with a tutor-led discussion:

- structure, writing style and content;
- sources and citation;
- methods and methodology;
- correct interpretation of data;
- introduction of bias (researcher bias, reactivity bias, selection bias and measurement bias, for example);
- validity and reliability (quantitative research);
- accuracy, credibility and trustworthiness (qualitative research);
- usefulness and impact.

➜ Related activities

Activity 21: Reading, critiquing and questioning

Activity 49: Getting the most from the library

Activity 52: Evaluating sources

Activity 59: Learning how to question

....

➜ Preparatory reading

Preparatory reading for students is not required for this activity. However, all the books listed below can be recommended to students who want to follow up the issues raised.

....

➜ Further reading

Browne, M. and Keeley, S. (2014) *Asking the Right Questions: a Guide to Critical Thinking*, 11th edition. Boston, MA: Pearson Education.

Chong Ho Shon, P. (2015) *How to Read Journal Articles in the Social Sciences*, 2nd edition. London: Sage.

Cottrell, S. (2017) *Critical Thinking Skills: Effective Analysis, Argument and Reflection*, 3rd edition. Basingstoke: Palgrave Macmillan.

Holosko, M. (2006) *Primer for Critiquing Social Research: a Student Guide*. Belmont, CA: Wadsworth Publishing Co., Inc.

Williams, K. (2014) *Getting Critical*, 2nd edition. Basingstoke: Palgrave Macmillan.

Activity 63

Section 9　Group work

Activity • • • • • • • • • ➔ 64

Establishing study groups

The activity

Introduce the idea of a study group to your students. The purpose of the group is to help students to become more confident with their studies through gaining support, encouragement and help from their peers. Explain that the group is informal and that it is not assessed. Ask students how often they would like to meet: this can be weekly, fortnightly, monthly or remain flexible depending on student preference. Ensure that you choose a time of day when all your students can attend.

Study groups tend to work best if there are no more than eight participants. If you have a large class of students and they are all interested in joining a study group, set up several different groups. Membership of each can be determined by you or by the students themselves. Be aware that existing friendship groups might encourage and support each other very well, but may be lacking in diversity, whereas students with different skills, talents, experiences and traits who have never met may find it harder to build friendships and offer appropriate support. A good balance is the key to a successful group.

Decide whether or not to make attendance compulsory: you might find it useful to ask all students to attend the first session so that they can determine whether the study group will be of interest and of use, and then make future attendance voluntary (students can also choose to attend depending on the topic that is to be discussed). Some students are able to undertake the required level of study without the support of their peers, so these students should not be forced into attendance. Others do not realise that the study group will be of interest or benefit until they actually attend a session.

When the group meets, lead the discussion yourself. First, ask students to discuss and agree a 'code of conduct' or a 'code of behaviour' that includes issues such as courtesy and respect, domination, digression and confidentiality. Second, discuss purpose and expectations: what are the reasons for joining the group? What do students hope to gain by joining? Third, brainstorm a list of topics that students would like to cover in future meetings. This varies, depending on your student cohort and their level of study, but can include the following:

- general study skills such as improving academic reading and writing;
- skills that students struggle with, such as maths, statistics and data visualisation (see Activities 34, 35 and 77);
- discussion and comparison of personal notes from lectures and seminars, to ensure that students take effective notes and get the most out of lectures, or to provide feedback and information for students who have missed a lecture due to illness, for example;
- topics specific to the course, such as an assessed piece of work that has been assigned;
- specific research methods (for those studying at advanced level).

The aim of the first session is to encourage students to return next time. Ask students to decide on a suitable topic for the next session (based on your brainstorm) so that they can plan and prepare. Also, find out whether students would like you to continue running the group or whether they would prefer to run the group themselves. This depends on the abilities, personalities and preferences of students. In cases where study groups are meeting without tutor input it is useful to check on the group every now and again to make sure that it is running smoothly, that goals are being met and that the discussions are staying on track.

Key issues

Study groups can be useful for students who are unconfident about their ability to study at the required level. They can also be useful for students who need to undertake work at a more advanced level and find it beneficial to have support from their peers. Discussions enable students to share knowledge, exchange ideas, overcome problems, raise concerns or offer advice and support to others.

When establishing a study group it is important to ensure that all group members are clear about the purpose of the group and know how to behave. Topics should be relevant, of interest and aimed at the right level, and all group members should feel that attendance is of personal benefit and that the study group meets their needs and expectations. The meeting space should be appropriate, informal and free from disturbances and distractions, and there should be a competent person available to lead, coordinate, facilitate or manage the group. Times and dates of meetings should be advertised clearly and meetings arranged at a time that suits everyone who wishes to attend. If it is not possible to find a suitable time (or location) you could consider establishing an online study group instead (see Activity 67).

➜ Related activities

Activity 18: Establishing academic reading groups

Activity 25: Establishing academic writing circles

Activity 65: Getting the most out of group work

Activity 67: Introducing online study groups

➜ Preparatory reading

All three papers cited below provide useful preparatory reading for tutors for this activity. Preparatory reading for the first meeting is not required for students.

➜ Further reading

Herner-Patnode, L. (2009) 'Educator study groups: a professional development tool to enhance inclusion', *Intervention in School and Clinic*, 45 (1): 24-30.

Lizzio, A. and Wilson, K. (2005) 'Self-managed learning groups in higher education: students' perceptions of process and outcomes', *British Journal of Educational Psychology*, 75: 373-90.

Rybczynski, S. and Schussler, E. (2010) 'Student use of out-of-class study groups in an introductory undergraduate biology course', *CBE Life Sciences Education*, 10 (1): 74-82.

Activity 64

Activity · · · · · · · · · · · · ➔ 65

Getting the most out
of group work

**Student
handout
page 330**

TUTOR NOTES

Purpose: This activity helps students to get the most out of group work. It is a self-guided individual exercise that should be given to students to work on before they take part in their first group project. It asks them to think about the words 'compassion', 'encouragement' and 'respect' in relation to group work, to find and summarise relevant references and to provide a one-sentence tip or piece of advice that will help students to work effectively in groups.

Type: Self-guided individual exercise followed by tutor-led discussion.

Alternative type(s): Student-centred digital resource.

Level: Elementary.

Duration: Students need to spend one or two hours during independent study working on the exercise. Fifty minutes to one hour of contact time is required to discuss responses, expand on issues raised and introduce the group project. If you choose the digital resource option you need to spend a few minutes setting up and monitoring the digital resource.

Equipment/materials: If the digital resource option is chosen you need to set up a suitable digital platform and students need the required access details.

Learning outcome: By the end of this activity students will have a deeper understanding of how to work effectively in groups and will feel confident about getting the most out of group work as their course progresses.

The activity

This activity should take place before your students begin their first group project. Give the Student Handout to your students to work on as a self-guided individual exercise during independent study. Ask them to complete the work ready for your next teaching session when you will lead a discussion on their responses. The questions in the Student Handout provide a useful structure for your class discussion. Once the discussion is complete, divide your students into groups and introduce your group project. If time is available groups can spend a few minutes getting to know each other and raising questions they may have about their group project (and discussing a code of conduct: see key issues).

It is possible to run this activity as a student-centred digital resource if you do not have the contact time available. Ask your students to work through the questions contained in the Student Handout and then upload their responses onto the digital platform that has been set up for this purpose. Students should be encouraged to review and comment on their peers' responses. Give a deadline by which time all responses must be uploaded and spend a little time monitoring posts to ensure that all information is timely, correct, supportive and encouraging. This builds a useful resource that students can access when they undertake group work as their course progresses.

Key issues

There are a variety of issues that can be raised during the tutor-led discussion and these depend, in part, on your student cohort, their subject of study and the type of group work undertaken. Examples include:

- Groups will be more effective if members act with compassion and respect, and if they understand how encouragement can have an influence on group members and their work within the group.
- Focusing on compassionate action within groups:

  o noticing when problems occur and working towards a solution;
  o helping to deal with dominant members or monopolisers;
  o gentle encouragement of non-contributors;
  o respectful challenging of ideas;
  o offering support and encouraging peer learning;
  o listening to others;
  o providing positive and constructive feedback (also connected to encouragement);
  o understanding group dynamics and avoiding conflict (see Activity 71).

- Focusing on encouragement within groups:

  o encouragement as a motivator;
  o encouragement for growth and improvement (for the group as a whole and for individuals within a group);
  o understanding the connection between collaboration and encouragement;
  o knowing how, when and why encouragement should be used in group work;
  o understanding the difference between praise and encouragement.

- Focusing on respect within groups:

  o respecting views, opinions, wishes and feelings;
  o listening and taking others seriously;
  o engaging in respectful intellectual debate;
  o encouraging and supporting others to act with respect.

When you introduce your group project, discuss why group work is undertaken and the benefits that are to be gained, such as:

- increased efficiency and productivity;
- improved performance;
- peer support and encouragement;
- wider and deeper coverage of topics;
- skills development;
- personal development;
- improved relationships;
- development of social networks.

Encourage groups to develop a code of conduct, contract or code of behaviour that covers the topics listed above, along with more practical issues such as confidentiality, meeting times, mobile phones, work allocation, expectations, goals and so on.

➔ **Related activities**

Activity 7: Fostering collaborative learning and interaction

Activity 8: Becoming part of a learning community

Activity 45: Presenting in groups

Activity 66: Producing group assignments

Activity 71: Understanding group dynamics and avoiding conflict

....

➔ **Preparatory reading**

Monson, R. (2017) 'Groups that work: student achievement in group research projects and effects on individual learning', *Teaching Sociology*, 45 (3): 240–51, first published 31 March 2017, https://doi.org/10.1177/0092055X17697772. This paper provides interesting preparatory reading for tutors.

Students need to find two references as part of this activity, which provides useful preparatory reading (see the Student Handout).

....

Activity 65

➜ **Further reading**

Kahn (2009) and Levin (2005) can be recommended to students who wish to follow up the issues raised in this activity, whereas Gastil (2010) is an interesting read for tutors.

Gastil, J. (2010) *The Group in Society.* Thousand Oaks, CA: Sage.

Kahn, W. (2009) *The Student's Guide to Successful Project Teams.* New York: Psychology Press.

Levin, P. (2005) *Successful Teamwork! For Undergraduates and Taught Postgraduates Working on Group Projects.* Maidenhead: Open University Press.

Activity 65

Activity · · · · · · · · · → 66

Producing group assignments

The activity

Divide your students into groups and explain the activity to them. They will be given a group assignment that they must work on, together, to complete ready for the next session. When you next meet you will evaluate the group assignment in a tutor-led discussion. This can include an evaluation of how well group members worked together, the methods used to work together and the overall success of the assignment, for example. It can also include problems encountered and methods that can be used to overcome problems (it is important to stress that students must not attack group members on a personal level: see below).

Once this evaluation is complete students will be required to develop an action plan that will help them to complete group assignments successfully as their course progresses. This can be done in the last 20 minutes of your session in the form of a tutor-led discussion or a brainstorm, for example.

Key issues

When choosing an assignment for this activity, choose a type and topic that will challenge your students and raise important issues that can be discussed when you next meet. Do not mark or assess the assignment at this stage, but illustrate to students during the class discussion how you would go about assessing the assignment. This will help them to think about what is required from a group assignment in the future (content, type, standard and level of work required, for example).

When you lead your class discussion it is important to discuss a code of conduct or a code of behaviour before you begin so that individuals are not named, criticised or blamed if the group has not worked well together. Students should remain courteous, respectful and honest. If problems were encountered they should be discussed on a general rather than personal level, with attention placed on how the problem can be overcome in future group assignments. You will need to monitor the discussion carefully so that you can stop any potential problems from arising.

Questions that can be posed during the tutor-led discussion include the following:

- How well did group members work together? Why was this? (whether positive or negative)
- What group dynamics were displayed (see Activity 71)?
- Were group members happy with the allocation of tasks?
- Did they encounter any problems when working together? Did they manage to overcome the problems and, if so, how?
- Did they encounter any conflict? If so, what action was taken to deal with it? Was this action successful (see Activity 71)?
- Are all group members satisfied with the finished assignment?
- Could anything have been done differently or could anything have been done better?
- What has been learnt that will help them to work on group assignments in the future?

Once this evaluation has taken place (usually after about 30 to 40 minutes) lead a class discussion or run a brainstorm that will help students to develop an action plan for successful group assignments. Issues raised can include:

- fostering compassion, encouragement and respect (see Activity 65);
- the importance of listening and letting others speak;
- respecting views, opinions, wishes and feelings;
- negotiation and delegation;
- taking care not to bully, cajole or force someone into doing something they do not want to do;
- understanding group roles;
- the importance of completing allocated tasks;
- understanding when to ask for help and seek support (and noticing when group members need help and support, and giving it, where appropriate);
- dealing with difficult group members sensitively and positively;
- avoiding conflict.

➜ Related activities

Activity 7: Fostering collaborative learning and interaction

Activity 8: Becoming part of a learning community

Activity 64: Establishing study groups

Activity 65: Getting the most out of group work

Activity 71: Understanding group dynamics and avoiding conflict

....

➜ Preparatory reading

All three books listed below can be recommended to students as preparatory and follow-up reading for this activity.

....

➜ Further reading

Hartley, P. and Dawson, M. (2010) *Success in Groupwork*. Basingstoke: Palgrave Macmillan.
Kahn, W. (2009) *The Student's Guide to Successful Project Teams*. New York: Psychology Press.
Levin, P. (2005) *Successful Teamwork! For Undergraduates and Taught Postgraduates Working on Group Projects*. Maidenhead: Open University Press.

Activity 66

Activity · · · · · · · · · · · ➜ 67

Introducing online study groups

> **TUTOR NOTES**
>
> **Purpose:** This activity establishes an online directory that enables students to list relevant online study groups, find and join suitable groups and/or put out calls for members to join a new online study group. It provides a useful digital resource for students to access if they are interested in joining, or establishing, an online study group.
>
> **Type:** Online directory.
>
> **Alternative type(s):** None.
>
> **Level:** Elementary, intermediate and advanced.
>
> **Duration:** Tutors need to spend a few minutes setting up and introducing students to the resource.
>
> **Equipment/materials:** A suitable online platform for the directory and access for all students.
>
> **Learning outcome:** By the end of this activity students will have built an online directory that will enable them to find out about, join or establish online study groups, which will help them to participate in, and benefit from, online collaboration and peer-to-peer learning as their course progresses.

The activity

Set up an online directory, using a suitable digital platform. Make some initial entries, if you feel this will help your students to understand what is required (relevant online study groups run by your faculty or department or subject-specific groups set up by students, for example). Provide a link to the online study group with a short description of the group and its purpose. Ask your students to make similar entries so that you can build a useful resource on which students can draw throughout their course. Explain that this resource will be built over a period of time: if students encounter a study group that is of personal use they should place it in the directory, and if students feel it would be useful to set up an online group for a particular module or subject, they can use the directory to put out a call for members.

Some students have not come across online study groups and may need a little more information before they get involved. When you introduce the activity, lead a class discussion about online study groups, drawing on the understanding and experiences of those students who have taken part in online study groups previously. Online study groups:

- help to connect students from vast geographical regions and encourage collaborative and peer-to-peer learning among a diverse range of cultures, social groups and countries;
- enable students to ask questions, answer questions and discuss topics;
- encourage the sharing of knowledge, understanding and resources;
- provide support, encouragement and friendship;
- help students to learn, study and develop.

Use the discussion to highlight potential problems and strategies to deal with these problems. For example, some online study groups become a waste of time, an irrelevant distraction or a platform for personal attack and criticism. To avoid this, students should ensure that they are clear about the purpose of the study group and that it matches their learning goals (and that there is compatibility between members' learning goals). They should also ensure that topics are relevant, of interest and aimed at the right level. Taking part in the group should be of personal benefit to members, and the needs and expectations of group members should be met. All members should try to foster compassion, encouragement and respect (see Activity 65).

Key issues

Some students utilise online study groups a great deal, finding them a useful way to discuss topics and learn from their peers. Others, however, do not take part in online study groups, believing them to be a distraction and a waste of time. This is a voluntary activity that enables students to use the resource if they feel it will be of personal benefit. It is a simple way to build a useful resource that can be accessed by students when required.

This activity can be expanded by joining it together with Activity 68, which asks students to produce reviews of online collaboration tools. The directory can be combined with reviews to build a useful student-centred digital resource that will encourage further online collaboration and peer-to-peer learning.

➜ Related activities

Activity 7: Fostering collaborative learning and interaction

Activity 64: Establishing study groups

Activity 68: Using online tools for collaborative study

Activity 71: Understanding group dynamics and avoiding conflict

➜ Preparatory reading

The papers listed below provide useful preparatory reading for tutors who want to read about research into online study groups. Students do not need to undertake any preparatory reading for this activity.

➜ Further reading

Chapman, D., Storberg-Walker, J. and Stone, S. (2008) 'Hitting reply: a qualitative study to understand student decisions to respond to online discussion postings', *E-Learning and Digital Media*, 5 (1): 29-39, first published 1 January 2008, https://doi.org/10.2304/elea.2008.5.1.29. This is an interesting paper for all tutors using activities that require students to read, and respond to, online posts.

Cunha Jr, F., Kruistum, C. and Oers, V. (2016) 'Teachers and Facebook: using online groups to improve students' communication and engagement in education', *Communication Teacher*, 30 (4): 228-41, published online 9 September 2016, http://doi.org/10.1080/17404622.2016.1219039. This paper illustrates how online groups can improve communication between teachers and students in Brazil.

Johnson, G. (2006) 'Online study groups: reciprocal peer questioning versus mnemonic devices', *Journal of Educational Computing Research*, 35 (1): 83-96, first published 1 July, 2006, https://doi.org/10.2190/1G67-HLL5-4172-083U. This paper provides interesting information about pedagogy, attitudes and behaviour in online study groups.

Activity 67

Activity · · · · · · · · · · · → 68

Using online tools for collaborative study

> **TUTOR NOTES**
>
> **Purpose:** This activity asks students, in groups, to test, evaluate and produce reviews of online tools that can be used for collaborative study. These reviews are brought together to build a useful student-centred digital resource that can be accessed by students when required.
>
> **Type:** Student-centred digital resource.
>
> **Alternative type(s):** Student reviews (as a PDF).
>
> **Level:** Elementary, intermediate and advanced.
>
> **Duration:** Groups need to spend one or two hours testing, evaluating and uploading reviews.
>
> **Equipment/materials:** A suitable digital platform and access for all students.
>
> **Learning outcome:** By the end of this activity students will know more about the online tools that are available for collaborative study and will have a useful resource that will help them to assess, evaluate and choose online collaboration tools as their course progresses.

The activity

Divide your students into small groups and present them with a list of online tools that can be used for collaborative study (video production, file management, note-taking and chat tools, for example: see below). Ask each group to choose a tool, until all tools have been chosen. Examples of tools are given below, but you may need to adapt this list, depending on your subject and level of study, the tools that are freely available at your institution and the number of student groups.

Ask students, in their groups, to test, evaluate and produce a review of their chosen tool. Once they have done this the review should be posted on a suitable digital platform so that you can build a useful digital resource to be made available throughout your students' course. Ask groups to produce useful and insightful information that will help their peers to evaluate whether or not the tool would be of use to them. This can include information about how to access the tool, ease of use, usefulness to course and/or studies, cost (if relevant) and how effective it is as a collaboration tool, for example. Give a deadline by which time all reviews should be uploaded. Encourage students to add to the resource and post comments as their course progresses and as they get the chance to use different tools. Monitor reviews and posts from time to time to ensure that information is correct, supportive and useful.

You can extend this activity by combining it with Activity 67, which builds a directory of online study groups. The two activities together produce a useful student-centred digital resource that will help students to benefit from online collaboration and peer-to-peer learning as their course progresses.

It is possible to collect together reviews and compile them into a PDF that is sent to all students if you do not want to set up a digital resource. If you choose this option, ask groups to imagine that they have been asked by their student newspaper to review their chosen tool and produce a piece for the next edition (give a specific deadline). Collect the reviews together, read through them, edit if necessary and convert to a PDF that can be emailed to your students or placed on your VLE/intranet for future reference.

Key issues

There are a wide variety of tools that can be reviewed in this activity. Some examples are given below. However, tools can change quickly and some of these may not be available when you run this activity. Also, find out what tools are available from your university, or for your subject area, as there may be specialist tools available that are not listed here. Before you run this activity check that it is free for groups to test the tool and that they will not be required to pay anything for access (the tools below are free, offer free trials or are available through most universities at time of writing, but this can change over time). The list has been ordered alphabetically:

- 99 Chats (www.99chats.com) for setting up four-way chats that can include up to 99 people;
- Blackboard collaborate (http://www.blackboard.com/online-collaborative-learning/blackboard-collaborate.html) for online learning, web conferences and real time classes;
- Canva (www.canva.com) for creating, collaborating on and sharing slides, posters, flyers and infographics;
- Citeulike (www.citeulike.org) for managing and sharing scholarly references;
- Crocodoc (https://crocodoc.com) for taking, making and sharing notes;
- Dropbox (www.dropbox.com) for storing, sharing and using files;
- Evernote (https://evernote.com) for capturing, organising and sharing notes;
- Google Drive (www.google.com/drive) for file storage, sharing and collaboration;
- Prezi (https://prezi.com) for creating presentations and collaborating with groups of up to ten people;
- Scrible (www.scrible.com) for researching, capturing, sharing and bookmarking;
- Sketch (www.sketchapp.com) for digital designing, synchronising, sharing and updating;
- WeVideo (www.wevideo.com) for collaborative video creation;
- WordPress (https://wordpress.org) for creating websites, blogs and apps, and inviting contributions and changes;
- Wunderlist (www.wunderlist.com) to-do lists for students working on the same project.

➜ **Related activities**

Activity 7: Fostering collaborative learning and interaction

Activity 64: Establishing study groups

Activity 67: Introducing online study groups

Activity 71: Understanding group dynamics and avoiding conflict

➜ **Preparatory reading**

The papers listed below provide useful preparatory reading for tutors who are interested in research covering online tools and collaborative study. Students will carry out preparatory work when they research and review their chosen collaborative tool.

➜ **Further reading**

Chapman, D., Storberg-Walker, J. and Stone, S. (2008) 'Hitting reply: a qualitative study to understand student decisions to respond to online discussion postings', *E-Learning and Digital Media*, 5 (1): 29–39, first published 1 January 2008, https://doi.org/10.2304/elea.2008.5.1.29. This is an interesting paper for all tutors using activities that require students to read, and respond to, online posts.

Kiili, C., Laurinen, L., Marttunen, M. and Leu, D. (2012) 'Working on understanding during collaborative online reading', *Journal of Literacy Research*, 44 (4): 448–83, first published 6 September 2012, https://doi.org/10.1177/1086296X124 57166. This paper provides insight into how students work together in a collaborative online reading project.

Activity 68

Smith, S. and Chipley, L. (2015) 'Building confidence as digital learners with digital support across the curriculum', *Journal of Educational Technology Systems*, 44 (2): 230–9, first published 9 December 2015, https://doi.org/10.1177/0047239515617469. This paper is relevant for tutors who are encouraging the use of digital tools for collaborative learning.

Tutors who are interested in using a learning platform that enables students to annotate readings and respond to others' comments and questions about text may find Perusall of interest (https://perusall.com/).

Activity 68

Activity • • • • • • • • • • ➜ 69

Surviving virtual group work

Student
handout
page 331

TUTOR NOTES

Purpose: This activity helps students to survive virtual group work by introducing them to a number of real-life scenarios that they must work through with their group members to find acceptable and workable solutions. 'Virtual group work', for the purpose of this activity, is defined as a number of students working together on a specific project in a virtual work environment, using IT and software to communicate and work together.

Type: Scenarios for group discussion (in class).

Alternative type(s): Group exercise during independent study.

Level: Elementary, intermediate and advanced.

Duration: Fifty minutes to one hour of contact time. If the group exercise option is chosen, students need to spend one or two hours working with their group members during independent study.

Equipment/materials: None required.

Learning outcome: By the end of this activity students will have a greater understanding of how to undertake virtual group work and will feel more confident about working on virtual projects, knowing how to recognise and overcome problems if they occur.

The activity

Divide your students into groups and ask them to work through the scenarios presented in the Student Handout. This will take up to 40 minutes. When the groups have finished, lead a class discussion on the issues raised. If contact time is not available you can ask groups to work through the scenarios during independent study.

Key issues

The following issues can be raised by the scenarios provided in the Student Handout.

Scenario 1

1. When preparing and planning for a project students should:

   a. Build a sense of community. Try to bond with team mates (share information, begin a discussion, identify points of common interest).

   b. Discuss worries and concerns about taking part in the project and learn from the experiences of those who have already done this type of work.

   c. Discuss worries and concerns about technology. Agree a strategy that will see the more experienced helping the less experienced.

d. Identify tasks. Work out what is required to meet goals. Illustrate relevance of tasks and how individual tasks connect with the whole exercise/assignment.

e. Identify the work that is involved. Be specific. Ensure that every group member understands what is required.

2. Discussions should include:

a. agreeing on roles, responsibilities and behaviours;

b. agreeing on contact details and communication protocol;

c. finding a communication strategy that works for every group member;

d. the importance of fostering compassion, encouragement and respect (see Activity 65).

3. Problems that could occur include:

a. Individuals do not pull their weight (solution: agree on tasks; monitor work and check on progress; address problems as they occur; offer help and encouragement; identify concerns and work together on acceptable solutions).

b. Technology failure, misuse or abuse (solution: ensure technology is available, suitable and can be accessed and used by all team members; try to find expert help if failure should occur; agree on a code of conduct/behaviour at the start).

c. The team does not gel and cannot work together (solution: choose team members wisely; address problems as soon as they occur; foster compassion and respect; seek help from tutors if problems persist).

Scenario 2

1. Students can adopt the following strategies:

a. meet face-to-face if it is a local virtual group to discuss issues sensitively and to find solutions;

b. listen carefully to concerns (taking care to hear all points of view);

c. find out if there is something important that has stopped or prevented one student from working;

d. reach consensus on ways to address problems.

2. Students can work together if they:

a. discuss existing tasks and ensure that everyone knows what they must do and by what date;

b. reach agreement on how they should behave within the group;

c. remain motivated and help others to remain motivated, offering encouragement and support.

3. This problem could be prevented if:

a. team members are chosen carefully;

b. team members are all motivated to do their best;

c. everyone understands their roles and responsibilities;

d. tasks are allocated carefully and everyone is happy with the allocation;

c. all team members are clear about deadlines;

f. everyone adheres to a negotiated code of conduct or code of behaviour.

Scenario 3

1. Successful team leaders should:

a. foster trust, respect, compassion and empathy;

b. encourage open dialogue;

c. provide constructive and effective feedback;

d. have good negotiating and delegating skills;

e. encourage cohesion;

f. clarify goals and establish a common purpose or vision;

g. remain motivated and help to motivate others;

h. provide direction and clear instructions that everyone can understand.

2. Team members should have:

a. the required knowledge, understanding and skills or the ability and motivation to acquire these as the project progresses;

b. the ability to work together with team mates, and use the required technology (or gain the ability to use this technology);

c. the ability and motivation to work independently on allocated tasks;

d. awareness of and sensitivity to other cultures, nationalities, organisations and groups;

3. Issues to consider include:

a. availability, cost and maintenance of technology at the various global locations;

b. cultural sensitivity (when using particular communication methods, types and approaches, for example);

c. language issues;

d. time zones.

Scenario 4

1. The group could handle this issue by:

a. stating they do not need a team leader and can work together, equally on the project;

b. suggesting they do need a team leader but that this should be put to the vote (so that a more experienced, less dominant person can be chosen);

c. suggesting that they begin the project without a leader and reassess midway through, or if they encounter any problems;

d. suggesting another, more experienced person as team leader and giving a justification as to why more experience is important on a virtual project;

e. going ahead with the person who wishes to be leader.

2. Some groups need team leaders, some do not. Students should be encouraged to talk about their previous experiences and provide examples of when groups have worked well with and without team leaders.

3. The groups should follow the steps outlined in the first answer in Scenario 1 as these will help them to work successfully on their virtual project.

Activity 69

→ Related activities

Activity 7: Fostering collaborative learning and interaction

Activity 68: Using online tools for collaborative study

Activity 71: Understanding group dynamics and avoiding conflict

Activity 98: Collaborating and cooperating ethically

→ Preparatory reading

The articles listed below provide interesting preparatory reading for tutors. Students do not need to undertake preparatory reading for this activity (they should be encouraged to discuss and learn from personal experience).

→ Further reading

Hazari, S. and Thompson, S. (2015) 'Investigating factors affecting group processes in virtual learning environments', *Business and Professional Communication Quarterly*, 78 (1): 33–54, first published 15 December 2014, https://doi.org/10.1177/2329490614558920. This paper provides interesting reading for tutors who are interested in perceptions of group work in online classes.

Martins, L. and Shalley, C. (2011) 'Creativity in virtual work: effects of demographic differences', *Small Group Research*, 42 (5): 536–61, first published 28 February 2011, https://doi.org/10.1177/1046496410397382. This paper considers how demographic differences, the nature of interaction processes and technical experience affect creative processes in short-term virtual work interactions.

Schouten, A., van den Hooff, B. and Feldberg, F. (2016) 'Virtual team work: group decision making in 3D virtual environments', *Communication Research*, 43 (2): 180–210, first published 11 November 2013, https://doi.org/10.1177/0093650213509667. This paper reports on how three-dimensional virtual environments support shared understanding and group decision making.

Activity 69

Activity • • • • • • • • • • ➔ 70

Working within international teams

Student handout page 333

TUTOR NOTES

Purpose: This activity helps students to understand how to work effectively and efficiently within an international team. It asks them to imagine that they are applying for a distinguished scholarship. As part of the application process they must produce an essay that illustrates 'best practice' when working within an international team.

Type: Essay (written assignment).

Alternative type(s): Vlogs and blogs.

Level: Advanced (this activity is aimed at students who may be required to work with international colleagues in the present or future).

Duration: Students need to spend a few hours during independent study working on their essays.

Equipment/materials: None required.

Learning outcome: By the end of this activity students will have researched and produced an essay on best practice within international teams, which will help them to feel more confident and knowledgeable about working effectively within an international team as their course and career progresses.

The activity

Give the Student Handout to your students. This asks them to imagine that they are applying for a distinguished scholarship that will enable them to work on a research project within an international team. As part of the application process they must produce an essay that discusses issues of 'best practice' when working within international teams. Give a deadline by which time essays need to be handed to you. If appropriate, you can compile the essays together as a useful resource for students to access if they intend to work within an international team. Decide whether or not to make this an assessed piece of work.

It is possible to ask students to produce a vlog or blog instead of an essay if you feel that a less formal approach is suited to your students and to this topic. Give a deadline by which time vlogs and blogs must be posted and encourage discussion among students. Monitor posts to ensure that information is correct, constructive and supportive.

Key issues

This activity is useful for students studying at advanced level who are intending to work within an international team or who may be thinking about this for their future employment. Asking students to think specifically about 'best practice' helps them to focus on important collaborative issues such as choosing the right team members; ensuring everyone has the same aims, objectives and goals; agreements on ownership of intellectual property and equipment; preparing joint bids and joint funding applications; adhering to author protocols on published material and sharing of potentially sensitive information, for example. It also helps them to focus on how to build a good working relationship, which can include issues such as management and leadership, communication, networking and understanding (social, cultural and organisational, for example).

➔ **Related activities**

Activity 7: Fostering collaborative learning and interaction

Activity 69: Surviving virtual group work

Activity 71: Understanding group dynamics and avoiding conflict

Activity 98: Collaborating and cooperating ethically

➔ **Preparatory reading**

Jonsen, K., Butler, C., Mäkelä, K., Piekkari, R., Drogendijk, R., Lauring, J., Lervik, J., Pahlberg, C., Vodosek, M. and Zander, L. (2012) 'Processes of international collaboration in management research', *Journal of Management Inquiry*, 22 (4): 394-413. This paper provides insight into working in international teams based on a reflexive, auto-ethnographic approach and provides useful preparatory reading for both tutors and students.

The Organisation for Economic Co-operation and Development (OECD) has produced *A Report on Opportunities, Challenges and Good Practices in International Research Cooperation between Developed and Developed Countries* (https://www.oecd.org/sti/sci-tech/47737209.pdf). This document contains some pertinent information about good practice in international cooperation and provides useful preparatory reading.

➔ **Further reading**

Huang, F., Finkelstein, M. and Rostan, M. (2014) *The Internationalization of the Academy: Changes, Realities and Prospects*. Dordrecht: Springer. This book provides a good overview of internationalisation, with chapter 7 dealing specifically with internationalisation in research.

Kwiek, M. (2015) 'The internationalization of research in Europe', *Journal of Studies in International Education*, 19 (4): 341-59. This paper considers the impact of international research on individual research productivity in 11 European countries and illustrates the benefits that can be gained from international collaboration. It is useful further reading for both tutors and students.

Activity 70

Activity • • • • • • • • • • → 71

Understanding group dynamics and avoiding conflict

Student handout page 334

TUTOR NOTES

Purpose: This activity is an entertaining way to raise awareness of issues associated with group dynamics and avoiding conflict when students are working together in groups. It asks students, in groups, to produce a light-hearted video that illustrates problems with group dynamics and conflict. These are viewed and discussed in class, with students working together to find solutions to the problems illustrated in the videos.

Type: Video production with tutor-led viewing and discussion.

Alternative type(s): Videos can be uploaded for online viewing and discussion, if contact time is not available.

Level: Elementary, intermediate and advanced.

Duration: Students need to spend a few hours in their groups researching the topic and producing their video. Up to two hours of contact time is required to view and watch videos (the amount of time depends on the number of videos produced).

Equipment/materials: Students require access to video production equipment and software. You need suitable presentation equipment to show the videos in class.

Learning outcome: By the end of this activity students will have a raised awareness of problems that can occur with group dynamics and understand how to recognise, and address, these problems so that conflict can be avoided in group work as their course progresses.

The activity

Divide your students into groups and give each group a copy of the Student Handout. This asks them to work with their group members to produce a video that illustrates problems with group dynamics and conflict that can occur when working in groups. They are asked to keep the video light-hearted and to be creative and imaginative when producing their video. When you next meet you will watch each video in turn, spending a little time after each one to discuss the issues raised and to find solutions to the problems illustrated.

The videos should be no longer than ten minutes and the discussion should take up to ten minutes for each video viewed. Ensure that you have enough contact time available to view all videos (student groups can contain a larger number of members if you only have an hour of contact time). If contact time is not available, ask students to upload their videos onto the relevant digital platform for online viewing and discussion. Monitor videos and posts to ensure that the information presented is correct, constructive and supportive.

Key issues

Students provide humorous, entertaining and imaginative videos that introduce a wide variety of problems (some groups concentrate on one particular issue, whereas others cover a number of issues within one video). Problems tend to be exaggerated to make them light-hearted or humorous. These can include:

- dominant speakers;
- digressions;
- disruptive members;
- break-away groups;
- arguments (opposite points of views and an unwillingness to compromise, for example);
- disagreement on tasks;
- disagreement on whether a group leader is required and problems with the group leader if one is chosen/ puts themselves forward;
- group members not pulling their weight;
- individuals wanting to work on their own and resenting having to work in groups;

- individuals not taking the work seriously;
- group members not listening to each other;
- negative comments and no encouragement;
- not taking deadlines seriously;
- antagonism towards other group members;
- unconfident, shy or nervous group members who find it hard to interact or speak in a group setting;
- insensitivity and lack of empathy and compassion for other group members (those that are overloaded with work or family commitments that make group work difficult, for example).

➜ Related activities

Activity 7: Fostering collaborative learning and interaction

Activity 64: Establishing study groups

Activity 65: Getting the most out of group work

Activity 69: Surviving virtual group work

Activity 98: Collaborating and cooperating ethically

➜ Preparatory reading

Behfar, K., Mannix, E., Peterson, R. and Trochim, W. (2011) 'Conflict in small groups: the meaning and consequences of process conflict', *Small Group Research*, 42 (2): 127–76, first published 13 December 2010, https://doi.org/10.1177/1046496410389194. This paper provides information about how process conflict negatively affects group performance.

Chapman, K., Meuter, M., Toy, D. and Wright, L. (2006) 'Can't we pick our own groups? The influence of group selection method on group dynamics and outcomes', *Journal of Management Education*, 30 (4): 557–69, first published 1 August 2006, https://doi.org/10.1177/1052562905284872. This paper provides interesting reading for tutors who need to decide between self-selecting or random selection of group members and the influence that this selection has on group dynamics and outcomes. You need to decide whether or not to have self-selecting groups for this activity, and these issues can be raised during your tutor-led discussion.

➜ Further reading

All three books listed below can be recommended to students who want to know more about how to work successfully in groups.

Hartley, P. and Dawson, M. (2010) *Success in Groupwork*. Basingstoke: Palgrave Macmillan.

Kahn, W. (2009) *The Student's Guide to Successful Project Teams*. New York: Psychology Press.

Levin, P. (2005) *Successful Teamwork! For Undergraduates and Taught Postgraduates Working on Group Projects*. Maidenhead: Open University Press.

Activity 71

Section 10

IT, assistive learning and e-learning

Activity • • • • • • • • • • ➜ 72

Gaining confidence with IT for academic study

Student handout page 335

TUTOR NOTES

Purpose: This activity helps students to become more confident with their use of information technology (IT) for academic study by asking them to discuss some real-life statements, suggest solutions to the stated problems and develop an action plan that they can implement as their course progresses. It is aimed at students studying at elementary level who are unconfident with IT and is of particular use to adult returners who may be anxious about using new technology and software during their studies.

Type: Workshop.

Alternative type(s): Group exercise during independent study; one-to-one support session.

Level: Elementary.

Duration: One hour for the workshop and ongoing student time to implement their action plan.

Equipment/materials: None required for the workshop. Students will need access to the relevant IT facilities so that they can proceed with their action plan.

Learning outcome: By the end of this activity students will feel more confident with the use of IT during their academic studies and will have developed an action plan that they can implement to help them get the most out of IT as their course progresses.

The activity

Invite together students who could benefit from this workshop. Divide them into small groups and give each group a copy of the Student Handout. This presents several real-life statements that have been made by students who are new to using IT for academic study. It asks groups to discuss the statements and suggest solutions to overcome the stated problems. Once students have discussed all the statements and identified solutions, they should work with their group members to develop an action plan that will help them to get the most out of IT during their academic studies. Allocate up to 40 minutes for the group discussion, up to 15 minutes to develop an action plan and up to five minutes to sum up and conclude the workshop.

This activity works well because it introduces the anxieties, concerns and worries that students may be experiencing, but does not require them to discuss or confess their own feelings, unless they wish to do so during the discussion. It enables students to discuss these issues with other students in their group, bounce ideas off each other, learn from those with more experience and/or confidence and provide practical and effective solutions to the stated problems. They go on to develop an action plan that will help them to build their confidence and get the most out of IT during their studies.

It is possible to run this activity as a group exercise during independent study if contact time is limited. You can also run this activity as a one-to-one support session if an individual student needs specific help.

Key issues

The following issues can be raised during this activity, depending on your students, their previous and present experiences and their level of understanding:

1. A student is displaying a lack of confidence in using technology. This can lead to anxiety and worry about things that may never happen (such as the student thinking that she will 'break' the computer). The student could take the following action:

   a. enrol on a 'computers for the terrified course';
   b. get help and advice from younger relatives in an informal, relaxed environment;
   c. foster cooperation and collaboration with more experienced fellow students;
   d. seek advice and encouragement from tutors;
   e. practise at every opportunity.

2. A student is displaying a lack in confidence, nervousness and a sense of not fitting in or not being the same as other students. This student should not worry about what others are thinking: they are probably more concerned with their work or haven't even noticed the new arrival. Again, this student needs to develop his confidence and can adopt the strategies described above. He could also try using the room when it's less busy, find a smaller space or go with a supportive friend.

3. A student seems overwhelmed by the pace of change. However, students should embrace new technology. It should be viewed as a fantastic aid to academic study, rather than as a problem. New developments should not be feared or dismissed. Students can learn the basics that are then transferable to many different technologies. Action includes:

   a. cultivate an open and enquiring attitude towards changing technology;
   b. find out what is available to help with your studies and keep up-to-date with new developments (seek information and advice from fellow students, tutors, library staff and IT technicians);
   c. keep an eye on courses, modules and free online tutorials that will help you to get to grips with new software, technology and equipment.

4. A student can be helped by technology as it provides the opportunity to view, understand and use data in a huge variety of ways. If figures are daunting and confusing, she can try data visualisation tools (see Activity 77). Software can help with data analysis and make the process much quicker and easier. Action includes:

   a. seek advice from relevant members of staff;
   b. read books, journals and magazines;
   c. view online tutorials that are abundant and free to access;
   d. use help buttons that are provided with specific tools;
   e. enrol on workshops or courses.

5. Technological literacy is an important skill to develop for studies, work and life in general. Although a student is feeling 'left behind' he should use his academic studies to gain in confidence and take the opportunity to use a wide variety of technology that is available for his use, with the help and support of knowledgeable members of staff. Action includes:

   a. understand the benefits (learning can take place anytime, anywhere and collaboratively; there is 24-hour access to immediate information; it is possible to store and access huge amounts of data; there is access to multiple communication channels and social networks that can support and encourage learning);
   b. learn from the kids;
   c. keep up-to-date where possible.

6. Technology can help with academic studies in so many ways. It gives access to a wide variety of learning resources such as multimedia, online libraries, databases, repositories and journal articles. It helps us to collect, view, analyse and present data. It enables us to collaborate, network and learn from others, and disseminate, share and discuss our academic work with our peers. Technology cuts down time-consuming work and can make studies more efficient. Action includes:

   a. go on all orientation tours (library, IT facilities, etc.) when you begin your course;
   b. obtain information, help and advice from relevant helpdesks, members of staff and websites;
   c. practise using tools and software and seek advice if you encounter any problems.

➜ Related activities

Activity 34: Maths for unconfident adults

Activity 73: Making the most of IT facilities and support

Activity 75: Getting the most out of online learning

Activity 77: Using data visualisation tools and software

Activity 72

➜ Preparatory reading

Wikibooks provides a free online book called 'Computers for Beginners' (https://en.wikibooks.org/wiki/Computers_for_Beginners). This book can be recommended to students who are new to computers and is also useful preparatory reading for this exercise as it helps to remind tutors of the areas with which students might struggle when using computers.

Students can be directed to 'Webwise' from the BBC in the UK (www.bbc.co.uk/webwise) for general information about getting connected and developing online skills to make the most of mobiles, tablets, computers or interactive television. There is also a useful booklet that helps students to get online and use the internet (http://downloads.bbc.co.uk/connect/BBC_First_Click_Beginners_Guide.pdf).

➜ Further reading

Clarke, A. (2011) *How to Use Technology Effectively in Post-Compulsory Education*. Abingdon, Oxon: Routledge. This book is aimed at tutors in the lifelong learning sector who wish to employ technology in their teaching. It provides a useful overview of the variety of technologies available and gives practical examples of how they can be used to teach adults (and how adults can use the technology to learn).

Erwig, M. (2017) *Once Upon an Algorithm: How Stories Explain Computing*. Cambridge, MA: MIT Press. This book provides a fresh approach to computer science by relating complex issues to a variety of well-known stories. It provides interesting reading for tutors and can be recommended to students who have little technical knowledge of the subject.

Activity 72

Activity · · · · · · · · · · ➔ 73

Making the most of IT facilities and support

The activity

Contact your computer services department/IT department to organise a session called 'making the most of IT support and facilities'. Most will run a session in a PC lab/specialist computing room to offer advice and guidance on the equipment that is available to students. They will discuss what is available, illustrate how to access equipment, provide a brief demonstration and supply information about further support, training and courses that are available, if required. They may also provide a tour of relevant facilities, time permitting. If your IT department does not run this type of session, book the appropriate PC lab or specialist computing room and run the session yourself.

This activity can be used for students at all levels of study: make sure that the IT technician/member of support staff is aware of the level of study and pitches their session accordingly. It is of particular use to students studying at elementary level who are new to your university and for students studying at intermediate or advanced level who need to find out more about facilities, equipment and software that will help with their dissertation or thesis, for example.

Key issues

This activity provides a practical, hands-on demonstration of equipment, facilities and software that are available for students. It introduces students to the hardware and software, illustrating how to access appropriate computing equipment (including location and booking) and software that are available on the institution's network. This can include information on how to print and photocopy (including issues of copyright), netbooks and laptops available for loan, connecting to the Wi-Fi network, citing references, bibliographic software, statistical software and data mining software, for example (depending on level of study). More information about data analysis techniques is provided in Activity 84, more information about software for research is provided in Activity 74 and more information about library facilities is provided in Activity 49.

It is useful to ask an experienced IT technician/software specialist to run this session because they can keep abreast of the most recent developments in hardware and software acquisition and design and can offer the most up-to-date advice about workshops, training and courses.

➔ Related activities

Activity 49: Getting the most from the library

Activity 72: Gaining confidence with IT for academic study

Activity 74: Using software for research

Activity 84: Introducing data analysis techniques

....

➔ Preparatory reading

Ask students to read the relevant section on the university website in preparation for this activity, so that they can find out what equipment and facilities they would like to know more about and can prepare relevant questions before the session takes place.

....

➔ Further reading

The person running this session will recommend further reading (paper or online documents that explain how to locate, access and use relevant hardware and software, for example).

Activity 73

Activity · · · · · · · · · · · · → 74

Using software for research

The activity

Ask your students to imagine that they have been approached by the editor of a software magazine to produce a review of a particular software package (you will assign a software package to each student to ensure good coverage). The type of software assigned depends on subject and level of study: see below. The review must be interesting and useful for other students, containing detailed information that will help their peers to assess the usefulness and user-friendliness of the software. Explain that all the reviews will be compiled into one resource, which will be sent as a PDF to all students. This will enable them to read each review and decide, for themselves, which software will be of use to them as their course progresses. You can ask students to undertake this activity on an individual basis or in small groups, depending on your student cohort. Provide a deadline by which time all reviews should be received.

Examples of software that can be assigned to students are given below. Add to, delete and alter this list as appropriate (when new software enters or disappears from the market, for example). If you have a large number of individual students (or groups) you can assign software packages more than once: reviews usually highlight different aspects of software so repetition tends to be avoided. Check that packages are still available and are free to use before assigning software.

It is possible to ask students to produce their reviews as vlogs or blogs that are uploaded onto a suitable digital plat-form for their peers to view/read and discuss if this better suits your students. Give a deadline by which time all vlogs and blogs should be uploaded and check that all uploaded material is suitable, constructive and useful.

Key issues

The broad title of this activity is deliberate as it enables tutors to decide what software to use in the activity. For example, if you are teaching students at elementary level, perhaps adult returners who are unfamiliar with software that can help with assignments, you can ask them to review citing, referencing and bibliography software such as:

- BibMe (www.bibme.org);
- Citation machine (www.citationmachine.net);
- Citavi (www.citavi.com);
- Cite This For Me (www.citethisforme.com);
- Citefast (www.citefast.com);
- Docear (www.docear.org);
- EndNote (http://endnote.com);
- Mendeley (www.mendeley.com);
- OttoBib (http://www.ottobib.com);
- Recipes4Success (http://recipes.tech4learning.com);
- RefWorks (www.refworks.com).

Alternatively, you could ask students to review software that helps them to collaborate with their peers (see Activity 68):

- Crocodoc (https://crocodoc.com);
- Dropbox (www.dropbox.com);
- Evernote (https://evernote.com);
- Google Drive (www.google.com/drive);
- Scrible (www.scrible.com);
- WeVideo (www.wevideo.com);
- WordPress (https://wordpress.org);
- Wunderlist (www.wunderlist.com).

If your students are studying at intermediate or advanced level and are interested in software for statistical analysis, you could ask students to review the following (depending on what is available at your institution):

- SPSS (www.ibm.com/spss);
- Minitab (www.minitab.com);
- Stata (www.stata.com);
- StatCrunch (www.statcrunch.com);
- SAS (www.sas.com);
- JMP (www.jmp.com);
- R (www.r-project.org).

Or you could ask students to review software for qualitative data analysis (depending on what is available at your institution):

- NVivo (www.qsrinternational.com/nvivo);
- ATLAS.ti (http://atlasti.com);
- MAXQDA (www.maxqda.com);
- ANTHROPAC (www.analytictech.com/anthropac/anthropac.htm);
- LibreQDA (https://libreqda.github.io);
- hyper RESEARCH (www.researchware.com).

Alternatively, you could ask students to review software from all the above categories to obtain a much wider coverage, if appropriate.

➜ Related activities

Activity 68: Using online tools for collaborative study

Activity 73: Making the most of IT facilities and support

Activity 77: Using data visualisation tools and software

Activity 84: Introducing data analysis techniques

....

➜ Preparatory reading

The Software Sustainability Institute (www.software.ac.uk) 'cultivates better, more sustainable, research software to ena-ble world-class research'. It works with researchers, developers and funders to identify key issues and best practice in

Activity 74

scientific software. The website contains an interesting and useful blog that covers up-to-date and pertinent issues. There is also a useful list of resources for students using software for their research [accessed 9 November 2017].

....

Further reading

The following books can be recommended to students studying at intermediate and advanced level if they are interested in data analysis software.

Bazeley, P. (2013) *Qualitative Data Analysis, Practical Strategies*. London: Sage.

Kent, R. (2015) *Analysing Quantitative Data*. London: Sage.

Miles, M., Huberman, M. and Saldana, J. (2014) *Qualitative Data Analysis: a Methods Sourcebook*, 3rd edition. Thousand Oaks, CA: Sage.

Paulus, T., Lester, J. and Dempster, P. (2013) *Digital Tools for Qualitative Research*. London: Sage.

Silver, C. and Lewins, A. (2014) *Using Software in Qualitative Research: a Step-by-Step Guide,* 2nd edition. London: Sage.

Activity 74

Activity · · · · · · · · · · ➔ 75

Getting the most out of online learning

The activity

The first way to run this activity is as a tip exchange for students who are currently studying on an online course. Set up a suitable digital platform on which to run the tip exchange and invite your students to post tips as their online course progresses. Call the tip exchange 'getting the most from online learning'. Tips should be useful and offer helpful advice that will enable students to get more out of their online learning. Monitor posts from time to time to ensure that all tips are supportive, encouraging and useful. Students should be reminded to post tips as soon as they think of them throughout their course, which will build a useful student-centred digital resource on which students can draw as their online course progresses.

The second way to run this activity is as a brainstorming session for students who are currently studying face-to-face (on a classroom-based course) who may need to study online in the future (on a compulsory online module or on a voluntary online course that is of interest, for example). Invite these students together for a session in which you brainstorm the question 'how can I get the most out of online learning?' Write their answers on your screen/board/flipchart without judgement, analysis or reflection. If students are unfamiliar with the brainstorming technique ask them to give any answer they can think of in relation to the question. They are not going to be judged and they should not judge or critique the answers given by other students (even if they do not agree with another's contribution). Each answer they give will be written down: the goal is to share ideas and learn from each other. Students can, on occasions, take a few minutes to think about this topic before becoming more spontaneous with their suggestions.

Once the brainstorm is complete (after about 20 minutes) discuss the issues raised with your students, combining, expanding on and improving ideas (see key issues). Do this for a further 20 minutes until you feel that the discussion has run its course. Once the discussion is complete, ask your students to work on an individual basis to develop a personal action plan that will help them to get the most out of online learning, based on the issues that have been raised during the brainstorm and discussion. Students should refer back to their action plans as their course progresses so that they can get the most out of online learning.

Key issues

Examples of brainstorming ideas and tips that have been raised in this activity are given below (some have been shortened or amalgamated):

- identify goals;
- check there is a match between goals and learning outcomes;
- stay focused on goals;
- understand course requirements;
- understand technology requirements;
- become familiar with technology;
- obtain reliable internet access;
- back up everything using reliable storage;
- create a study space free from distractions and disturbances;
- keep family members away from important work and technology;
- turn off phones and email alerts;
- log off social networking sites;
- create and stick to a study plan (see Activity 10);
- maintain motivation (see Activity 14);
- understand how to work independently (see Activity 15);
- mark all important assignment dates on a calendar (use an effective calendar system);
- manage time effectively (see Activity 11);
- meet all deadlines (allowing for technology glitches);
- engage with the online community;
- participate in discussions and activities;
- complete all work, even if it is not assessed;
- foster cooperation and collaboration (see Activity 7);
- ask for help when required (from peers and tutors);
- ask for clarification when something is unclear;
- review and revise work on a regular basis;
- establish an online study group for peer support and encouragement (see Activity 67);
- listen to, and act on, all tutor feedback (see Activity 48);
- be compassionate and respectful (see Activity 65);
- be mindful of your online tone when disagreeing with others;
- write in clear sentences to avoid misunderstandings;
- remain culturally and socially sensitive.

➜ Related activities

Activity 67: Introducing online study groups

Activity 68: Using online tools for collaborative study

Activity 69: Surviving virtual group work

Activity 78: Copyright infringement and plagiarism of electronic material

➜ Preparatory reading

Harasim, L. (2017) *Learning Theory and Online Technologies*, 2nd edition. New York: Routledge. This book provides information about online environments for learning, evaluation of student online learning and research into online learning. It is useful preparatory reading for tutors who are interested in these issues.

Means, B. (2014) *Learning Online: What Research Tells Us About Whether, When and How*. New York: Routledge. This book provides a useful discussion of different learning technologies, their implementation and research into them. It is useful preparatory reading for tutors interested in these issues.

Activity 75

➜ Further reading

Lehman, R. and Conceição, S. (2014) *Retaining and Motivating Online Students: Research-based Strategies and Interventions that Work*. San Francisco, CA: Jossey-Bass. This is a useful book for tutors who develop online courses.

Talbot, C. (2016) *Studying at a Distance: a Guide for Students*, 4th edition. Maidenhead: Open University Press. This book can be recommended to students who wish to find out more about distance and online learning.

Activity 75

Activity · · · · · · · · · · → 76

Making the most of assistive technology

The activity

Contact the specialist member of staff within your university who deals with assistive technology. This could be an Assistive Technology Officer, a Disability Officer or a specialist member of library or IT staff, for example. Ask them to organise a session called 'making the most of assistive technology'. Most will run a session in the specialist assistive technology suite or in the library/LRC to demonstrate the equipment, materials, software, facilities and services that are available and to offer advice and guidance on how to access and use equipment. The duration of the session depends on the number of students present, their individual needs and the type of equipment that is available. If such a person is not available, lead a tour, talk and demonstration yourself. If you choose to do this, obtain advice and guidance from IT officers and practise using the equipment before you run your session. Useful references and sources of information are given below.

The session can be run with a group of students from different levels of study and from different courses, or on a one-to-one basis. When arranging the session, ensure that it is at a date and time that all students can attend and make sure that the venue is accessible. Some students with a high level of need may require ongoing support, advice and guidance with assistive technology as their course progresses. Universities have a specialist support unit or member of staff that can offer this type of support: frequent liaison will ensure that the needs of your student(s) are met.

Key issues

The term 'assistive technology' in higher education refers to any technology, materials or equipment that can be used by students with disabilities to aid their studies. This includes:

- digital voice recorders, dictaphones and audio note-takers;
- reading pens and digital text scanners to capture, extract and reproduce printed information;
- screen readers, screen magnifiers and video magnifiers;
- digital wireless communications systems, loops and audio devices;
- dyslexia-friendly software and apps (focused reading mode and dyslexia-friendly font, for example);
- time management and organisation tools:

  o mind-mapping software to help with planning, organisation and revision;

  o planning and motivation apps and software;
  o task management tools;
  o timer and activity loggers;
  o distraction blockers;
- reading and writing tools:

  o spelling and grammar proofreading software;
  o text-to-speech software for proofing;
  o citing and bibliographic apps and software;
- ergonomic keyboards, mice and screens;
- ergonomic chairs, desks and foot support;
- electronic height adjustable desks.

The specialist members of staff will explain what equipment is available and for whom (students in the UK may have to be registered with the disability service or be in receipt of Disabled Students Allowances to access equipment, for example). Equipment may be available for purchase, hire or short-term loan and booking procedures will be explained. The specialist member of staff will demonstrate how equipment works, how it can be of benefit and give details of workshops, seminars or leaflets that are available to provide more information, advice and guidance. Information about specialist support staff availability and help desk support will also be given in the session, along with details of other professional services that may be of use, such as counselling, welfare, IT and medical services.

➜ Related activities

Activity 49: Getting the most from the library

Activity 72: Gaining confidence with IT for academic study

Activity 74: Using software for research

....

➜ Preparatory reading

The RNIB in the UK has a useful online guide to assistive technology that can be accessed at http://www.rnib.org.uk/information-everyday-living-using-technology-beginners-guides/beginners-guide-assistive-technology. This provides useful preparatory work for students and tutors who are new to this topic.

   YouTube (www.youtube.com) has some informative videos on various types of assistive technology, including examples, demonstrations and evaluations (search 'assistive technology'). These provide useful preparatory work for tutors who intend to run this session without the help of a specialist.

....

➜ Further reading

Bouck, E. (2017) *Assistive Technology*. Thousand Oaks, CA: Sage. This is a comprehensive and interesting book for tutors who wish to know more about assistive technology, including background, frameworks, methods and types.

Patti, A. and Garland, K. (2015) 'Smartpen applications for meeting the needs of students with learning disabilities in inclusive classrooms', *Journal of Special Education Technology*, 30 (4): 238–44. This paper discusses one type of assistive technology (the Smartpen) and provides an interesting example of how it can be of benefit in the classroom.

Activity 76

Using data visualisation tools and software

Student handout page 336

TUTOR NOTES

Purpose: This activity introduces students to data visualisation tools and software. It provides advice and guidance about using these tools and/or software through the development of a student-centred, digital resource. The activity utilises the knowledge and experiences of tech-savvy students who can share information and advice with their peers.

Type: Student-centred digital resource.

Alternative type(s): Self-guided individual exercise.

Level: Elementary, intermediate and advanced.

Duration: A few minutes of tutor time to set up a suitable digital platform. Up to one hour of contact time to introduce the activity and explain requirements. Students need to spend several hours finding data, testing the tool, posting their review and contributing to the discussion.

Equipment/materials: A suitable digital platform on which to build the resource and the required access details for all students.

Learning outcome: By the end of this activity students will have tried, tested and critiqued a data visualisation tool and/or software and will have developed a useful student-centred resource on which they can draw throughout their course, when required.

The activity

Introduce the topic of 'data visualisation' to your students. The amount of time you spend on this varies, depending on the level and subject of study and the amount of introductory information required by your students. Possible discussion points include issues such as how we see what we see, how we perceive what we see and how we make judgements about what we see (drawing conclusions, making generalisations and developing models and hypotheses, for example). Specific questions that can be asked include:

- How do we understand a visualisation?
- How do we respond to a visualisation?
- How is understanding and response connected to audience (who is viewing, when, where and how)?
- How is understanding and response connected to type of visualisation (what has been produced, how, why and in what form)?

Once you have introduced the topic, give your students a copy of the Student Handout. This asks them to identify, test, review and critique a data visualisation tool and/or software chosen by them or from the given list. Students can undertake this activity individually or in small groups (this is useful if you feel some students might struggle with this activity and could, therefore, benefit from the support of group members). If you want to ensure a wide coverage of the listed tools you can allocate a different tool to each group/individual. However, this tends to be unnecessary because most students try several tools before finding one with which they are happy. Students from a non-scientific background tend to choose the easier website tools, whereas those with a science background are happy to test the more complex software (where programming and/or coding is required, for example). Students need access to data that they can use to test the tool/software. They can do this by following the links provided in the Student Handout or you can provide data for them to use.

Once they have identified, tested, reviewed and critiqued their chosen tool/software, they should post the information on the relevant digital platform (including links or uploaded data visualisations, where appropriate). Students should be encouraged to review, discuss and ask questions about the examples posted by fellow students so that a useful resource can be developed. Give a deadline for the posting of information, to ensure that all students take part in this activity. Monitor the posts to check that information is correct and constructive, and post questions, dilemmas and discussion points, if these are not forthcoming from students.

It is possible to run this activity as a self-guided individual exercise during independent study, if you do not want to set up the digital resource. The exercise can be followed by a discussion in class, if time is available.

Key issues

There are different types of data visualisation, including mathematical visualisation, scientific visualisation, information visualisation and domain-specific visualisation such as medical imaging, business intelligence and geographical information systems. You can use any type of visualisation for this activity, depending on the level and subject of study and the requirements of your students. The Student Handout has been produced with information visualisation in mind, but can be adapted, if required.

All the websites provided in the list, at time of writing, provide free trials or are free to use. Some of the software listed also provides free trials. Other software will be available only through your institution. However, this is subject to change, so it is important to check all websites before undertaking this activity. Alternatively, find out what tools and software are available at your institution and produce a new list for your students.

You can also direct students to relevant modules or workshops at your institution, or to free online courses that will help to build their understanding and use of data visualisation. There are various MOOCs (massive open online courses) available covering this subject and details of these can be obtained from the following MOOC platforms:

- FutureLearn (www.futurelearn.com)
- Coursera (www.coursera.org)
- edX (www.edx.org)
- open2study (www.open2study.com)

→ Related activities

Activity 38: Introducing data mining

Activity 39: Finding and using datasets

Activity 74: Using software for research

....

→ Preparatory reading

Part 1 of Kirk (2016) provides good preparatory reading for tutors. You may also find it useful preparation to practise using some data visualisation tools/software, if you have not already done so.

....

→ Further reading

The following books can be recommended to students who wish to follow up the issues raised in this activity.
Evergreen, S. (2016) *Effective Data Visualization: the Right Chart for the Right Data*. Thousand Oaks, CA: Sage.
Kirk, A. (2016) *Data Visualisation: a Handbook for Data Driven Design*. London: Sage.
Ware, C. (2013) *Information Visualization: Perception for Design*. Waltham, MA: Elsevier.
Yau, N. (2013) *Data Points: Visualization that Means Something*. Indianapolis, IN: Wiley Publishing, Inc.

Activity 77

Activity • • • • • • • • • • • → 78

Copyright infringement and plagiarism of electronic material

Student handout page 338

TUTOR NOTES

Purpose: This activity helps students to understand what is meant by copyright infringement and plagiarism of electronic material by asking them to plan, produce and upload a video or podcast that teaches their fellow students about these issues. Students have the opportunity to review, discuss and provide feedback on videos produced by their peers.

Type: Video/podcast production.

Alternative types(s): Group exercise followed by group presentation.

Level: Elementary and intermediate.

Duration: Several hours during independent study for students to plan, produce and upload their video, and up to an hour to review and provide feedback on the videos produced by their peers. Tutors need to spend an hour or two monitoring the videos, discussion and feedback. If the group presentation option is chosen, students need several hours during independent study to produce their presentations and 50 minutes to one hour of class time to make their presentations.

Equipment/materials: Students need access to video recording equipment and access to the relevant digital platform on which to upload their video or podcast. They will need access to presentation equipment, if this option is chosen.

Learning outcome: By the end of this activity students will know what is meant by copyright infringement and plagiarism of electronic materials, recognise when it might have occurred in the work of others and understand how to avoid it in their own academic work. They will also have a useful collection of videos/podcasts on which to draw, when required.

The activity

Divide your students into small groups and give each group a copy of the Student Handout. This asks them to produce a video or podcast that teaches their fellow students about copyright infringement and plagiarism of electronic materials. They are to upload the video on the relevant digital platform (it can be an internal or external platform, depending on your preference).

Students should review, discuss and provide feedback on each group's video/podcast so that they can gain a deeper understanding of what is meant by these issues, recognise when these problems occur in the work of others and know how to avoid them in their own work. Monitor the videos, discussion and feedback to ensure that the information given is correct, supportive and encouraging. Sometimes students can post misleading or unreliable information that will need correcting or deleting, or they can actually breach copyright or plagiarise in their video/podcast. Give a deadline by which time all videos and podcasts should be uploaded and feedback be received.

It is possible to ask groups to make an in-class presentation, rather than a video or podcast, if you have time available and if it better suits your student cohort. Save a little time at the end of presentations for feedback, questions and answers.

Key issues

This activity works well because students must first understand, and become familiar with, what is meant by copyright infringement and plagiarism of electronic materials before they can teach their fellow students in their video or podcast (see Activity 95 for detailed definitions of copyright infringement and plagiarism, along with related terms such as public domain, Creative Commons licence and fair use). Some students studying at elementary level have not come across these terms and need to take time in their groups to research and discuss the issues and reach agreement on what they mean. Others have come across the terms, but are not familiar with specific details: some believe, for example, that they can cut and paste text if they reword it slightly, or that it is acceptable practice to use information found on the internet because it is 'publicly available'.

This activity utilises a student-centred approach to highlight issues of deliberate and unintentional copyright breaches and plagiarism, in addition to providing advice and guidance about how to recognise these problems and avoid them in their own work. The focus, structure, content and method of delivery are a group choice: students tend to produce informative, creative and imaginative videos or podcasts that help to maintain enthusiasm and encourage learning among peers.

→ Related activities

Activity 30: Citing, referencing and producing a bibliography

Activity 51: Using primary and secondary sources

Activity 56: Referencing, copyright and plagiarism

Activity 94: Recognising and avoiding academic malpractice

....

→ Preparatory reading

PlagiarismAdvice.org (www.plagiarismadvice.org) was set up as the Plagiarism Advisory Service in the UK in 2002 by the Joint Information Systems Committee (JISC). The original aim of the service was 'to address growing concerns about plagiarism and the authenticity of student work'. A wide range of resources, including teaching resources, research papers, student leaflets and information about plagiarism detection software, is available on this site.

Visit the PlagiarismAdvice YouTube channel (www.youtube.com/user/Plagiarismadviceorg) for videos of presentations and conference keynote sessions at plagiarismadvice.org by global academics (these are a few years old, but are still relevant).

More information about copyright in the UK can be obtained from the Government information website (www.gov.uk/topic/intellectual-property/copyright).

....

→ Further reading

The following books can be recommended to students if they need more information about citing, referencing and plagiarism.

Neville, C. (2010) *The Complete Guide to Referencing and Avoiding Plagiarism*, 2nd edition. Maidenhead: Open University Press.

Pears, R. and Shields, G. (2013) *Cite Them Right: the Essential Referencing Guide*, 9th edition. Basingstoke: Palgrave Macmillan.

Williams, K. (2009) *Referencing and Understanding Plagiarism*. Basingstoke: Palgrave Macmillan.

Activity 78

Section 11

Research projects and dissertations

Activity • • • • • • • • • → 79

Producing a research proposal

The activity

Invite together a group of students who feel that they need help to produce a research proposal. These could be students who are about to embark on their dissertation for undergraduate study, or those who are planning their thesis for postgraduate study, for example. The students that join the group could be from one course and one level or from a range of courses and levels. The group should not be too large: eight to 12 participants is ideal (even numbers are desirable so that students can be paired together). Explain the purpose and format of the structured support group. First, you will meet in a 50 minute or one hour session to discuss the structure, style, content and purpose of research proposals and talk about worries and concerns that students may have about producing their proposal at the required level (see key issues).

At the end of this session you will pair students together so that they can provide help, support and encouragement for their partner in the second stage of this activity. This stage requires students to produce a draft research proposal. When they have produced a draft copy of their work they should swap with their partner for constructive feedback, support and encouragement, before producing their next version. The duration of this stage depends on the course and level of study (these can differ considerably: if you have a group of students from different levels you will need to choose a duration that is suitable for everyone). Students can also meet other group members on an informal basis as the activity progresses, if they feel that support and encouragement from other group members would be of benefit.

The final stage of this activity requires the group to reconvene for another 50 minute or one hour session to discuss their proposals, talk about any other worries and concerns they may have and build a plan of further action to improve on, and finalise, their proposals.

It is possible to run this activity as a one-to-one support session with individual students, if you have time available and it better suits your students. You will need to be available to offer support throughout the activity if this option is chosen.

Key issues

Your first session should introduce students to research proposals, discuss their purpose and illustrate the structure preferred by your institution, if relevant. You can also discuss worries and concerns that students may have about producing a research proposal at the right level. This can include, for example, the required level of critical analysis; creating, interpreting and advancing knowledge; demonstrating new insight or developments; implications for policy and practice; impact and so on. You can also help students to think about workable timetables, budgets and the resources that will be required for their project.

Students are then required to work on their proposals with the help and support of their partner. Proposals can vary depending on level of study, subject and institutional preferences. However, all proposals should be clear, well-written, well-justified in terms of topic and method, and have a clear timetable and well-developed budget. The following sections should be included and can be discussed when you meet for your next session (or you can produce a handout to give to students as they work on their proposal):

- Title: this should be short and explanatory. It can hint at the research question, methodology and research population.
- Background: this section should contain a rationale for the research. This discussion should be placed within the context of existing research and/or within personal experience or observation.
- Aims and objectives: the aim is the overall driving force of the research and the objectives are the means by which to achieve the aim. The aims and objectives must relate to the research question and demonstrate how this will be answered.
- Methodology: this section describes the proposed research methodology and provides a justification for its use. It should include any relevant ethical issues raised by the proposed research (this section will need to be very detailed for students studying at advanced level).
- Research methods: these are the tools that are used to collect data and answer the research question (samples, numbers of people to be contacted, methods of data collection and methods of data analysis, for example).

It should also include ethical issues related to data collection and analysis such as informed consent and data protection.
- Timetable: this should include the amount of time required for background research, questionnaire or interview schedule development and testing, data collection, data analysis and report writing, for example.
- Budget and resources: this section should provide plenty of detail about costs, materials and equipment if students intend to apply for funding for their project.
- Research impact: this section highlights the expected impact of the research and is of particular importance for students who are applying for funding.
- Dissemination: this section demonstrates how others are going to know about the results of the research. This can be through producing a thesis and providing a copy for the university library, journal papers (including deposits in open access repositories), conference papers, internal and external seminars, blogs, lectures, chapters for books and entire books, for example.
- References and bibliography.

The following questions can be addressed during your sessions or produced into a handout for students to use when they review their partner's proposal.

1. Is the research question of sufficient importance?
2. Has the originality of the topic been demonstrated?
3. Will the research add to existing knowledge or generate new knowledge on this topic?
4. Has comprehensive knowledge of the background literature and the research topic been demonstrated?
5. Are the aims and objectives clear, succinct and unambiguous?
6. Are the aims and objectives realistic in terms of what can be achieved during the research (available resources, time, access to participants, for example)?
7. Do the aims and objectives support the methodology?
8. Is the connection between epistemological standpoint, theoretical perspective and methodological position stated clearly and well-defined (this relates to students studying at advanced level)?
9. Has the chosen methodology been well justified and reasons given for why other methodologies were not

chosen? Have methodological limitations been highlighted (this relates to students studying at advanced level)?
10. Does the adopted approach match the issues to be addressed?
11. Is the proposed timescale appropriate and realistic? Is the overall plan achievable in the time available?
12. Is information about the data collection method(s) sufficiently detailed?
13. Is information about the data analysis method(s) sufficiently detailed?
14. Is there enough information about required resources and budget, in particular for those students who are applying for funding? Are all costs, equipment and materials relevant and justified?
15. Is it clear how the results are to be disseminated?
16. Has the expected impact of the research been demonstrated?

Activity 79

➔ Related activities

Activity 80: Choosing research topics and methods

Activity 85: Producing a dissertation

Activity 99: Undertaking ethical research

Activity 100: Knowing about data protection

➔ Preparatory reading

The books listed below provide useful preparatory reading for this activity and can be recommended to students who wish to be part of this structured support group. You may also find it useful to direct students to your institutional guide-lines, if available, to ensure that all students are clear about rules and regulations before they begin their proposal.

The Sage Research Methods video collection (http://methods.sagepub.com/Video) provides information about all stages of the research process and can be recommended to students who are in the process of planning their research.

➔ Further reading

Denicolo, P. and Becker, L. (2012) *Developing Research Proposals*. London: Sage.
Denscombe, M. (2012) *Research Proposals: a Practical Guide*. Maidenhead: Open University Press.
Punch, K. (2016) *Developing Effective Research Proposals*, 3rd edition. London: Sage.

Activity 79

Activity • • • • • • • • • • → 80

Choosing research topics and methods

> **TUTOR NOTES**
>
> **Purpose:** This activity helps students to define, focus, clarify and move forward with their choice of research topics and methods by utilising collaborative dialogue techniques following the Socratic Method.
>
> **Type:** Collaborative dialogue.
>
> **Alternative type(s):** One-to-one support session.
>
> **Level:** Intermediate and advanced (this activity is for students who are beginning to plan their dissertation or thesis).
>
> **Duration:** Students need to spend a few hours during independent study finding out about the Socratic Method and thinking about questions that can be asked to help their partner focus and clarify ideas. They also need to spend some time thinking about their own research topic and methods, if they have not already done so. You need 50 minutes to one hour of contact time for the collaborative dialogue session and class discussion.
>
> **Equipment/materials:** None required.
>
> **Learning outcome:** By the end of this activity students will have thought about, focused in on, defined, developed and discussed the topic and methods for their dissertation or thesis, which will enable them to move forward with planning their research.

The activity

Ask your students to prepare for this activity by finding out about the 'Socratic Method'. They are going to use this technique to help their fellow students define, focus, clarify and move forward with their choices about topics and methods. They will need to think about the type of questions they can ask and pay attention to how the questions are asked (see key issues). Students will also need to spend some time thinking about the topic and methods that they are considering for their own research (for their dissertation or thesis), if they have not already done so. Some students will know what they want to research and will have a good idea of the methods they intend to use, whereas others may have no idea and might be struggling to think of a suitable topic and appropriate methods. This activity is suitable for students at all stages of this decision-making process and can be used in a wide variety of subjects.

When you next meet, divide your students into pairs. Ask one student to give a brief summary of their research topic and methods choices so far, including any difficulties they may be experiencing when making their choices. The other student should listen to this summary, asking questions when appropriate to help the first student focus in on their choices, clarify thoughts and develop further insight into the appropriateness of their choices. The pairs of students should do this for up to 20 minutes before reversing roles and continuing with the dialogue for another 20 minutes.

Using the Socratic Method students can choose to ask questions that perform the following functions (these can be developed into a Student Handout if you feel your students need more guidance in this activity):

- help to clarify choices that have been made so far;
- probe existing knowledge about the topic;
- probe rationale and justification for the research;
- query any evidence presented (justification and background knowledge, for example);
- probe relevance of the suggested topic;
- test viewpoint, perspective, knowledge and experience;
- ask about alternative topics or alternative methods;

- query implications of the research;
- query consequences of the research;
- query the suitability of methods and the match between topic and methods;
- query appropriateness of methods to methodology (for students studying at advanced level);
- probe ethical issues and awareness.

Encourage your students to be thought-provoking, challenging and stimulating, but not discourteous, aggressive or offensive when they ask their questions. They should try to keep the discussion focused and intellectually responsible, enabling and encouraging a deeper understanding of research topics and methods. Follow their collaborative dialogue with a tutor-led discussion on the issues raised, if time is available.

It is possible to run this activity as a one-to-one support session if you feel that a particular student needs specific help and guidance when choosing a research topic and methods. Use the Socratic Method in your session so that you can help your student to define, focus, clarify and move forward with his or her choices.

Key issues

The 'Socratic Method' is a technique that is used to draw individual answers and encourage fundamental insight into the issue that is being discussed. It is also referred to as 'method of elenchus' or 'Socratic debate'. Using this technique, a problem (or issue) is broken down into a series of questions that are asked to help students justify beliefs, clarify their thoughts and think about the extent of their knowledge. The aim of the Socratic Method is to help students process, interpret and analyse information and build a deeper understanding of the issue under discussion.

This method is of particular use when discussing research topics and methods because it helps students to:

- understand how they have arrived at their particular topic and/or methods (or why they are having difficulty arriving at a topic and/or methods);
- identify possible assumptions;
- determine their underlying beliefs or extent of their knowledge;

- decide whether their topic and/or methods are appropriate;
- identify weaknesses or potential problems;
- refine and narrow ideas, thoughts, beliefs or hypotheses;
- think about what else they need to consider as they plan their research.

➜ Related activities

Activity 79: Producing a research proposal

Activity 85: Producing a dissertation

Activity 86: Working with supervisors and personal tutors

Activity 99: Undertaking ethical research

....

➜ Preparatory reading

Trepanier, L. (ed.) (2018) *The Socratic Method Today: Student-Centered and Transformative Teaching in Political Science.* Abingdon, Oxon: Routledge. This book provides useful preparatory reading for tutors who are interested in detailed information about the Socratic Method.

The Sage Research Methods video collection (http://methods.sagepub.com/Video) provides information about all stages of the research process and can be recommended to students as both preparatory and follow-up work.

....

Activity 80

➜ **Further reading**

The following books can be recommended to students who are embarking on a research project.

Bell, J. (2014) *Doing Your Research Project*, 6th edition. Maidenhead: Open University Press.
Cottrell, S. (2014) *Dissertations and Project Reports: a Step by Step Guide*. Basingstoke: Palgrave Macmillan.
O'Leary, Z. (2017) *The Essential Guide to Doing Your Research Project*, 3rd edition. London: Sage.
Thomas, G. (2017) *How to Do Your Research Project: a Guide for Students*, 3rd edition. London: Sage.
Walliman, N. (2011) *Your Research Project: Designing and Planning Your Work*, 3rd edition. London: Sage.

Activity 80

Activity · · · · · · · · · · · → 81

Improving interview techniques

The activity

Ask your students to prepare for this activity by undertaking some background reading on interviewing for research purposes (see further reading). Once they have done this they should search online for videos of research interviews. This activity requires them to find what they perceive to be one example of an effective research interview and one example of a poor research interview. They must critique each interview, explaining why they consider one to be effective and the other to be poor. Once they have done this they should upload a link to each video, along with their critique, onto the digital platform that has been set up for this purpose. You can ask students to undertake this activity on an individual basis, in pairs or in small groups, depending on what best suits your student cohort. Give a deadline by which time all links and critiques should be uploaded.

This activity builds a useful student-centred digital resource that students can access if they decide to use interviews for their research. You will need to monitor the resource from time to time to ensure that information posted is correct, constructive, supportive and encouraging. You should also look out for breaches of copyright, plagiarism, slander or libel (it is advisable to use an internal platform for this activity).

It is possible to run this activity as a workshop, if this better suits your student cohort. Invite together a group of students who are intending to use interviews in their research. These could be from one course and level or from different courses and levels. Find or produce two videos of research interviews (one effective and one poor) that you can show to your students. Lead a discussion on each, asking students to identify why one is an effective interview and why the other is a poor interview. Once you have done this ask students to work on an individual basis to produce an action plan that will help them to improve their interview technique. Spend a little time at the end of the session discussing action plans and summing up the workshop.

Key issues

Examples of the type of issues that can be raised by this activity are provided below.

Effective interviews

- A good explanation of the purpose of the research and style or type of interview;
- well-constructed questions;
- a logical order of questions;
- open questions that encourage longer answers (in semi-structured or unstructured interviews);
- interviewer listens actively and responds to what is being said;
- interviewer probes effectively for more information;
- interviewer displays confidence and has built rapport;
- seating arrangements look comfortable and enable dialogue without the need to move or strain;
- unobtrusive use of the recording device;
- questions are relevant to the topic;
- interviewer keeps the interview on topic;
- interviewer provides an effective summary and asks for clarification;
- interviewer concludes the interview politely and effectively.

Poor interviews

- Poorly worded, double-barrelled, confusing, leading or irrelevant questions;
- no probing for more information, or probes are too leading;
- seating arrangements are confrontational;
- rapport has not been established;
- interviewer is fidgeting, getting distracted and not listening to answers;
- interviewer keeps interrupting;
- no eye-contact and poor body language;
- interviewer gets distracted with the recording device or draws attention to the device;
- interviewer says something that has no relevance to what the interviewee is saying;
- questions are asked that have already been answered;
- interviewee veers off topic and the interviewer is unable to steer them back to the topic;
- summary or conclusion is not provided.

➜ Related activities

Activity 40: Becoming an active listener

Activity 41: Improving listening skills

Activity 82: Designing questionnaires

Activity 83: Running focus groups

....

➜ Preparatory reading

Tutors should search for, and view, some online research interview videos as preparatory work for this activity. Some are available that demonstrate poor interview technique, followed by effective interview techniques: you will need to check that students are not merely copying what is already available. All the books listed in further reading provide useful preparatory work for students for this activity.

If you are interested in using alternative activities that will help students to learn how to conduct interviews, consult Dawson, C. (2016) *100 Activities for Teaching Research Methods*. London: Sage.

....

Activity 81

➜ Further reading

The following list provides a selection of books on different types of interviewing, which can be recommended to students, depending on their methodological choices and level of study.

Brinkmann, S. and Kvale, S. (2015) *InterViews: Learning the Craft of Qualitative Research Interviewing*, 3rd edition. Thousand Oaks, CA: Sage.

Fujii, L. (2018) *Interviewing in Social Science: a Relational Approach*. New York: Routledge.

Gillham, B. (2005) *Research Interviewing: the Range of Techniques*. Maidenhead: Open University Press.

Gubrium, J. and Holstein, J. (eds) (2003) *Postmodern Interviewing*. Thousand Oaks, CA: Sage.

King, N. and Horrocks, C. (2010) *Interviews in Qualitative Research*. London: Sage.

Kvale, S. (2007) *Doing Interviews*. London: Sage.

Mann, S. (2016) *The Research Interview: Reflective Practice and Reflexivity in the Research Processes*. Basingstoke: Palgrave Macmillan.

Rubin, H. and Rubin, I. (2012) *Qualitative Interviewing: the Art of Hearing Data*, 3rd edition. Thousand Oaks, CA: Sage.

Seidman, I. (2013) *Interviewing as Qualitative Research: a Guide for Researchers in Education and the Social Sciences*, 4th edition. New York: Teachers College Press.

Activity 81

Designing questionnaires

TUTOR NOTES

Purpose: This activity is an entertaining and informative way to help students to design a questionnaire for their dissertation or thesis. It asks them, in groups, to produce a questionnaire in which flaws, defects and faults have been incorporated deliberately. The 'game' element is that other groups must detect the flaws, defects and faults. Therefore, groups should make them subtle and as difficult to detect as possible.

Type: Game.

Alternative type(s): None.

Level: Intermediate and advanced. This activity is aimed at students who are starting to think about the research methods they wish to use for their dissertation or thesis.

Duration: Students need to spend a few hours, in their groups, during independent study researching, discussing and producing their questionnaire. You need one to two hours of contact time, depending on the number of student groups.

Equipment/materials: Students need to produce their questionnaire in a format that can be viewed by their peers in class (projections from laptops, phones or tablets, for example). Connectors, adaptors and projectors should be made available for their use or you can do this for them, if appropriate (see below).

Learning outcome: By the end of this activity students will know how to spot flaws, defects and faults in their own questionnaires and in those designed by others, which will help them to feel more confident and knowledgeable about designing, using and critiquing questionnaires as their course progresses.

The activity

Divide your students into groups. Four or five groups are a good number: if you only have a small number of students (doctoral students, for example) ask that they undertake this activity on an individual basis. Ask the groups to design a questionnaire and to think about how it will be administered. The subject, structure, type, content, length of questionnaire and type of respondent is a group choice. However, within their questionnaire they must deliberately incorporate a number of flaws, defects and faults. They should try to make these subtle and difficult to detect.

   Once groups have produced their questionnaire they should ensure that it is suitable for projecting to the rest of the class when you next meet (using laptops, phones or tablets, for example). If your students are unable to do this, ask that they hand the questionnaires to you so that you can ensure that they are suitable for projection (operate the equipment for students when you meet, if necessary). If suitable equipment is not available, produce several paper copies of each questionnaire to give out to students.

When you next meet, introduce the 'game' element of the activity by explaining that students must detect the flaws, defects and faults that have been introduced into questionnaires. Work through each questionnaire in turn, asking groups to confirm that all flaws have been detected (and to be honest about whether additional, unintentional flaws have been detected: see below). If you are happy to turn this into a competition, the winner is the group that has made their flaws, defects and faults the hardest to detect or that has been the most creative, inventive or enlightening (students can vote on the winning group, if appropriate). Sum up the game with a discussion on the issues raised.

Key issues

This activity works well because students must first of all research and discuss together issues of questionnaire construction, design and administration, before considering problems that can occur when undertaking these tasks. An interesting aspect to this activity is that, on occasions, student groups spot a flaw or mistake that has not been incorporated deliberately: students are unaware of the problem until it is highlighted by their peers. This helps students to become more aware of potential problems when constructing, designing and administering questionnaires and when critiquing questionnaires produced and used by others.

Students tend to be inventive, creative and enlightening in this activity, producing a variety of questionnaires that illustrate, and generate discussion on, different problems. Examples of these are given below.

Questionnaire design

- The topic and questions are irrelevant to the lives, attitudes and beliefs of the respondents.
- The questionnaire is:

  - monotonous;
  - difficult to follow;
  - unclear, long-winded and cluttered;
  - too short (and will not generate meaningful data)
  - does not follow a logical order.
- Filter questions have not been used so respondents are unable to skip irrelevant questions or sections.

Question construction

- Questions are:

  - confusing and too long;
  - not relevant to the research topic;
  - worded in a way that assumes knowledge or makes it seem that a certain level of knowledge is expected;
  - double-barrelled, negative or leading;
  - full of jargon and technical words;
  - written in a way that contains some type of prestige bias (questions that could embarrass or force respondents into giving a false answer).

- Words that have been used have:

  - multiple meanings;
  - emotional connotations;
  - vague meanings such as 'often' and 'sometimes'.
- Opinions have been created artificially by asking someone a question they know nothing about, or they do not care about.
- Respondents are forced into an answer (all possible answers have not been included in a closed question, for example).

Administering a questionnaire

- Self-administered questionnaires produced in English are to be given to respondents who cannot speak or read English.
- Instructions are too complicated.
- Respondents are not told about:

  - the purpose of the questionnaire;
  - why the questionnaire has been produced and who has produced it;
  - what will happen to the results;
  - how long the questionnaire will take to complete;
  - issues of anonymity, confidentiality, privacy and data security.
- A deadline for questionnaire completion and return is not included.
- Return postage is not included (if relevant).

→ Related activities

There are no related activities provided in this book. However, if you feel that your students could benefit from undertaking more activities on constructing, designing and administering questionnaires, and on improving response rates, consult Dawson (2016).

Activity 82

➜ Preparatory reading

Dawson (2016) *100 Activities for Teaching Research Methods*. London: Sage. This book contains additional activities and
information covering questionnaire construction, design and response and provides useful preparatory reading for
tutors who feel they need more information about this topic before running this activity.

➜ Further reading

The following books can be recommended to students who are thinking about designing a questionnaire for their dissertation or thesis.

Bradburn, N. (2004) *Asking Questions: the Definitive Guide to Questionnaire Design*. San Francisco, CA: John Wiley &
Sons, Inc.

Cox, J. and Cox, K. (2008) *Your Opinion Please: How to Build the Best Questionnaire in the Field of Education*. Thousand
Oaks, CA: Corwin Press.

Ekinci, Y. (2015) *Designing Research Questionnaires for Business and Management Students*. London: Sage.

Gillham, B. (2007) *Developing a Questionnaire*, 2nd edition. London: Continuum.

Activity 82

Activity • • • • • • • • • → 83

Running focus groups

Student
handout
page 339

TUTOR NOTES

Purpose: This activity helps students to understand more about how focus groups are run (and used in research) by asking them to produce reviews of two online focus group demonstrations for a fictitious university magazine. The reviews are compiled into a useful resource that can be accessed by students when required.

Type: Student reviews.

Alternative type(s): Vlogs or blogs.

Level: Intermediate and advanced.

Duration: Students need to spend one or two hours during independent study finding and viewing demonstrations and producing and handing in their reviews. Tutors need to spend a few minutes compiling and uploading the completed PDF of reviews. If the vlogs and blogs option is chosen you need to spend a few minutes setting up a suitable digital platform on which vlogs and blogs can be uploaded and up to an hour to monitor posts.

Equipment/materials: Tutors need access to a PDF converter. Tutors and students need access to the relevant digital platform if the vlogs and blogs option is chosen.

Learning outcome: By the end of this activity students will have a greater awareness of the focus group method and understand more about how focus groups are run. They will have produced a collection of focus group reviews that can be accessed if they decide to use focus groups for their research project.

The activity

Give your students a copy of the Student Handout. This provides information about the focus group method and then goes on to ask students to imagine that they have been asked to choose and review two online focus group demonstrations for a university magazine. You can ask them to do this individually or in groups, depending on your student cohort. Give a deadline by which time their reviews should be submitted. Once received, proofread, edit and sort as necessary, then compile into a PDF that is sent to all students. This can be used by students to help them understand more about the focus group method and will be a useful resource for students who may be thinking about using focus groups for their research project.

An alternative way to run this activity is to ask students to produce their reviews as vlogs or blogs, which can be posted on a suitable digital platform for their peers to access. Again, this can be done individually or in groups, depending on your student cohort. Provide a deadline by which time all vlogs and blogs should be received. Monitor posts from time to time to ensure that information is correct, useful and constructive.

Key issues

This activity tends to produce a wide variety of reviews of different styles, structures, length and content. Some students concentrate specifically on the role of the moderator, whether they have performed well and how they could improve, for example. Others look at the overall group, illustrating how people interact, how they communicate and how they are encouraged to remain on topic. Others talk about the focus group method and how their chosen demonstrations help to highlight advantages, disadvantages and potential problems, for example. The Student Handout is not specific in terms of what should be included in reviews as this tends to encourage a wider variety and type of review. However, if you feel that your students may struggle with this activity you can pose specific questions for them to address in their reviews.

➜ Related activities

Activity 40: Becoming an active listener

Activity 41: Improving listening skills

Activity 71: Understanding group dynamics and avoiding conflict

Activity 80: Choosing research topics and methods

➜ Preparatory reading

There are a wide variety of focus group demonstrations available online (the search term 'focus group demonstration' finds some good groups). You may find it useful preparatory work to view some of these demonstrations prior to this activity.

➜ Further reading

The following books provide useful further reading for both tutors and students.

Barbour, R. (2007) *Doing Focus Groups*. London: Sage.
Kruegar, R. and Casey, M. (2015) *Focus Groups: a Practical Guide for Applied Research*, 5th edition. Thousand Oaks, CA: Sage.
Liamputtong, P. (2011) *Focus Group Methodology: Principle and Practice*. London: Sage.
Stewart, D. (2015) *Focus Groups: Theory and Practice*, 3rd edition. Thousand Oaks, CA: Sage.

Activity 83

Activity · · · · · · · · · · → 84

Introducing data analysis techniques

The activity

Divide your students into small groups at the end of a teaching session. Allocate one data analysis technique to each group (a list of techniques is provided below, but you can modify this list depending on the size of your student cohort, the subject you are teaching and the level of study). Ask your students to produce and prepare, in their groups, a presentation of no more than ten minutes on the data analysis technique they have been allocated. They must make this presentation to their peers when you next meet. Encourage your students to be as interesting, creative and informative as possible so that their peers can learn from their presentation. They can use any presentation equipment and materials that they choose and these should be made available for their use.

When you next meet allocate up to 15 minutes for each presentation and associated questions from peers. If contact time is limited or, if you prefer, you can ask students to produce a video of their presentation that can be uploaded on the relevant digital platform for peer review, discussion and feedback. This will build a useful bank of videos on which students can draw throughout their course, if required. Monitor the videos and posts to ensure that information is correct, supportive and constructive.

Key issues

The following list provides examples of the type of data analysis technique that you could allocate to students (some are basic whereas others are more complex). You can add to, delete or modify the list, depending on your subject and level of study:

- content analysis;
- discourse analysis;
- social network analysis;
- narrative analysis;
- conversation analysis;
- comparative analysis;
- thematic analysis;
- time interval data analysis;
- descriptive statistical analysis;
- inferential statistical analysis;
- frequency distribution;
- cross tabulation;
- correlation analysis;
- regression analysis;
- text analytics;
- predictive analytics;
- necessary condition analysis;
- longitudinal data analysis.

This list contains a mix of qualitative and quantitative techniques: it is useful to include both so that students can be introduced to techniques they may not have considered, or of which they are unaware (if they are approaching the activity from a particular methodological standpoint, for example).

Students are asked to work in groups in this activity because some of the data analysis techniques are quite complex: the groups hold in-depth discussion, work through the complexities and help each other to understand and get to grips with the technique. Asking students to work in groups also helps to filter out misinformation or incorrect information. However, you will need to monitor each presentation carefully to ensure that students are presenting (or posting) accurate and correct information to their peers.

→ Related activities

Activity 38: Introducing data mining

Activity 39: Finding and using datasets

Activity 74: Using software for research

Activity 77: Using data visualisation tools and software

→ Preparatory reading

Some of the discussions, papers and reports about data analysis on ResearchGate (www.researchgate.net/topic/Data-Analysis) provide interesting and useful preparatory reading for this activity (this is a social networking site for researchers to share information, ask questions and connect with researchers around the world). Academia.edu (www.academia.edu) is another social networking site for researchers, which contains interesting and useful information about data analysis techniques. These sites are useful for tutors and can be recommended to students studying at advanced level.

→ Further reading

The following books can be recommended to students if they need to follow up some of the issues raised in this activity.

Flick, U. (ed.) (2014) *The Sage Handbook of Qualitative Data Analysis*. London: Sage.
Kent, R. (2015) *Analysing Quantitative Data*. London: Sage.
Miles, M., Huberman, M. and Saldana, J. (2014) *Qualitative Data Analysis: a Methods Sourcebook*, 3rd edition. Thousand Oaks, CA: Sage.
Treiman, D. (2009) *Quantitative Data Analysis: Doing Social Research to Test Ideas*. San Francisco, CA: John Wiley & Sons, Inc.
Vogt, W., Vogt, E., Gardner, D. and Haeffele, L. (2014) *Selecting the Right Analyses for Your Data: Quantitative, Qualitative, and Mixed Methods*. New York: Guildford Press.

Activity 84

Activity • • • • • • • • • • → 85

Producing a dissertation

The activity

Invite together a group of students who feel they need extra help with producing their dissertation. This is a voluntary workshop for students who would like help in moving forward: if students need more structured support you can run Activity 79, which helps them to plan and produce a proposal for their dissertation or thesis with help and support from group members.

Begin the workshop by asking students about any worries and concerns they have about producing their dissertation (this can be done as a short, ten-minute brainstorm if you feel that students might be reluctant to share worries and concerns with others: a brainstorm enables them to give suggestions without attributing them to themselves). Once you have done this, talk to students about what is required from a dissertation. This can include the purpose, structure, length, academic level and specific content, for example (see key issues). When the discussion has concluded, ask students to work for ten to 15 minutes on an individual action plan that will help them to move forward with their dissertation. Lead a class discussion for the remaining few minutes, enabling students to discuss any further issues that are of importance, before summing up the issues raised during the workshop.

Key issues

Worries and concerns that can be raised by students include:

- producing work at the right academic level;
- carrying out research;
- analysing data;
- remaining motivated;

- overcoming distractions;
- working independently;
- writing a long report.

The following issues can be discussed when considering requirements:

- Students should produce dissertations in the correct structure and format (this varies, depending on subject and university, but should include the following):

  o a title page to include the title, student name, the name of university, the degree for which the dissertation is submitted and the date of submission;
  o an abstract that summarises context, methods, results and conclusions;
  o acknowledgements;
  o a table of contents to include chapter headings (numbered sequentially), subheadings and page numbers;
  o a list of figures, diagrams, graphs, etc. (if relevant);
  o an introduction;
  o background literature;
  o research methods (and methodology, if studying at advanced level);
  o results and conclusions (this could include how results relate to other research in the field, the relevance and impact of findings and information about how the research could be continued, for example);
  o references and bibliography;
  o appendices, if relevant.
- Dissertations should be written at the right level. Writing should be clear and concise and students should display technical detail and subject knowledge. Students must

have a thorough understanding of all technical terms used in their dissertation.
- Students should avoid informalities, conversational language, generalisations and opinions (unless they fit with their methodology). They should ensure that their style is in keeping with required standards (supply examples of work that has been written at the required standard, if appropriate).
- Students should not make sweeping generalisations such as 'academics state' or 'scholars suggest'. They should be specific with references, giving exact names and dates.
- In some cases bullet points or a series of numbered points may provide the best way to explain a finding. However, students should use these techniques sparingly: dissertations should provide a connected and convincing argument, rather than a list of observations and facts.
- Findings should be highlighted and well-signposted for examiners.
- Students should check for spelling mistakes, grammatical errors and typing mistakes, ensuring that work is produced to the highest standard possible. Peers can offer to proofread each other's work, if it helps.
- Dissertations should demonstrate a student's ability to carry out independent research and present their work in a coherent document.

Action plans can include:

- Read around the subject, in particular, areas that are causing concern (data collection and analysis, for example).
- Find out about additional training, workshops or short courses that will help to improve areas of concern.
- Work with a friend to provide mutual support.
- Seek help and feedback from tutors, when required (and listen to feedback).

- Produce a research plan with specific action and deadlines to be achieved.
- Make a commitment to use social media less, read email once a day and not be distracted by texts, games or other technology.
- Make a commitment to ask peers and family members to respect study time and not cause distractions (and an agreement to respect the study time of their peers).

➜ **Related activities**

Activity 28: Producing an effective argument

Activity 32: Overcoming difficulties with writing

Activity 79: Producing a research proposal

Activity 80: Choosing research methods and topics

Activity 86: Working with supervisors and personal tutors

Activity 85

➜ Preparatory reading

Students do not need to carry out preparatory work for this activity, other than thinking about and planning their dissertation. The books listed below can be recommended after the workshop for students who need more information and advice about producing a dissertation.

➜ Further reading

Cottrell, S. (2014) *Dissertations and Project Reports: a Step by Step Guide*. Basingstoke: Palgrave Macmillan.
Greetham, B. (2014) *How to Write Your Undergraduate Dissertation*, 2nd edition. Basingstoke: Palgrave Macmillan.
Walliman, N. (2014) *Your Undergraduate Dissertation: the Essential Guide for Success*, 2nd edition. London: Sage.
Williams, K. (2103) *Planning Your Dissertation*. Basingstoke: Palgrave Macmillan.

Activity 85

Activity · · · · · · · · · · → 86

Working with supervisors and personal tutors

Student handout page 340

TUTOR NOTES

Purpose: This activity asks students, in groups, to consider a comprehensive list of tutor and student roles and responsibilities, which they must place on a Venn diagram. It enables students to think about, discuss and work out connections between individual roles and responsibilities within the tutor/student relationship.

Type: Group exercise followed by tutor-led discussion.

Alternative type(s): None.

Level: Elementary, intermediate and advanced.

Duration: Fifty minutes to one hour of contact time.

Equipment/materials: Several large pieces of card or paper, about A1 size (594 × 841 mm or 23.4 × 33.1 inches) and several marker pens.

Learning outcome: By the end of this activity students will have a greater understanding of roles and responsibilities when working with personal tutors and supervisors, which will enable them to work effectively together and build a good working relationship as their course progresses.

The activity

Divide your students into small groups and give each group a large piece of card or paper, a marker pen and a copy of the Student Handout. This asks them to draw a Venn diagram, in which the universal set is 'roles and responsibilities' and two sets are labelled 'personal tutor' and 'student'. If you intend to use the term 'supervisor', perhaps because you are working with postgraduate students, alter the Student Handout accordingly.

A list of possible roles and responsibilities is provided in the Student Handout, which asks students to discuss, and reach agreement on, where to place each item on the Venn diagram (you can add to or delete items on the list, as appropriate). Students can decide that some items from the list cannot be placed within either set and they can decide to add further items that have not been included in the list, if appropriate.

When students have finished this exercise (it usually takes 20–30 minutes) lead a class discussion on the issues raised. This can include the following questions:

1. How easy was it to reach agreement on where to place items?
2. Has each group produced a similar diagram or are there significant differences? If so, what are they and why are they so different?
3. Were there any items that could not be placed in either set or at the intersection? Why?
4. Did students add any other items? If so, what were they and where were they placed?
5. Were students unclear about any items?
6. Were students surprised by the results?
7. Do students have any questions about working with personal tutors/supervisors?

Key issues

This activity encourages students to think more deeply about how they work with personal tutors/supervisors. There are items on the list that they may not have considered and it is only by thinking about the items, discussing where to place them and reaching agreement that they are able to understand significance and connections that will help them to build a better working relationship with personal tutors/supervisors. It is also useful for students to think about and discuss the overlapping roles in the relationship. They often express surprise to find that so many roles and responsibilities are placed at the intersection. This helps them to understand that the personal tutor/supervisor and student relationship is a partnership in learning with shared responsibilities.

➜ Related activities

Activity 47: Engaging with lecturers and tutors

Activity 48: Getting the most from tutor feedback

➜ Preparatory reading

The books listed below provide useful preparatory and further reading for tutors for this activity. Students do not need to undertake any preparatory work for this activity.

➜ Further reading

Bullock, K. and Wikeley, F. (2004) *Whose Learning: the Role of the Personal Tutor*. Maidenhead: Open University Press.
Neville, L. (2007) *The Personal Tutor's Handbook*. Basingstoke: Palgrave Macmillan.
Wisker, G., Exley, K., Antoniou, M. and Ridley, P. (2008) *Working One-to-One with Students: Supervising, Coaching, Mentoring, and Personal Tutoring*. New York: Routledge.

Activity 86

Section 12

Revision, examinations and tests

.

Activity • • • • • • • • • • → 87

Understanding the reasons for assessment

Student
handout
page 341

TUTOR NOTES

Purpose: This activity helps students to think more deeply about the meaning and purpose of assessment by asking them, in groups, to work through a series of questions covering this topic. This is followed by a tutor-led discussion on the issues raised.

Type: Group exercise followed by tutor-led discussion.

Alternative type(s): Self-guided individual exercise.

Level: Elementary.

Duration: Fifty minutes to one hour of contact time. Students need to spend an hour or so working through the questions during independent study if the self-guided individual exercise option is chosen.

Equipment/materials: None required.

Learning outcome: By the end of this activity students will have a raised awareness about the meaning and purpose of assessment in higher education and will understand the relevance to teaching, learning, performance and personal development.

The activity

Divide your students into small groups and give them a copy of the Student Handout. This asks them to discuss, with their group members, a series of questions about assessment in higher education. Once they have done this for 20 to 30 minutes, lead a class discussion on the issues raised. This can include a discussion about the different types of assessment (formative, summative, diagnostic, dynamic and criterion assessment, for example). If you do not have the contact time available you can ask students to work through the questions on an individual basis during independent study.

It is possible to combine this activity with Activity 88, which is a brainstorm that asks students to list different methods that are used to assess students. It goes on to discuss, in detail, specific assessment methods that will be used on their course and address questions or concerns that students may have about how they will be assessed. If you choose to follow with Activity 88, delete Question 6 on the Student Handout and replace with the brainstorm and discussion described in Activity 88. Both activities should be run near the beginning of your course so that students understand the need for assessment and are well-prepared for the assessment methods they are likely to encounter.

Key issues

The questions provided can generate discussion on the following:

1. Assessment is the process of evaluating, judging, rating, testing or marking someone or something. In higher education this could be a student's work, a tutor's teaching, a course or a university, for example. There are different types of assessment that can be used in higher education, including formative, summative, diagnostic, dynamic and criterion assessment. All assessment methods should be valid, reliable, relevant and transparent.

2. The purpose of assessment in higher education is to:

   a. provide a link between teaching and learning;
   b. help tutors to assess whether they are teaching what they think they are teaching;
   c. enable tutors to find out whether students are learning what they are supposed to be learning;
   d. help tutors to evaluate the effectiveness of their teaching, find out what works well and work out whether anything can be done differently;
   e. enable tutors to promote better and more effective learning;
   f. help students to work out how well they are progressing;
   g. help students to work out what else they need to learn;
   h. help both students and tutors to work out whether learning outcomes are being met;
   i. help with internal and external quality control.

3. The assessment of students can help tutors by:

   a. providing feedback that helps them to understand what students already know, what they need to know and what has to be taught;
   b. providing feedback on how well students are progressing and helping them to plan what they need to do next;
   c. helping them to set standards by enabling them to determine what is required to demonstrate understanding, knowledge and mastery;
   d. helping to describe standards through the production of assessment criteria that enables them to see how well a student has achieved learning outcomes;
   e. helping them to evaluate their teaching by enabling them to see how well students are performing (and how well students can integrate and apply their skills, knowledge and understanding).

4. Assessment can help students by:

   a. improving motivation and performance by enabling them to see how they are progressing;
   b. helping them to work out what else they need to learn to succeed on their course;
   c. enabling them to build on their strengths and learn from their mistakes;
   d. giving a sense of purpose and satisfaction;
   e. giving a clear idea of the standard they should aim for and encouraging them to produce better work;
   f. enabling them to continue with their learning;
   g. encouraging personal development and growth;
   h. providing qualifications, awards and certification required for future education and employment.

5. Assessment can help course leaders/administrators and universities by:

   a. acting as a quality insurance mechanism by providing data for both internal and external quality checks, to ensure that the course and institution are operating at required levels;
   b. quantifying achievement, rewarding achievement and providing data for selection for further education or employment;
   c. enabling course and institutional comparison (league tables, for example);
   d. safeguarding academic standards and quality in higher education.

6. Methods of assessment that might be used on a university course include tests, examinations, written assignments, group projects, questionnaires, self-assessment, peer assessment, experiments, oral presentations, dissertations, theses and portfolios of student work (see Activity 88). Discussions about effectiveness tend to be based on perceptions, previous experience and personal preference: it is interesting for students to find out that their peers may have different experiences and perceptions of assessment methods.

→ **Related activities**

Activity 47: Engaging with lecturers and tutors

Activity 48: Getting the most from tutor feedback

Activity 86: Working with supervisors and personal tutors

Activity 88: Knowing about the different methods of assessment

Activity 87

➜ **Preparatory reading**

The Higher Education Academy (HEA) in the UK provides information about key research into assessment, teaching resources and assessment events (https://www.heacademy.ac.uk/individuals/strategic-priorities/assessment). This provides useful preparatory reading for tutors, along with the books listed below. Preparatory reading for students is not required for this activity.

➜ **Further reading**

Bloxham, S. and Boyd, P. (2007) *Developing Effective Assessment in Higher Education: a Practical Guide*. Maidenhead: Open University Press.

Bryan, C. and Clegg, K. (eds) (2006) *Innovative Assessment in Higher Education*. Abingdon, Oxon: Routledge.

Samball, K., McDowell, L. and Montgomery, C. (2013) *Assessment for Learning in Higher Education*. Abingdon, Oxon: Routledge.

Secolsky, C. and Denison, B. (eds) (2018) *Handbook on Measurement, Assessment, and Evaluation in Higher Education*, 2nd edition. New York: Routledge.

Activity 87

Activity · · · · · · · · · · ➜ 88

Knowing about the different methods of assessment

The activity

Brainstorm with your students the question 'What are the different methods that are used to assess students?' Write their answers on your screen/board/flipchart without judgement, analysis or reflection. Students can, on occasions, take a few minutes to think about this topic before becoming more spontaneous with their suggestions. If students are unfamiliar with the brainstorming technique ask them to give any answer they can think of in relation to the question. They are not going to be judged and they should not judge or critique the answers given by other students (even if they do not agree with another's contribution). Each answer they give will be written down: the goal is to share ideas and learn from each other.

Once the brainstorm is complete (this usually takes ten to 15 minutes) pick out the methods of assessment that will be used on your course. Lead a class discussion on each of these methods, explaining more about the method and its purpose, inviting questions and asking about concerns students may have about the method and how it will be used.

It is possible to run this activity as a group exercise, rather than a brainstorm if this better suits your student cohort. Divide your students into small groups and ask them to think about the different methods that can be used to assess students. Once they have done this for ten or 15 minutes, lead a class discussion on the particular methods of assessment that will be used on your course, inviting questions from students, where appropriate.

This activity can be combined with Activity 87, which helps students to understand the reasons for assessment. If you decide to combine both activities, delete Question 6 in Activity 87 and replace with the brainstorm or group exercise described above. Both activities should be run near the beginning of your course so that students understand the need for assessment and are well-prepared for the assessment methods they will encounter.

Key issues

The following assessment methods can be mentioned in the brainstorm:

- multiple choice tests;
- online quizzes;
- end-of-year examinations;
- written assignments;
- group projects;
- questionnaires;
- self-assessment;
- peer assessment;
- experiments;
- poster presentations;
- oral presentations;
- dissertations;

- theses;
- oral examinations;
- viva voce;
- portfolios of student work;
- reflective portfolios;
- work practice competencies/portfolios;
- role plays;
- class debates;
- class discussion;
- case studies;
- scenarios;
- problem solving.

The tutor-led discussion should discuss any of the above methods that will be used during the course. This can include a discussion of what, why, when and how the method will be used, with questions invited from students. These questions often centre around more unusual assessment methods (or methods that students have not encountered previously) and methods that assess group work (the criteria that will be used and how problems with people not pulling their weight will be addressed, for example). Also, some students, such as adult returners, may be concerned about taking end-of-year examinations, in particular, when they have not taken an exam for many years or have had bad experiences in the past (Activities 89, 90, 91 and 92 will be of use to these students).

➜ Related activities

Activity 47: Engaging with lecturers and tutors

Activity 48: Getting the most from tutor feedback

Activity 86: Working with supervisors and personal tutors

Activity 87: Understanding the reasons for assessment

....

➜ Preparatory reading

The Higher Education Academy (HEA) (https://www.heacademy.ac.uk/individuals/strategic-priorities/assessment) in the UK provides information about key research into assessment, teaching resources and assessment events. This is useful preparatory reading for tutors, along with the books listed below. Preparatory reading for students is not required for this activity.

    The Quality Assurance Agency for Higher Education in the UK has produced a guide called *Understanding Assessment: its Role in Safeguarding Academic Standards and Quality in Higher Education, a Guide for Early Career Staff*, which can be downloaded at http://www.qaa.ac.uk/en/Publications/Documents/understanding-assessment.pdf.

....

➜ Further reading

Bloxham, S. and Boyd, P. (2007) *Developing Effective Assessment in Higher Education: a Practical Guide*. Maidenhead: Open University Press.

Bryan, C. and Clegg, K. (eds) (2006) *Innovative Assessment in Higher Education*. Abingdon, Oxon: Routledge.

Heywood, J. (2000) *Assessment in Higher Education: Student Learning, Teaching, Programmes and Institutions*. London: Jessica Kingsley.

Samball, K., McDowell, L. and Montgomery, C. (2013) *Assessment for Learning in Higher Education*. Abingdon, Oxon: Routledge.

Suskie, L. (2009) *Assessing Student Learning: a Common Sense Guide*, 2nd edition. San Francisco, CA: Jossey-Bass.

Activity 88

Activity · · · · · · · · · · · ➔ 89

Revising effectively

TUTOR NOTES

Purpose: This activity is for students who feel that they need the support, guidance and encouragement of their peers when revising for exams. It is a voluntary activity that works well for adult returners who have not revised for an exam for many years or for students who are unsure about how to revise or unconfident about their ability to revise effectively at the required level.

Type: Peer support group.

Alternative type(s): None.

Level: Elementary and intermediate.

Duration: The amount of time taken on this activity depends on student preferences and needs (see below).

Equipment/materials: A quiet space to meet, free from distractions and disturbances.

Learning outcome: By the end of this activity students will have revised effectively with the support, guidance and encouragement of their peers, which will help them to feel well-prepared and more confident about taking their exams.

The activity

Invite together a group of students who feel that they could benefit from taking part in a revision group. This should be done fairly early in your course so that students can start to understand the benefits of revising throughout their course (revising lecture notes and preparing for subsequent lectures, for example) in addition to revising for end-of-course exams. Students who express an interest in this activity tend to be adult returners who have not taken an exam for a long time, or students who feel unconfident about their ability to revise effectively at the level required for their university study. Other students see revision as a personal, individual process and are not interested in taking part in this type of revision group. This activity, therefore, is voluntary: you may find that some student cohorts are not interested in establishing revision groups.

If you do have students who are interested (five to seven students is a good number) bring them together to discuss the following issues:

1. What do students want to get out of the group? What are their expectations and goals? Can agreement be reached on these?
2. What type of group would they like (this could be face-to-face, online or a mixture of both)?
3. Can they agree on a code of conduct? How should students behave within the group and what behaviours are unacceptable? This can include issues such as attendance,

honesty, respect, listening to each other, providing mutual support, voluntary attendance and withdrawing from the group, for example.

4. How often would they like to meet, when and where? Is this acceptable to every member of the group?
5. How much tutor involvement would they like? Most groups are happy to work on their own with minimal

tutor input and this should be encouraged for students studying at higher education level.

6. What preparation work should be undertaken for the first session (reading, questions and tips, for example)? Students will need to make plans for the next time they meet at the end of each session.

7. What structure and content of meeting would students like? Does this need to be agreed in advance, or would groups like to adapt and change to student needs as their meetings progress? Examples include:
   a. asking group members to explain a specific topic to others;
   b. sharing mnemonics;
   c. revising a particular topic in advance and discussing in-depth during the meeting;
   d. creating or using existing exam questions and practising answering together;
   e. giving a 'one minute' talk on a particular topic, from each group member;
   f. using memory cards to test each other;
   g. allocating and revising different topics, with each student giving a short talk on their topic;
   h. peer teaching (topics are allocated in advance).

Once this meeting has taken place, leave the revision group to meet and revise according to what they have agreed. Check group progress once they have met a few times to ensure that all group members are happy and that the group is moving towards meeting its shared goals. Answer questions and offer advice at this stage, if required.

Key issues

Revision groups can work well because they enable students to:

- discuss topics from different perspectives and approaches;
- bounce thoughts and ideas off one another;
- solve problems together;
- share tips and advice;
- offer mutual support and encouragement;
- share useful resources, revision notes and timetables;
- work collectively on answers to difficult questions;
- work together on a cooperative basis, rather than on a competitive basis;
- increase productivity;
- gain in confidence;
- improve exam performance.

Some revision groups work better than others and you may find that some fold fairly quickly because students find that they are not benefiting personally from taking part in the group. The groups that do work well have very positive feedback, with students deciding to form new groups for their next end-of-year exams, and continuing throughout their studies.

→ Related activities

Activity 87: Understanding the reasons for assessment

Activity 88: Knowing about the different methods of assessment

Activity 90: Preparing for an exam

Activity 91: Taking an exam

Activity 92: Improving exam marks

Activity 93: Coping with stress

→ Preparatory reading

The books listed below provide information about revision techniques and can be recommended to students as both preparatory and further reading.

→ Further reading

Becker, L. (2010) *14 Days to Exam Success*. Basingstoke: Palgrave Macmillan. In most cases revising in 14 days should not be recommended. However, this book does have some useful information on revision techniques.

Cottrell, S. (2007) *The Exam Skills Handbook*. Basingstoke: Palgrave Macmillan.

Tracey, E. (2006) *The Student's Guide to Exam Success*, 2nd edition. Maidenhead: Open University Press.

Weyers, J. and McMillan, K. (2011) *How to Succeed in Exams and Assessments*, 2nd edition. Harlow: Pearson Education Ltd.

Activity 89

Preparing for an exam

Student
handout
page 342

TUTOR NOTES

Purpose: This activity helps student to prepare for exams by asking them to discuss, in groups, four questions that relate to preparing for exams (covering academic, psychological, physical and practical preparation). This is followed by a tutor-led discussion on the issues raised.

Type: Group exercise followed by tutor-led discussion.

Alternative type(s): Self-guided individual exercise.

Level: Elementary.

Duration: Fifty minutes to one hour.

Equipment/materials: None required.

Learning outcome: By the end of this activity students will have thought about, and discussed, how to prepare for exams academically, psychologically, physically and practically, which will help them to be prepared for, and feel more confident about, taking exams as their studies progress.

The activity

Divide your students into groups and give each group a copy of the Student Handout. This requires them, in their groups, to work through four questions that ask them to think about how they should prepare for exams academically, psychologically, physically and practically. Once they have completed this task (this usually takes about 20 minutes), lead a class discussion on the issues raised.

   This activity can be run together with Activities 91 and 92, which gives complete coverage of the topic (preparing for, taking and succeeding in exams). If you choose this option you will need about two hours of contact time. Ask students to answer the questions from this activity in groups, before moving on to run the discussion and brainwave outlined in Activity 91. When this is complete, run the brainstorm outlined in Activity 92. Follow all three activities with a tutor-led discussion on the issues raised. You may find that some information is repeated, but this helps to reinforce student learning. Alternatively, you can use a pick and mix approach, mixing the two most relevant activities together.

   It is possible to run this activity as a standalone, self-guided individual exercise, if contact time is not available. Give students a copy of the Student Handout and ask them to work through the questions on an individual basis during independent study. Answer any questions they may have from this activity the next time you meet, if you have time available.

Key issues

The following issues can be raised by this activity:

1. Students can prepare academically by:
    a. cultivating fundamental skills throughout the course, such as time management, note-taking, reading and

writing and a productive approach to learning, which can all aid revision;
    b. utilising both short- and long-term revision strategies (avoiding cramming);

c. creating a revision strategy that suits the way they like to learn (time of day and individual learning strategy preferences, for example);

d. creating a revision plan and timetable;

e. developing a checklist and ticking off items when complete;

f. developing a revision routine;

g. setting revision targets and goals;

h. joining a revision group (see Activity 89);

i. obtaining and practising with old exam papers;

j. practising answering questions within time limits;

k. holding discussion, debates and conversations with others;

l. thinking ahead and revising topics that will be covered;

m. identifying key ideas, understanding key information, organising ideas and developing memory.

2. Students can prepare psychologically by:

a. building personal confidence through comprehensive revision;

b. providing rewards when targets are reached;

c. trusting in personal ability;

d. focusing on work and ignoring distractions;

e. recognising that some anxiety is normal;

f. seeking help when required (peers, family, tutors or specialists, for example);

g. remaining positive;

h. eliminating negativity;

i. controlling stress levels (see Activity 93);

j. learning from mistakes and accepting that there is always room for improvement (perfectionism is not the goal);

k. identifying areas of concern and addressing each in turn.

3. Students can prepare physically by:

a. remaining healthy;

b. eating well;

c. taking plenty of exercise;

d. getting plenty of sleep;

e. relaxing and sleeping well the night before exams (avoiding last-minute revision);

f. taking plenty of revision breaks;

g. avoiding too much alcohol;

h. avoiding drugs.

4. Students can prepare practically by:

a. becoming familiar with university rules and regulations;

b. understanding rights in terms of illness, disability and late arrival;

c. getting organised for exams (knowing the venue, reliable transport options, collecting together items required and deciding on comfortable clothing, for example);

d. finding the correct ID to take to the exam (usually the student card);

e. collecting together permitted equipment (pens, calculators and bottles of water with all labels removed, for example);

f. discarding non-permitted items (smart watches, phones and bags, for example);

g. understanding the format of the exam and knowing in advance what to expect.

➜ Related activities

Activity 87: Understanding the reasons for assessment

Activity 88: Knowing about the different methods of assessment

Activity 89: Revising effectively

Activity 91: Taking an exam

Activity 92: Improving exam marks

Activity 93: Coping with stress

....

➜ Preparatory reading

The books listed below can be recommended as both preparatory and follow-up reading to students who want more information about exams.

....

➜ Further reading

Cottrell, S. (2007) *The Exam Skills Handbook*. Basingstoke: Palgrave Macmillan.

Tracey, E. (2006) *The Student's Guide to Exam Success*, 2nd edition. Maidenhead: Open University Press.

Weyers, J. and McMillan, K. (2011) *How to Succeed in Exams and Assessments*, 2nd edition. Harlow: Pearson Education Ltd.

Activity 90

Activity • • • • • • • • • • → 91

Taking an exam

Student handout page 343

TUTOR NOTES

Purpose: This activity provides student-centred tips, advice and guidance about taking exams through the use of small group discussion and class brainwave. This enables students to discuss, share and remember useful information and advice about taking exams in an entertaining and creative way.

Type: Brainwave.

Alternative type(s): Tip exchange (student-centred digital resource).

Level: Elementary.

Duration: Fifty minutes to one hour of contact time for the group discussion and brainwave. If the tip exchange option is chosen you need to set up the resource and spend a little time monitoring it over the duration of the course. Students will spend a few minutes posting and reading tips.

Equipment/materials: A suitable digital platform and access for all students if the tip exchange option is chosen.

Learning outcome: By the end of this activity students will feel more prepared, knowledgeable and confident about taking exams, having discussed and shared tips and advice with their peers.

The activity

Divide your students into small groups. The number and size of groups will depend on the size of your class. Ideally, you need five or six groups with three or more students in each. Give each group a copy of the Student Handout. This asks them to discuss and develop a list of useful tips and advice about taking exams that they can share with their peers in this activity.

When all groups have developed their list (usually after about 20 minutes) the brainwave can begin. This is a variation on the brainstorming method. It enables students to share their information in an entertaining way, while listening to others, thinking quickly and memorising what has come before. Each answer is given quickly, without judgement or criticism from other members of the class.

Using this technique you instruct one member of the first group to stand up and offer a tip or piece of advice. Then a member of the second group stands up and gives a different example, then a member of the third group and so on. The groups do not have to make their contribution in any particular order: you can point randomly at the groups to keep students alert.

This continues until a member from each group has spoken and given an example. The brainwave can continue on, starting again at the first group (with a different member speaking, if appropriate) until all ideas are exhausted and/or tips are beginning to be repeated. Use your judgement about whether tips are repeated: you will find that some tips and pieces of advice are similar, but are described in a slightly different way (see list, below). You can choose to let these stand because they encourage students to think about the issues from slightly different perspectives. If you have time you can conclude with a discussion on the issues that have been raised during the brainwave.

It is possible to run this activity together with Activities 90 and 92. The three activities together provide complete coverage of the topic (preparing for, taking and succeeding in exams) and will take about two hours to complete. Alternatively, you can use a pick and mix approach, combining the activities from Section 12 that are most suitable for your student cohort.

This activity can be run as a tip exchange if you do not have the contact time available. Set up a suitable digital platform on which to build the tip exchange and ask students to contribute when they think of any advice or tips that will help their peers to take exams. Develop the tip exchange fairly early in the course so that students can start to think about the issues well before exams are encountered, adding to the resource whenever they think of something new. Monitor the resource from time to time to ensure that information is correct, constructive and encouraging.

Key issues

The following list provides a snapshot of the type of tips that are given in the group brainwave:

- get plenty of sleep;
- don't cram the night before;
- revise throughout your course;
- eat a healthy breakfast;
- drink plenty of water;
- know where the venue is;
- arrive in good time;
- read the paper carefully;
- follow all instructions;
- know how many questions you need to answer;
- read all questions before deciding which to answer;
- answer the question that you know most about first;
- eliminate questions you know nothing about;
- answer the right number of questions;
- time each question;
- manage your time effectively;
- move on if you get stuck and return at the end if you have time;
- leave blank spaces to return to if necessary;
- rest your arm if it hurts while thinking of your answer;
- don't panic;
- relax;
- remain confident;
- don't dwell on how badly you are doing;
- don't look at others and worry that they are writing more than you;
- keep focused on the specific question you are working on, then move to the next and keep focused;
- don't get distracted;
- try to write neatly and legibly (practise beforehand);
- keep a little time to read through each answer at the end;
- remain positive after the exam and move on to the next.

➜ Related activities

Activity 87: Understanding the reasons for assessment

Activity 88: Knowing about the different methods of assessment

Activity 89: Revising effectively

Activity 91: Taking an exam

Activity 92: Improving exam marks

Activity 93: Coping with stress

....

➜ Preparatory reading

The books listed below can be recommended as preparatory and further reading to students who want to read more about taking exams.

....

➜ Further reading

Cottrell, S. (2007) *The Exam Skills Handbook*. Basingstoke: Palgrave Macmillan.

Evans, M. (2010) *How to Pass Your Exams: Proven Techniques for Any Exam that will Guarantee Success*, 4th edition. Oxford: How to Books.

Tracey, E. (2006) *The Student's Guide to Exam Success*, 2nd edition. Maidenhead: Open University Press.

Weyers, J. and McMillan, K. (2011) *How to Succeed in Exams and Assessments*, 2nd edition. Harlow: Pearson Education Ltd.

Activity 91

Activity · · · · · · · · · ➜ 92

Improving exam marks

The activity

Brainstorm with your students the question 'how can I improve my exam marks?' Write their answers on your board/ flipchart without judgement, analysis or reflection. Some students may be unfamiliar with the brainstorming technique. If this is the case, ask them to give any answer they can think of in relation to the question. They are not going to be judged and they should not judge or critique the answers given by other students (even if they do not agree with another's contribution). Each answer they give will be written on your board: the goal is to come up with a comprehensive list of tips, advice and techniques that will help students to improve their exam marks.

Once the brainstorm is complete (this usually takes up to 20 minutes) discuss the issues raised with your students. Do this for a further 20 minutes until you feel that the discussion has run its course. Once the discussion is complete ask your students to work on an individual basis to develop a personal action plan that will help them to improve their exam marks, based on the issues that have been raised during the brainstorm and discussion.

It is possible to run this activity as a group exercise followed by a class discussion, if you do not want to hold a brainstorm. Divide your students into small groups and ask them to discuss how they can improve their exam marks. Once they have done this lead a class discussion on the issues raised.

This activity can be run together with Activities 90 and 91, if contact time is available and it suits your student cohort. Run the group exercise given in Activity 90, followed by the discussion and brainwave described in Activity 91, followed by the brainstorm described above. All these activities together will take around two hours to complete and provide complete coverage of the topic (preparing for, taking and succeeding in exams). There may be some repetition, but this helps to reinforce student learning.

Key issues

Brainstorming should generate free-flowing ideas, promote creative thinking, encourage participation and interaction, pool knowledge and illustrate what students already know about passing exams. This is of particular use in classes where some students have experience of passing exams and others do not. Students often find it less threatening and more constructive to learn from their fellow students rather than be told about revision and exam techniques by a tutor.

The following list provides examples of the type of issue that can be raised during this brainstorm (and that can be included in students' plans for action).

Revision

- carry out systematic revision throughout your course;
- start revision in plenty of time;
- draw up a revision timetable;
- use online revision tools but don't get distracted;
- revise in short bursts and take plenty of breaks;
- review and reinforce what you are revising;
- form and make use of a revision group if this suits you, personally;
- don't cram before exams: relax and unwind instead.

Practise

- obtain and work through copies of previous exam papers (try some under mock conditions);
- attend examination sessions if they are run by your tutor/college/university;
- practise answering specific questions on topics of interest;
- run practice sessions with your fellow students;
- if practice shows a gap in your knowledge, fill it;
- practise relaxation exercises and techniques to control stress and nervousness.

During the exam

- be prepared and know what to expect;
- know what you can and can't take into the examination room;
- read all instructions carefully;
- work out how much time you have for each question;
- check all sides of the exam paper to make sure that you haven't missed any information;
- write as clearly and as legibly as possible;
- keep an eye on the time, only spend the required time on each answer and then move on;
- answer all required questions;
- be confident and stay positive.

→ **Related activities**

Activity 89: Revising effectively

Activity 90: Preparing for an exam

Activity 91: Taking an exam

Activity 93: Coping with stress

→ **Preparatory reading**

The Open University has some useful tutorials on revising for exams, revision techniques, taking exams and managing stress (www2.open.ac.uk/students/skillsforstudy/revising-and-examinations.php). These provide useful preparatory reading for this activity and can be recommended to your students if you feel they need further help and advice.

Activity 92

➜ **Further reading**

The following books can be recommended to students who want to know more about improving exam marks.

Evans, M. (2010) *How to Pass Your Exams: Proven Techniques for Any Exam that will Guarantee Success,* 4th edition. Oxford: How to Books.

Tracey, E. (2006) *The Student's Guide to Exam Success,* 2nd edition. Maidenhead: Open University Press.

Weyers, J. and McMillan, K. (2011) *How to Succeed in Exams and Assessments,* 2nd edition. Harlow: Pearson Education Ltd.

Activity 92

Activity • • • • • • • • • • → 93

Coping with stress

The activity

Choose a suitable digital platform on which you can build the digital resource. Ensure that all students have access to this platform and that it is available throughout their course. Call it 'Coping with Stress' and ask students to provide advice, guidance, information and tips about how students can cope with stress during their studies. They should be encouraged to establish a support network through this digital resource. This can include fellow students, alumni, tutors, specialist staff and experts who can offer advice, guidance and help to students who are trying to cope with stress (digital or face-to-face). Ask students to be useful, practical and enlightening. Explain that the digital resource and support network will be available for everyone throughout their course so that, if they experience stress at any time during their studies, they can access this resource for help and advice.

It is useful to ask students to build this digital resource and support network themselves because they are able to provide relevant, up-to-date information that fellow students will understand and be able to access. However, you may need to remind students to post information and you may also find it useful to post some of your own advice (perhaps to get the resource started or to encourage more entries). Examples of the type of post that you can include are given below.

This activity has been developed as a digital resource and support network (rather than taking up contact time) because the topic may not be of personal relevance to all students in your group. Some students progress through their course without ever feeling stressed and, therefore, will not find this activity useful. Others, however, find it invaluable and post questions, offer advice and meet up to support and encourage each other. The level of involvement should be an individual choice and students should not be forced to take part if they do not wish to do so. You will need to monitor posts from time-to-time to ensure that students are being constructive, encouraging and helpful.

Key issues

The following list provides examples of the type of information that can be posted (the type, amount and standard of post tends to depend on subject, level of study and student motivation).

- Information about counselling staff, welfare officers and medical staff who can help, along with contact details and times.
- Information about relevant training sessions, seminars and workshops.
- Details of any existing, and relevant, student support groups.
- Information about mental health helplines and national charities that can help with mental health.
- Specific questions from students (these can be answered by other students or you could ask that a specialist member of staff responds, if required).
- Information from an expert about the signs of stress (physical, behavioural and psychological) and when and why it is important to seek help.
- Information from an expert about the causes of stress including physical, mental, emotional or environmental factors.
- Practical tips and advice about ways to reduce stress. These can be from students and experts and can include:

  o talk about your problems and anxieties with family, friends and/or tutors;
  o be selective in your tasks and drop everything that is not essential;
  o improve your time-management and organisational skills (details of training sessions can be posted: see Activities 11 and 13);
  o work out why you are feeling stressed and alter the situation that is causing the trouble;
  o think through stressful events before they happen and be well prepared;
  o recognise that you don't have to be a perfectionist all the time;
  o don't criticise yourself, or others, too much;
  o avoid competition and try to cultivate cooperation instead (see Activity 7);
  o escape from your worries for a while and take a break if possible;
  o allocate yourself recreation time and try to relax;
  o overcome anger and frustration with physical activity;
  o join a yoga or meditation class (times and costs can be posted).
- Useful websites, tools and apps that can be accessed by students to help them cope with stress. For example, Student Minds is a UK student mental health charity. There is a useful section about coping with the stress of examinations on their website (www.studentminds.org.uk/exam-stress.html).
- Themes covered by students studying at a more advanced level can include the transitional nature of college and university life, interpersonal relationships, stress and personal perception, confronting stress, positive reappraisal and planned problem solving, for example.

➔ Related activities

Activity 6: Recognising and overcoming imposter syndrome

Activity 7: Fostering collaborative learning and interaction

Activity 13: Overcoming organisation problems

Activity 98: Collaborating and cooperating ethically

....

➔ Preparatory reading

The NHS in the UK has some useful advice to give about coping with stress (www.nhs.uk/Conditions/stress-anxiety-depression/Pages/reduce-stress.aspx). Mind, a UK mental health charity, also has some useful and comprehensive information about the signs, causes and treatments of stress (www.mind.org.uk/stress). These two websites provide useful preparatory reading for this activity and can be posted on the digital resource so that students can access the information, if required.

....

Activity 93

➔ Further reading

Fricchione, G., Ivkovic, A. and Yeung, A. (eds) (2016) *The Science of Stress: Living Under Pressure*. Chicago, IL: University of Chicago Press. This book provides interesting reading for those interested in research about stress.

The following two books provide practical information for students and can be added to your digital resource.

Levin, P. (2007) *Conquer Study Stress!* Maidenhead: Open University Press.
Palmer, S. and Puri, A. (2006) *Coping with Stress at University: a Survival Guide*. London: Sage.

Activity 93

Section 13 Ethics and integrity

Activity • • • • • • • • • • ➔ 94

Recognising and avoiding academic malpractice

Student handout page 344

TUTOR NOTES

Purpose: This activity asks students to develop, in groups, three plausible scenarios that illustrate three different types of academic malpractice that are then discussed by their peers in class. It helps students to understand what is meant by academic malpractice, think about specific types of malpractice and discuss what can be done to avoid, reduce, rectify or eliminate malpractice.

Type: Student-developed scenarios for class discussion.

Alternative type(s): Student-developed scenarios for digital discussion.

Level: Elementary, intermediate and advanced (the level of study will be reflected in the type of scenarios developed).

Duration: Students need to spend a few hours in their groups developing their scenarios. You need 50 minutes to one hour of contact time for students to present and discuss their scenarios. If the digital option is chosen you need to spend a few minutes setting up, contributing to and monitoring the digital resource and students will spend a few hours developing, uploading and discussing scenarios.

Equipment/materials: A suitable digital platform on which to upload and discuss scenarios and the required access for all students, if this option is chosen.

Learning outcome: By the end of this activity students will understand more about what is meant by academic malpractice, will know about specific types of academic malpractice and will understand how to avoid, reduce, rectify or eliminate academic malpractice.

The activity

Divide your students into groups and give each group a copy of the Student Handout. This asks them to work in their groups, during independent study, to develop three scenarios that illustrate three different types of academic malpractice. They are free to choose the structure, style, content and context of scenario and they can decide whether to make each type of academic malpractice easy or difficult to detect. They should ensure that all scenarios are informative and plausible, enabling their peers to remain interested and learn from the activity.

When you next meet, ask each group to present their scenarios to their peers. Work through each scenario, asking students to detect the type of academic malpractice that has been illustrated and to discuss methods that can be used to avoid, rectify, reduce or eliminate each type of malpractice.

It is possible to ask groups to share and discuss their scenarios using a relevant digital platform, if contact time is not available. Give a deadline by which time all scenarios should be uploaded and encourage students to take part in a digital discussion about the types of academic malpractice that have been illustrated in scenarios and possible methods that can be used to avoid, reduce, rectify or eliminate the different types of malpractice. You should take part in the digital discussion, encourage contributions and monitor posts to ensure that information is correct, supportive and encouraging.

Key issues

This activity works well because students must first of all research and discuss what is meant by academic malpractice before considering the different types of malpractice and understanding how, when and why these occur in academia. This enables them to produce three interesting, informative and plausible scenarios that can be discussed in class. A wide range of student and staff malpractice can be covered, examples of which include:

- plagiarism (see Activities 56 and 78);
- copyright infringement (see Activity 78);
- cheating in exams;
- theft of materials;
- favouritism;
- inappropriate student/tutor relationships;
- taking credit for someone else's work;
- copying another's work;
- using essay mills/buying assignments;
- duplicate submission;
- falsification of results;

- fabrication of results;
- manipulation of data;
- bribery (accepting bribes and offering bribes, for example);
- sabotage of another's work;
- providing false information to tutors;
- lying about previous qualifications;
- bullying;
- disruptive behaviour;
- non-attendance;
- breaches of data protection (see Activity 100).

International students can provide an interesting dimension to this activity through providing scenarios that illustrate academic malpractice that may be widespread in their country, but not so prevalent in your own country. Also, students studying at different levels tend to highlight different types of malpractice (fabrication and falsification of results at advanced level and plagiarism and essay mills for those studying at elementary level, for example).

➜ Related activities

Activity 36: The use, abuse and misuse of statistics

Activity 56: Referencing, copyright and plagiarism

Activity 97: Detecting and addressing bias

Activity 98: Collaborating and cooperating ethically

Activity 100: Knowing about data protection

➜ Preparatory reading

Felaefel, M., Salem, M., Jaafar, R. et al. (2017) 'A cross-sectional survey study to assess prevalence and attitudes regarding research misconduct among investigators in the Middle East', *Journal of Academic Ethics*, published online 13 October 2017, http://doi.org/10.1007/s10805-017-9295-9. This paper discusses research misconduct in the Middle East and provides interesting preparatory reading for tutors.

Both books listed below provide useful preparatory reading for tutors who are interested in why students cheat.

Lang, J. (2013) *Cheating Lessons: Learning from Academic Dishonesty.* Cambridge, MA: Harvard University Press.
McCabe, D., Butterfield, K. and Treviño, L. (2017) *Cheating in College: Why Students Do it and What Educators can Do about it*, reprint edition. Baltimore, MD: Johns Hopkins University Press.

➜ Further reading

The following books can be recommended to students who want to find out more about understanding and avoiding plagiarism.

Neville, C. (2016) *The Complete Guide to Referencing and Avoiding Plagiarism*, 3rd edition. London: Open University Press.
Williams, K. and Carroll, J. (2009) *Referencing and Understanding Plagiarism*. Basingstoke: Palgrave Macmillan.

Activity 94

Activity •••••••••• → 95

Recognising ethical issues and dilemmas when using the internet

Student handout page 345

TUTOR NOTES

Purpose: This activity helps students to recognise ethical issues and dilemmas when using the internet by presenting a number of real-world scenarios and related questions for group discussion.

Type: Scenarios for group discussion.

Alternative type(s): Student worksheet.

Level: Elementary, intermediate and advanced (the level of study will be reflected in the discussion).

Duration: Fifty minutes to one hour of contact time for groups to discuss the scenarios and work through the related questions. Students need one or two hours during independent study if the worksheet option is chosen.

Equipment/materials: None required.

Learning outcome: By the end of this activity students will have a raised awareness of ethical issues and dilemmas when using the internet and know how to recognise, avoid or overcome such issues as their course progresses and in life in general.

The activity

Divide your students into groups and ask them to work through the scenarios and questions given on the Student Handout. Ask them to spend around ten minutes on each scenario. Once they have done this, lead a class discussion on the issues raised. This activity can be adapted into a student worksheet for students to work through on an individual basis during independent study, if contact time is limited.

Key issues

The following issues can be raised by the scenarios presented in the Student Handout.

Scenario 1

The student has sent an email that has a string of emails attached in which is it possible that copyright has been infringed (copyrighted work has been redistributed, reproduced, duplicated or communicated to others without permission). Although the student is not the one to have infringed copyright directly, she may still have infringed copyright indirectly by redistributing, reproducing and communicating copyrighted material to others. This is referred to as secondary infringement.

Copyright covers the creations of writers, artists, graphic artists, composers and musicians. Once the work has been created in a 'fixed and tangible form' copyright is established, even if there is no formal copyright notice. Work that is not protected by copyright includes ideas, concepts, principles, discoveries, titles, names, short phrases and slogans, contents lists and devices.

The student could have decided not to forward the string of emails or, alternatively, could have gone through each email carefully to check whether copyright had been infringed by the sender. If she found that this was the case she could have deleted the relevant email and only sent those that had not infringed copyright. Alternatively, she could have looked into issues of 'fair dealing' (UK) or 'fair use' (US) as it is possible to use these as a defence against copyright infringement.

Students can ensure that they do not infringe copyright by:

- understanding the law and knowing what copyright means (laws can differ from country to country);
- sending, publishing and using work that has already been passed into the public domain (and understand what is meant by 'public domain': see below);
- sending, using and publishing work that has been published under a Creative Commons licence and understand and abide by the terms of that licence (see below);
- understanding what is meant by 'fair dealing' (UK) and 'fair use' (US) and abide by the terms;
- understanding the difference between copyright infringement and plagiarism (see below).

Scenario 2

This student has plagiarised the work of someone else. He has not breached copyright because the work is in the 'public domain' (it is an essay on which no one holds the copyright). However, students should understand that, although this essay is in the public domain, it does not mean that it is freely accessible for them to copy, even if they do alter a few words. If they do this they have plagiarised the work of another person. 'Public domain' is a legal term that refers to works on which rights have been forfeited, waived or expired. These rights, however, can be country-specific (the works might be in the public domain in one country, but subject to rights in another).

'Plagiarism' involves taking the thoughts, ideas, words, arguments, results or conclusions of another person and using them as if they were one's own, without acknowledgement or consent. It also applies to media such as graphs, illustrations, web pages and computer codes. 'Copyright' grants the creator exclusive rights to publish, reproduce and distribute the work for a number of years. It is infringed if another person does this without seeking permission, even if the work is referenced correctly. Therefore, this student has plagiarised because he has tried to pass the work off as his own (even though he altered a few words here and there) but has not breached copyright because the work was not protected by copyright.

Students can avoid plagiarism by:

- understanding what is meant by plagiarism (and understanding the difference between copyright infringement and plagiarism);
- knowing how to reference, cite and quote correctly (see Activities 29 and 30);
- becoming familiar with their university rules and regulations regarding plagiarism;
- maintaining high ethical and moral standards when producing assignments.

Scenario 3

This student could include a statement at the end of each blog, such as 'the author grants a nonexclusive licence to use this work in any way'. Alternatively, she could look into a Creative Commons licence that makes the work available to the public for certain uses while copyright is still maintained (a 'No Rights Reserved' licence, for example). Students should look for this type of licence or statement on work they wish to use to check whether or not they need to seek permission. They should also find out more about Creative Commons licences so that they understand what they can, and cannot, do with the work of other people.

Scenario 4

A Code of Ethics for using the internet could include the following issues:

- avoiding plagiarism;
- avoiding copyright infringement;
- understanding and using Creative Commons licences;
- understanding 'fair dealing' or 'fair use' policy;
- treating others with respect, courtesy and decency;
- respecting anonymity and confidentiality;
- understanding and complying with issues of informed consent;
- understanding and complying with data protection legislation (see Activity 100);
- details of complaints procedures, help, advice or support;
- a list of unacceptable use or behaviours, along with possible sanctions/punishment for breaches.

Activity 95

The Code of Ethics could be sent to all students at the start of their course, with follow-up sessions or reminders to check that students are adhering to the Code of Ethics.

→ Related activities

Activity 30: Citing, referencing and producing a bibliography

Activity 78: Copyright infringement and plagiarism of electronic materials

Activity 94: Recognising and avoiding academic malpractice

Activity 99: Undertaking ethical research

Activity 100: Knowing about data protection

→ Preparatory reading

Information about copyright in the UK can be obtained from the Government information website (www.gov.uk/copyright) and in the US from the United States Copyright Office (www.copyright.gov). Information about Creative Commons licences can be obtained from https://creativecommons.org/licenses/. These websites provide useful preparatory reading for tutors and can be recommended to students as further reading.

→ Further reading

The following books can be recommended to students who need to follow up the issues raised in this activity.

Neville, C. (2010) *The Complete Guide to Referencing and Avoiding Plagiarism*, 2nd edition. Maidenhead: Open University Press.

Pears, R. and Shields, G. (2016) *Cite Them Right: the Essential Referencing Guide*, 10th edition. Basingstoke: Palgrave Macmillan.

Ransome, P. (2013) *Ethics and Values in Social Research*. Basingstoke: Palgrave Macmillan.

Williams, K. and Davis, M. (2017) *Referencing and Understanding Plagiarism*, 2nd edition. Basingstoke: Palgrave Macmillan.

Activity 95

Activity · · · · · · · · · · ➔ 96

Knowing about subjectivity and objectivity

Student
handout
page 347

TUTOR NOTES

Purpose: This activity helps students to know more about subjectivity and objectivity by asking them to develop questions about the topic that they can ask their peers in a student-developed question and answer session. Students are asked to develop meaningful and searching open questions that will help to stimulate thought, generate in-depth discussion and enable their peers to learn more about the topic.

Type: Student-developed question and answer session.

Alternative type(s): None.

Level: Elementary, intermediate and advanced (the level of study will be reflected in the type of question asked and in the ensuing discussion).

Duration: Students need to spend a little time during independent study researching and developing their questions. Fifty minutes to one hour of contact time is required for the question and answer session. This can be done using a relevant digital platform if contact time is not available. You will need to spend a few minutes building and monitoring the digital resource and students will spend a few minutes uploading and answering questions.

Equipment/materials: A suitable digital platform and access for all students if this option is chosen.

Learning outcome: By the end of this activity students will have gained a deeper insight into what is meant by subjectivity and objectivity, and will be able to relate and apply this understanding to their studies, research and life in general.

The activity

Give your students a copy of the Student Handout. This asks them to develop three open questions on the topic of subjectivity and objectivity that they can put to their peers in a question and answer session when you next meet. The goal is not to ask questions that have a right or wrong answer, but to ask questions that will stimulate thought and generate in-depth discussion. When students develop their questions they should also develop an answer so that, if their peers struggle with the question, they can lead the discussion to develop deeper insight into the issues involved. You can ask students to undertake this activity on an individual basis, in pairs or in small groups, depending on what is best for your student cohort (students studying at elementary level might feel more comfortable working with peers, whereas students studying at advanced level can undertake this activity on an individual basis, for example).

Students are asked to develop three questions. This number can be increased or reduced, depending on the number of students in your class (you will need to alter the Student Handout accordingly). It is useful to ask students to develop more than one question as it encourages them to think more deeply about the topic. However, students may not have chance to ask all their questions if some are complex and require detailed discussion. Therefore, you should invite students to take it in turns to ask one of their questions. If time is available they can take it in turns to ask their second question and then their third, if you still have time available.

It is possible to run this question and answer session digitally if you do not have the contact time available. Give a deadline by which time all questions must be uploaded and invite answers from your students, again giving a deadline by which time they should be posted. Decide whether to make this activity voluntary or compulsory and decide whether or not to assess questions and answers (students will need to be told about your assessment criteria, if you choose this option). Alternatively, you can ask students to vote on the best question and best answer.

Key issues

This activity encourages students to prepare for a session on subjectivity and objectivity in a creative and interesting way. Students must first of all think about what is meant by subjectivity and objectivity (and carry out appropriate research, if they are unsure) and then think about how they can ask searching and meaningful open questions that will generate in-depth discussion, stimulate thought and help their peers to learn about the topic. They must also be able to answer their own questions thoroughly and concisely and in a way that can be understood by their peers.

There are a wide variety of questions that can be asked in this activity depending on level and subject of study (advanced students might relate questions to methodology and epistemology, whereas elementary students might look to the wider world of journalism and politics, for example). Examples of questions include:

1. How can human beings be objective?
2. Is it possible to be truly objective?
3. Is the scientific method objective?
4. Is objectivity an unachievable ideal?
5. Does objective truth exist?
6. Must all things exist objectively?
7. How can we remain objective in our research?
8. Is objectivity in research desirable and possible?
9. Is objective observation in fieldwork possible?
10. Is it possible for journalists to be objective?
11. Should we be subjective or objective in assignments?
12. Can something be both objective and subjective at the same time?
13. What is the difference between subjective and objective thinking?
14. How do issues of objectivity and subjectivity relate to social media?
15. Are subjectivity and objectivity so very different?
16. How subjective are politicians and does this matter?
17. Why am I subjective?
18. Is there a place for subjectivity in scientific research?
19. Should subjective journalism be rebranded as advocacy or activism?
20. How is subjectivity influenced by science, politics, society and culture?
21. Is being called 'highly subjective' an insult?

➜ Cautionary note

You will see from the sample questions given above that students will not be able to agree on answers for some questions, as these depend on epistemological, ideological and political beliefs and/or on theoretical and methodological preferences. You will need to lead or monitor discussions carefully to ensure that students remain on topic and treat their peers with courtesy and respect.

➜ Related activities

Activity 36: The use, abuse and misuse of statistics

Activity 52: Evaluating sources

Activity 53: Finding truth and fact in mass information

Activity 54: Recognising statistics, facts, arguments and opinions

Activity 97: Detecting and addressing bias

➜ Preparatory reading

Letherby, G., Scott, J. and Williams, M. (2013) *Objectivity and Subjectivity in Social Research.* London: Sage. This book offers an interesting take on objectivity and subjectivity and provides useful preparatory reading for tutors and for students studying at advanced level.

Activity 96

→ **Further reading**

Steinberger, P. (2017) *The Politics of Objectivity: An Essay on the Foundations of Political Conflict*, reprint edition. Cambridge: Cambridge University Press. This book can be recommended to students who are interested in political conflict and objectivity.

The following papers provide further reading for tutors and students who are interested in these topics.

Chong, P. (2017) 'Valuing subjectivity in journalism: bias, emotions, and self-interest as tools in arts reporting', *Journalism*, first published 4 August 2017, https://doi.org/10.1177/1464884917722453.

Greiffenhagen, C. and Sharrock, W. (2008) 'Where do the limits of experience lie? Abandoning the dualism of objectivity and subjectivity', *History of the Human Sciences*, 21 (3): 70-93, first published 1 August 2008, https://doi.org/10.1177/0952695108093954.

Hegelund, A. (2005) 'Objectivity and subjectivity in the ethnographic method', *Qualitative Health Research*, 15 (5): 647-68, first published 1 May 2005, https://doi.org/10.1177/1049732304273933.

Activity 96

Activity • • • • • • • • • • • ➜ 97

Detecting and addressing bias

Student
handout
page 348

TUTOR NOTES

Purpose: This activity is an entertaining way to help students understand how to detect and address different types of bias. It asks them, in groups, to produce a short video or podcast in which they make a presentation on a topic related in some way to their course. However, within their presentation they must incorporate some type of bias. Students must then work together to detect the bias that has been incorporated, and work out strategies to address this bias.

Type: Video/podcast production with tutor-led viewing and discussion.

Alternative type(s): Student-centred digital resource.

Level: Elementary, intermediate and advanced (the level and subject of study will be reflected in the videos and ensuing discussion).

Duration: Student groups need to spend a few hours during independent study producing and uploading their video or podcast. This will be followed by 50 minutes to one hour of contact time to view and discuss videos/podcasts (more time will be required if you have a large number of students). If the digital resource option is chosen students need to spend several hours in their groups producing, uploading, viewing and posting comments on videos/podcasts. Tutors need to spend up to two hours setting up the resource, monitoring posts and adding to the discussion, where required.

Equipment/materials: Students need access to video/podcast production equipment and access to the relevant digital platform on which to upload their videos/podcasts.

Learning outcome By the end of this activity students will understand what is meant by bias, have a greater awareness of when it occurs and understand how to recognise and address bias in the work of others and in their own work.

The activity

Divide your students into groups and give them a copy of the Student Handout. This asks them, in groups during independent study, to produce a video or podcast on a topic relevant to their course, which they must upload ready for viewing and discussion when you next meet. Within their video/podcast they must deliberately incorporate some type of bias. This could be one type of bias or several types, depending on group preference. To do this effectively they must first of all understand what is meant by 'bias' and then get to grips with different types of bias that can be presented in text and speech.

Give a deadline by which time groups must upload their video/podcast. Once they have done this, view each one to check suitability for class viewing when you next meet. Sort them into order, perhaps to group together those that present similar types of bias, or to provide a logical structure for the class discussion, for example.

When you next meet show the videos, one at a time, to your students. After each video ask your students to detect bias that has been presented (confirming with the production group that the correct bias has been identified). If they are unable to do this, ask the production group to explain what bias is present. Once this has been done, discuss how each case of bias could be addressed.

It is useful to have at least four videos/podcasts to discuss as this enables various types of bias to be discussed during this session. Student videos should not be more than five minutes in length and each discussion should not last more than ten minutes. If you have a large number of students you may need to allocate more time to view and discuss videos. However, if contact time is not available, it is possible to ask students to post, view and discuss videos/podcast on a suitable digital platform. If this option is chosen, give a deadline by which time all videos should be uploaded and another deadline by which time comments and discussion should be complete. Monitor the digital resource from time to time to ensure that all students contribute and to check that information is correct, constructive and informative.

Key issues

Many types of bias can be discussed in this activity, depending on the subject and level of study. They include:

- personal bias that can include, for example, heterosexual bias, race bias, gender bias and class bias;
- bias in the way research has been designed and conducted that can include, for example, design bias, population definition bias, sampling frame bias, measurement bias and data analysis bias (these issues tend to be raised by postgraduate students who are engaged in research);
- bias in the way topics are discussed or reported that can include, for example, bias by omission, placement bias, mainstream bias, bias by story selection and treatment bias.

Students, on occasion, notice a type of bias in a video that was not intended by the groups producing the video. When this happens it provides an interesting and enlightening discussion on problems associated with recognising, detecting and addressing bias. You can also hold a discussion, if relevant, on whether it is possible to eliminate bias through diligent enquiry, or whether it is only possible to discuss, report and acknowledge bias (illustrating how this relates to epistemological and methodological standpoint).

➜ Related activities

Activity 21: Reading, critiquing and questioning

Activity 28: Producing an effective argument

Activity 36: The use, abuse and misuse of statistics

Activity 52: Evaluating sources

Activity 54: Recognising statistics, facts, arguments and opinions

Activity 96: Knowing about subjectivity and objectivity

....

➜ Preparatory reading

Chapter 6 of Hammersley (2000), titled 'Bias in Social Research', provides interesting preparatory reading for this activity.

....

➜ Further reading

The following books can be recommended to students who wish to follow up the issues raised in this activity.

D'Angelo, J. (2012) *Ethics in Science*. Boca Raton, FL: CRC Press.
Hammersley, M. (2000) *Taking Sides in Social Research: Essays on Partisanship and Bias*. London: Routledge.
Hammersley, M. (2013) *Media Bias in Reporting Social Research? The Case of Reviewing Ethnic Inequalities in Education*. Abingdon, Oxon: Routledge.
Manning, P. (2001) *News and News Sources: A Critical Introduction*. London: Sage.

Activity 97

Activity · · · · · · · · · · · · · → 98

Collaborating and cooperating ethically

Student handout page 349

TUTOR NOTES

Purpose: This activity helps to raise awareness of ethical collaboration and cooperation in academia by asking students, in groups, to develop three plausible scenarios that display unethical practice when collaborating and cooperating with others. These are presented to peers who must identify the unethical practice and discuss ways that it can be prevented, avoided or rectified.

Type: Student-developed scenarios for class discussion.

Alternative type(s): Student-developed scenarios for digital discussion.

Level: Elementary, intermediate and advanced (the level of study will be reflected in the type of scenarios developed and in the ensuing discussion).

Duration: Students need to spend one or two hours in their groups developing their scenarios. You need 50 minutes to one hour of contact time for students to present and discuss their scenarios. If the digital option is chosen you need to spend a few minutes setting up, contributing to and monitoring the digital resource and students will spend a few hours developing, uploading and discussing scenarios.

Equipment/materials: A suitable digital platform on which to upload and discuss scenarios and the required access for all students, if this option is chosen.

Learning outcome: By the end of this activity students will know how to recognise, prevent, avoid and rectify unethical practice when collaborating and cooperating with others, which will help them to collaborate and cooperate ethically as their studies progress and in future careers.

The activity

Divide your students into groups and give each group a copy of the Student Handout. This asks them to work in their groups, during independent study, to develop three scenarios that illustrate unethical practice when collaborating and cooperating with others in academia (peers or research colleagues, for example). They are free to choose the structure, style, content and context of scenarios and they can decide whether to make the unethical practice easy or difficult to detect. They should ensure that all scenarios are informative and plausible and that they are able to stimulate thought, generate in-depth discussion and enable their peers to learn from the activity.

When you next meet, ask each group to present their scenarios to their peers. Work through each scenario, asking students to detect the unethical practice that has been illustrated and to discuss methods that can be used to prevent, avoid or rectify demonstrated practices.

It is possible to ask groups to share and discuss their scenarios using a relevant digital platform, if contact time is not available. Give a deadline by which time all scenarios should be uploaded and encourage students to take part in a digital discussion about the unethical practice that has been illustrated in scenarios and possible methods that can be used to prevent, avoid or rectify demonstrated practices. You will need to take part in the digital discussion, encourage contributions and monitor posts to ensure that information is correct, supportive and encouraging.

Key issues

This activity requires students to research and discuss what is meant by ethical and unethical practice when collaborating and cooperating with others. For students studying at elementary level this could include ethical considerations involved in group project work and for students studying at advanced level it could involve working within research teams or with international researchers, for example. Students are able to develop creative, imaginative and memorable scenarios that stimulate thought, encourage in-depth discussion and help students to think about how problems can be prevented, avoided or rectified.

The following list provides summaries of some of the scenarios that have been developed for this activity:

- A student who is bossy, disrespectful and dominant, who tells others in the group what to do, doesn't listen and tries to take credit for all the work.
- A team leader that expects team members to work all hours, refuses requests for days off and holds meetings up to midnight.
- A supervisor insisting that his name goes on all team papers and publications as lead author, even though he has not written or contributed to any of the publications.
- A team member who decides to keep quiet about holding shares in the company that is funding the team research project.
- A student who compromises a group project by fabricating results and another student who discovers this action but decides to keep quiet.
- Unencrypted, non-anonymised personal data of research participants are kept on a memory stick by one team member, who regularly takes the memory stick home.
- A student suspects that a member of the group has copied work from another student. She decides it won't matter because the combined effort of group members will ensure originality.
- A team member makes jokes about the English-language ability of an international team member.
- A junior researcher is desperate to recruit participants and decides that the informed consent forms are off-putting for potential recruits, so she decides not to use them, even though other researchers on the team are adamant that they are used.
- A student uses social media to criticise group members and complain that they are not pulling their weight in the group project.

→ Related activities

Activity 7: Fostering collaborative learning and interaction

Activity 65: Getting the most out of group work

Activity 70: Working within international teams

Activity 86: Working with supervisors and personal tutors

Activity 99: Undertaking ethical research

....

→ Preparatory reading

The books listed below provide useful preparatory and further reading for tutors and students.

....

→ Further reading

The following books are useful for tutors and for students studying at advanced level who may be required to work on collaborative research projects:

Anderson, M. and Steneck, N. (eds) (2011) *International Research Collaborations*. New York: Routledge.
Bozeman, B. and Boardman, C. (2014) *Research Collaboration and Team Science: a State-of-the Art Review and Agenda*. New York: Springer.

Activity 98

Griffin, G., Bränström-Öhman, A. and Kalman, H. (eds) (2013) *The Emotional Politics of Research Collaboration*. New York: Routledge.

O'Rourke, M., Crowley, S., Eigenbrode, S. and Wulfhorst, J. (eds) (2013) *Enhancing Communication and Collaboration in Interdisciplinary Research*. Thousand Oaks, CA: Sage.

The following books can be recommended to students who need to collaborate and cooperate on group projects:

Kahn, W. (2009) *The Student's Guide to Successful Project Teams*. New York: Psychology Press.

Levin, P. (2005) *Successful Teamwork! For Undergraduates and Taught Postgraduates Working on Group Projects*. Maidenhead: Open University Press.

Activity 98

Activity · · · · · · · · · · → 99

Undertaking ethical research

The activity

Ask your students to prepare for this activity by finding out about the 'Socratic Method'. They are going to use this technique to help their fellow students identify, define, focus and clarify their thoughts about ethical issues associated with their proposed research. They need to think about the type of questions to ask, while paying attention to how the questions are asked (see below). Students also need to spend some time thinking about ethical issues associated with their own research, if they have not already done so.

   When you next meet, divide your students into pairs. Ask one student to give a brief summary of their research and potential ethical considerations. The other student should listen to this summary, asking questions when appropriate to help the first student focus in on ethical issues, clarify thoughts and develop further insight. The pairs of students should do this for up to 20 minutes before reversing roles and continuing with the dialogue for another 20 minutes.

   When using the Socratic Method students can choose to ask questions that perform the following functions (these can be developed into a Student Handout if you feel your students need more guidance with this activity):

- probe preliminary thoughts about ethical issues;
- pose ethical dilemmas;
- help to clarify ethical issues and dilemmas;

- test viewpoint, perspective, knowledge and experience of the student;

- help to identify ethical choices and decisions that have been made;
- probe rationale and justification for ethical choices and decisions;
- query scope, extent, appropriateness and suitability of ethical choices and decisions;

- query implications and consequences of ethical choices and decisions;
- ask about alternatives;
- raise new ethical issues.

Encourage your students to be thought-provoking, challenging and stimulating, but not discourteous, disrespectful or offensive when they ask their questions. They should try to keep the discussion focused and intellectually responsible, enabling and encouraging a deeper understanding of ethical considerations. Follow their collaborative dialogue with a tutor-led discussion on the issues raised, if time is available.

It is possible to run this activity as a one-to-one support session if you feel that a particular student needs specific support with ethical issues associated with their research (they are working with vulnerable people or those at risk, for example). Use the Socratic Method in your session so that you can help your student to identify, define, focus and clarify ethical dilemmas, choices and decisions.

Key issues

As we have seen in Activity 80, the 'Socratic Method' is a technique that is used to draw individual answers and encourage fundamental insight into the issue that is being discussed. It is also referred to as 'method of elenchus' or 'Socratic debate'. Using this technique, a problem (or issue) is broken down into a series of questions that are asked to help students justify beliefs, clarify thoughts and think about the extent of their knowledge.

The aim of the Socratic Method is to help students process, interpret and analyse information and build a deeper understanding of the issue under discussion. It is of particular use when considering ethical research because it helps students to:

- identify ethical requirements and considerations;
- consider potential ethical problems;
- decide whether their ethical choices and decisions are appropriate and suitable;
- determine their underlying beliefs, biases, assumptions and extent of their knowledge (and what else needs to be known);

- refine and narrow ideas, thoughts and beliefs;
- identify weaknesses in their research proposal and create solutions;
- improve their proposal;
- prepare for ethics committee submission and approval.

It is possible to follow this activity with a specialist talk given by a member of staff from your University Research Ethics Committee, who will be able to describe the ethical approval process to your students. An activity of this type can be found in Dawson (2016).

➜ Related activities

Activity 79: Producing a research proposal

Activity 80: Choosing research topics and methods

Activity 94: Recognising and avoiding academic malpractice

Activity 97: Detecting and addressing bias

Activity 100: Knowing about data protection

➜ Preparatory reading

Trepanier, L. (ed.) (2018) *The Socratic Method Today: Student-Centered and Transformative Teaching in Political Science*. Abingdon, Oxon: Routledge. This book provides useful preparatory reading for tutors who are interested in detailed information about the Socratic Method.

A publication called *Ethical Guidelines* has been produced by the Social Research Association in the UK and is available for download from their website (http://the-sra.org.uk). This is a full and comprehensive guide that covers all ethical issues for social researchers [accessed 22 November 2017].

Activity 99

Dawson, C. (2016) *100 Activities for Teaching Research Methods*. London: Sage.
Section 6 of this book contains 14 additional activities about ethical research, any of which can be combined with this activity.

....

➜ Further reading

The following books can be recommended to students who want to find out more about ethics in research.

Biggs, H. (2010) *Healthcare Research Ethics and Law: Regulation, Review and Responsibility*. Abingdon, Oxon: Routledge-Cavendish.

Comstock, G. (2013) *Research Ethics: a Philosophical Guide to the Responsible Conduct of Research*. New York: Cambridge University Press.

Israel, M. (2015) *Research Ethics and Integrity for Social Scientists*, 2nd edition. London: Sage.

Ransome, P. (2013) *Ethics and Values in Social Research*. Basingstoke: Palgrave Macmillan.

Wiles, R. (2013) *What are Qualitative Research Ethics?* London: Bloomsbury Academic.

Activity 99

Activity · · · · · · · · · → 100

Knowing about data protection

Student handout page 350

TUTOR NOTES

Purpose: This activity raises awareness of the issues involved in data protection by asking students to imagine that they have applied for a job as a data protection and compliance manager for a global finance company. They must prepare thoroughly for the interview, which involves finding out about all relevant data protection and compliance issues. Students must then role play the job interview in pairs, thus reinforcing what they have learnt in the individual exercise.

Type: Self-guided individual exercise followed by student role play.

Alternative type(s): Self-guided individual exercise.

Level: Intermediate and advanced (this activity is useful for students who are starting to think about potential data protection issues for their dissertation or thesis).

Duration: Students need to spend one or two hours during independent study researching information and preparing for their interview (and preparing questions to ask their interviewee). You need 50 minutes to one hour of contact time for students to role play their interviews and for a class discussion.

Equipment/materials: None required.

Learning outcome: By the end of this activity students will have a deeper understanding of data protection and compliance issues and will be able to apply this understanding to their own research, when required.

The activity

Give your students a copy of the Student Handout. This asks them to imagine that they are applying for a job as a data protection and compliance manager for a global finance company. They must prepare thoroughly for their interview, which involves finding out all they can about data protection and compliance issues.

When you next meet, students will be paired together to role play the job interview. Therefore, students must also prepare some interview questions that they can ask their partner in the role play. Allocate up to 40 minutes for the role play (up to 20 minutes per interview) and up to 20 minutes for a class discussion. This can be used to talk about the data protection and compliance issues that have been raised by the activity, and to relate them to students' research. It is possible to run this activity as a self-guided individual exercise without the role play, if contact time is not available.

Key issues

This activity provides an interesting and memorable way for students to learn about data protection. They must research what is meant by data protection and compliance and think about their practical application by considering the tasks that should be undertaken by a data protection and compliance manager within a global finance company. They must get to grips with the issues so that they can provide convincing and knowledgeable answers to questions asked by their partner in the role play. This learning is reinforced further by students asking questions in the role of interviewer and listening to answers from their partner.

A global finance company has been chosen for this activity because it encourages students to think about legal, regulatory and 'best practice' issues that they may not consider initially when thinking about data protection issues for their research. It also enables them to adopt a different role that is far removed from their university study: students tend to play roles that are entertaining, creative and memorable, and they have fun with this activity. The tutor-led discussion should be used to relate the information supplied in the role play back to their university study.

Issues that can be discussed in this activity include:

- Compliance with relevant data protection legislation in all countries in which the global finance company operates (the Data Protection Act 2018 in the UK, for example). In the UK this involves compliance with eight important principles of the Act, which state that data must be:
  - fairly and lawfully processed;
  - processed for limited purposes;
  - adequate, relevant and not excessive;
  - accurate and up-to-date;
  - not kept for longer than is necessary;
  - processed in line with the rights of the individual;
  - secure;
  - not transferred to other countries without adequate protection.
- Knowing about the General Data Protection Regulation (GDPR) from May 2018, which intends to strengthen and unify data protection for all individuals in the EU.

- Understanding relevant regulatory requirements concerning financial services (the Financial Conduct Authority in the UK for example).
- The storage, preservation and management of data:
  - with the highest regard for ethical standards;
  - within the law, regulation and recognised good practice;
  - with the highest regard for security.
- The development of a Data Management Plan (DMP) that describes what type of data will be generated and how. It sets out how data will be stored, preserved, shared and disseminated. It also includes information about security and possible restrictions, given the nature of the data (in this case, financial data, but this can be related to research data during the discussion).

➜ Related activities

Activity 94: Recognising and avoiding academic malpractice

Activity 99: Undertaking ethical research

....

➜ Preparatory reading

A guide to data protection in the UK can be obtained from the Information Commissioner's Office (ICO) website (https://ico.org.uk) and a guide to the GDPR can be obtained from EUGDPR website (http://www.eugdpr.org).

The Social Research Association (SRA) in the UK has produced a publication called *Data Protection Act 1998: Guidelines for Social Research*. It is a useful and detailed publication that covers all the issues relevant to social research such as data security, disclosure of personal data from research projects and data protection scenarios. A free PDF can be downloaded from the SRA website: www.the-sra.org.uk [accessed 10 November 2017] (It is anticipated that an updated version will be available soon).

....

➜ Further reading

The books listed below provide useful further reading for both tutors and students who wish to follow up issues raised in this activity.

Calder, A. (2016) *EU GDPR: a Pocket Guide*. Ely: IT Governance Publishing.

Carey, P. (2015) *Data Protection: a Practical Guide to UK and EU Law*. Oxford: Oxford University Press.

Craig, T. and Ludloff, M. (2011) *Privacy and Big Data*. Sebastopol, CA: O'Reilly Media, Inc.

Duncan, G., Elliot, M. and Salazar-Gonzalez, J. (2011) *Statistical Confidentiality: Principles and Practice*. New York: Springer.

Activity 100

Part 2   Student Handouts

Activity • • • • • • • • • • • • → 1

Bringing learning to life

STUDENT HANDOUT

Please read the following two paragraphs:

Learning is concerned with the whole person and can include our physical, mental, emotional and psychological development. Learning helps us to think about our identity, who we are, what we do (or want to do) and helps us to find our place in the world. It helps us to think about our past, present and future lives and reflect on how this is interconnected with our past, present and future learning.

Learning helps us to think about, develop and express our attitudes, values and ideals. It helps us to overcome problems, succeed in times of crisis and manage long-term difficulties. It can provide support, encouragement, companionship and increase independence, self-esteem and confidence. New skills are learnt and developed, helping us to work, socialise, improve relationships, improve health and well-being, and develop hobbies. What we learn can be captivating, tantalising and fascinating. Learning involves passion, intrigue and excitement and takes place throughout our lives.

Once you have read these two paragraphs, complete the following exercise:

1. Provide some examples of how learning has helped you to develop. Try to include your 'physical, mental, emotional and psychological' development.
2. Give examples of how learning has helped you to overcome a problem, deal with a crisis and/or manage long-term difficulties.
3. How can learning provide 'support, encouragement and companionship'?
4. How can learning increase 'independence, self-esteem and confidence'?
5. Provide examples of instances where your personal learning has been 'captivating, tantalising and fascinating'. Think about formal learning that has taken place in the classroom, and informal learning that has taken place in your life, perhaps over many years and in many different situations.
6. Provide examples of instances where your personal learning has involved 'passion, intrigue and excitement'. Again, consider both formal and informal learning.

Complete this exercise as fully and honestly as possible. Thinking about your learning in this way will help you to get more from your studies, help you to stay motivated, remain enthusiastic and enjoy your learning. This exercise is for your personal benefit: it will not be assessed or seen by your tutor or peers, unless you wish to discuss the issues that have been raised with someone after you have completed the exercise.

Learning outcome: By the end of this activity you will have an increased understanding of the benefits, improvements and personal development that can be gained from learning, and be able to relate this understanding to your past, present and future learning on your course and in your personal and professional lives.

Activity • • • • • • • • • • ➜ 2

Becoming a reflective learner

STUDENT HANDOUT

Work through the following questions, answering each as fully as possible.

1. This activity is called 'becoming a reflective learner'. What do you think this means?
2. In what ways will becoming a reflective learner help with your studies and with your life in general?
3. How can you become a reflective learner? What action do you need to take?

Once you have answered these questions, go on to develop a personal plan of action that will help you to become a reflective learner. This could include, for example:

- thinking about past and present learning experiences, including both positive and negative learning experiences and a critical appraisal of why they were positive or negative;
- considering personal motivation for learning;
- thinking about the benefits of learning;
- recognising and building on strengths;
- recognising, acknowledging and overcoming weaknesses;
- finding subjects, courses and teaching methods that inspire and build enthusiasm;
- discussing, sharing and cooperating with peers;
- putting thoughts, ideas and experiences into words (oral or written);
- keeping a reflective learning diary;
- recognising and thinking about personal change and development.

Write down your personal plan for action in a format that works for you. This could be a list of tasks to complete and tick off, a flow diagram of how you hope to proceed or a broad timetable of milestones you expect to reach as your course progresses, for example. This is a personal endeavour that will not be seen or assessed by your tutor. However, if you wish to discuss this activity, or are struggling to complete the activity, please contact me to arrange to discuss it further.

Learning outcome: By the end of this activity you will understand what is meant by reflective learning, know about the benefits that can be gained and will have developed a personal plan of action that will help you to become a reflective learner as your course progresses.

Activity · · · · · · · · · · · · ➜ 3

Learning to learn

STUDENT HANDOUT

Discuss the following questions with your group members:

1. What factors can stop you learning or make it difficult to learn? Think about both internal factors (to do with you, personally) and external factors (to do with others).
2. What factors help you to learn and help you to learn effectively?
3. When is learning successful and what makes this learning successful? Think of specific examples where your learning has been successful and discuss these with your group members.
4. What can you do to make your learning more effective?
5. What factors will help you, personally, to succeed in your learning?

Learning outcome: By the end of this activity you will understand what is required to promote effective and successful learning and will be able to relate this understanding to your personal learning on your course and in your personal and professional lives.

Activity · · · · · · · · · · · → 4

Developing metacognition

STUDENT HANDOUT

Consider the following statements that can be made about metacognition:

- the ability to think about learning;
- the ability to think about thinking;
- an awareness of what has been learnt and how it has been learnt;
- an awareness of what else needs to be learnt and how to go about learning it;
- an awareness of what is not known and the ability to find out that that is not known;
- the ability to manage one's personal learning;
- the ability to monitor one's learning;
- the ability to process information;
- the ability to express opinions about information;
- the ability to update personal knowledge;
- the ability to develop and implement new learning strategies;
- an awareness of personal strengths and weaknesses;
- the ability to carry out a detailed self-assessment;
- the ability to set and monitor goals;
- the ability to transfer knowledge learned in one context to another;
- the ability to engage in critical enquiry.

Start to keep a learning journal. This can be paper or digital, depending on your personal preference. Consider the list given above: all these statements relate to 'metacognition'. Your learning journal is a tool that you are going to use to develop metacognition.

For your first entry create a personal plan of action that will help you to develop metacognition. Use the list given above to help and guide you. Once you have developed your personal plan of action, begin to implement your plan as your course progresses. Make entries in your journal when appropriate: this could be when you suddenly become aware of a new skill or ability, when you achieve a goal, when you develop personal insight or encounter a 'eureka moment', for example. As metacognition develops you will find that you become more strategic in your approach to learning, more self-reliant, more productive and more successful with your learning. Keep aware of these changes, reflect on them and note relevant information in your journal.

Your journal is a personal endeavour that will help you to develop metacognition and get more from your course, your relationships and life in general. It is for your personal benefit, so remember to make entries throughout your course. The journal will not be assessed or seen by your tutor or peers, unless you feel that you would like to discuss the issues that have been raised as your course progresses.

Learning outcome: By the end of this activity you will have produced a personal plan of action and kept a learning journal that will help you to become more aware of, and develop, metacognition, which will be of benefit to your studies, relationships and life in general.

Activity • • • • • • • • • • • • • ➔ 9

Making the right
learning choices

STUDENT HANDOUT

Imagine that you have applied for a job as a student guidance worker. As part of your job interview you have been asked to role play a guidance session in which you help your client to make the right learning choices. You will not be affiliated to, or work for, any particular institution, so you can offer advice about any local, national and/or international educational provision that may be of interest to your client.

You are very keen to get this job so you want to do well in the role play. Make sure that you prepare thoroughly for the guidance session and carry out the necessary research. This could involve finding out about local, national and international education provision and knowing about costs, accommodation, travel and childcare, for example. You will also need to think about how to ask questions, probe for more information and listen to answers carefully so that you can offer useful and appropriate advice to your client.

When we next meet you will be divided into pairs to undertake the role play. Fifteen minutes will be allocated for the first session in which one student will be the guidance worker and the other the client. After 15 minutes the roles will be reversed so that both students have the chance to play guidance worker and client. Ensure that you are polite and courteous and that you treat your partner with respect, listening carefully to what is said.

When you are playing the role of client you can decide whether to play yourself or whether to make up a role. Some students have made up their mind about what, where, when and how to study so need to make up a role to have a constructive guidance interview. Others, however, find it a useful experience to discuss their learning options and possible choices with a 'guidance worker' during the role play.

Learning outcome: By the end of this activity you will have a deeper understanding of the issues involved in making the right learning choices and will be able to apply this understanding to your own choices, where relevant.

Activity • • • • • • • • • • • → 11

Managing time

STUDENT HANDOUT

Work with your group members to develop an idea for a time management app aimed at students. You only need to develop an idea for your app, not actually design the app. Once you have developed your idea you will pitch it to your classmates when we next meet. The best app will be chosen at the end of the session, so ensure that your app is innovative, creative, interesting and useful, and that it will help students to take control of their time while they are studying (you will need to develop a good understanding of time management issues to do this effectively).

There are various time management apps available on the market. However, it is important that you develop your own ideas, rather than copy existing apps. When we next meet and you pitch your ideas, other students will be able to spot if you have copied an existing app, so ensure that you discuss and come up with innovative and new ideas with your group mates.

Learning outcome: By the end of this activity you will have a greater understanding of how to manage your time effectively and will be able to apply this understanding to your studies as your course progresses.

Activity • • • • • • • • • • • ➔ 13

Overcoming organisation problems

STUDENT HANDOUT

Consider the real-life scenarios described below and discuss, with your group members, ways to overcome the organisation problems presented.

Scenario 1

Jane lives with her husband and two children aged 5 and 7. Both children are at school from 9 a.m. to 3.30 p.m. Jane has begun a full-time undergraduate course at her local university, paid for through personal savings and a part-time job. However, she has found that she has three lectures starting at 9 a.m. and two lectures starting at 3 p.m. during the week. Her husband works full-time, having to arrive at work at 8.30 a.m. and finish at 5.30 p.m. He is not very supportive of her studies and feels that it is her responsibility to ensure that the children are dropped off and collected from school at the appropriate times. What can Jane do? Is it possible to overcome these problems and organise her study around her children and their school?

Scenario 2

Adam's mind is 'all over the place' or so he feels. His room is a mess: files, paper, books, assignments and empty food and drink containers cover every surface. He has too many ideas and not enough time to get them all down. He's missed a couple of assignment deadlines and he has been warned that he could fail his course if he doesn't get his act together. But too much is happening. Everything is chaotic and it's hard to get a grip. Life moves quickly for Adam. There's a lot to do and not enough time. What can Adam do? How can he overcome his problems and become more organised so that he doesn't fail his course?

Scenario 3

Anna is upset that she failed her last assignment. She'd worked really hard on it, staying up for three nights in a row to get it perfect. She'd handed it in with moments to spare, but then she always does that because it's so hard to fit everything in and get all her work done on time. Her social life, social networking, games and sorting out her laptop are all important and take up a lot of time. What can Anna do? How can she organise herself better so that she doesn't fail another assignment?

Scenario 4

Geoff is 45 and has decided to return to college. He left school when he was 14 and has worked in manual jobs ever since, but now he has decided that it is time to get some more qualifications so that he can get a different job (one that doesn't make him feel tired and sore when he gets home at night). He is very nervous about returning to education, in particular, because he had bad experiences of school and didn't pass any exams when he was young. He was told that he was 'disorganised' and would 'never make anything of himself'. Geoff is very keen and wants to do well, but doesn't have a clue about how to organise his studies. He intends to work part-time and study part-time. What advice can you offer Geoff to help him overcome his anxieties and organise his studies?

Learning outcome: By the end of this activity you will have discussed and found solutions to a variety of organisation problems that you can learn from and relate to your own studies, if and when necessary.

Activity 13

Activity · · · · · · · · · · · → 15

Becoming an
independent learner

STUDENT HANDOUT

Discuss the following questions with your group members:

1. What does an independent learner do?
2. What skills, attributes and characteristics do you think are required to be an independent learner?

3. Do you have any concerns or worries about becoming an independent learner? If so, what are they and how can you overcome them?
4. What action do you need to take to become an efficient and effective independent learner?

Learning outcome: By the end of this activity you will feel more confident in your ability to study independently and will have developed an action plan that will help you to become an efficient and effective independent learner.

Reading academic texts effectively

STUDENT HANDOUT

Group 1

Your group is to discuss 'active reading'. What do you think is meant by this term? What does it entail? Why is it desirable to become an active reader? How do you, as students, become active readers? What advice and tips can you offer to other students to help them to become active readers?

Group 2

Your group is to discuss 'improving understanding' when you read. How can you improve your understanding of what you are reading? What strategies can you adopt to help you to understand academic texts? What tips and advice can you offer to your peers that will help them to understand complex texts (those full of jargon, technical terms and difficult ideas and arguments, for example)?

Group 3

Your group is to discuss 'improving efficiency' when you read. How can you make your reading more efficient? How is it possible to read all the required texts and not feel overwhelmed or lose understanding? What tips and advice can you offer your peers to help them to become more efficient with their reading?

Learning outcome: By the end of this activity you will be able to read academic texts more effectively by knowing how to read actively, improve understanding and become more efficient.

Activity · · · · · · · · · · · ➜ 17

Reading scientific material for unconfident adults

STUDENT HANDOUT

Read the scientific paper that has been given to you. As you read the paper, answer the following questions. We will use your answers as a basis for discussion in the workshop, where we will be able to discuss your worries and concerns, help you to feel more confident about reading scientific material and help you to develop strategies that you can use as your course progresses.

1. What are your initial thoughts and feelings when you look at the paper you have been given?
2. Is there anything you don't understand? If so, jot down some examples of things that you don't understand.
3. What are your thoughts and feelings when you have read the whole paper? Do these differ in any way from what you thought and felt when you first looked at the paper?
4. What would help you to feel more confident about reading the paper?
5. What specific action can you take to help you to understand scientific material?

Learning outcome: By the end of this activity you will understand how to approach scientific material and will feel more confident with your ability to read scientific material as your course progresses.

Adopting and adapting reading styles and strategies

STUDENT HANDOUT

Read through the following scenarios. Once you have done this work with your group members to develop a reading strategy for each scenario using the example reading styles and strategies listed below as a guide (several of these should be combined into one comprehensive strategy for each scenario). You can also add new styles and strategies, if you think of any that would be more appropriate for a particular scenario. When you have worked through each scenario, be prepared to discuss and provide a justification or rationale for each of your reading strategies.

Scenario 1

Greta is 35 years old and has decided to return to education. Her children have just started school and she feels it is the right time to study for a degree in English Literature. She has always enjoyed reading and thinks that this is the right degree for her. However, she has just been presented with her reading list and is overwhelmed by the amount, type and level of reading required. Her course starts in two months' time. What reading strategy should she adopt?

Scenario 2

Amy is in the third year of an engineering degree. She must produce a dissertation (a long essay on a particular subject) for her course, but has not decided on a topic. Her tutor has suggested that she finds out more about the topics in which she is interested, to find out about current research. She hasn't a lot of time available and needs to decide on a topic fairly quickly. What reading strategy should she adopt?

Scenario 3

Jamila is studying sociology and has just been presented with a scientific paper, full of complex figures, graphs and charts. She feels daunted but has been asked to read the paper for her next tutorial. What reading strategy should she adopt?

Scenario 4

Kobe is moving onto a master's degree after having successfully completed his undergraduate degree in geography. He intends to carry out research into perceptions of earthquake hazard in Egypt and has obtained funding from his university. Although he studied geography at undergraduate level, this particular topic is new to him. What reading strategy should he develop?

Scenario 5

Richard has always had trouble reading. He finds it hard to remain motivated and carry out the required reading for his course and his marks are suffering. His tutor has told him that he must read more and that he is in danger of failing his course if he doesn't do this. Richard doesn't want to fail so has agreed to try to improve his reading (and his attitude towards reading). What reading strategy should he adopt?

Scenario 6

Feng is studying psychology. He is from China and English is his second language. He's finding it difficult to adapt to Western education, in particular, the requirement for critical appraisal. What reading strategy should he adopt?

Scenario 7

Greg has his first-year exams in two weeks' time. His revision is going well but he feels his knowledge is lacking in one crucial topic. What reading strategy should he adopt?

Examples of reading styles and strategies

- Preview;
- prepare;
- skim;
- scan;
- contextualise;
- appraise critically;
- check facts;
- follow-up references;
- read around the subject;
- read primary texts;
- read secondary texts;
- compare and contrast with related texts;
- recognise positionality (of author and reader);
- recognise bias (of author and reader);
- evaluate personal response;

- activate prior knowledge;
- make predictions;
- define technical terms;
- visualise;
- infer meaning;
- ask questions;
- prioritise information;
- summarise;
- read in spare time;
- read translations;
- read for understanding;
- read intensively;
- read extensively;
- read to deadlines.

Learning outcome: By the end of this activity you will have a raised awareness of different reading styles and strategies and will know how these can be adopted and adapted, depending on reading purpose, subject and level of study.

Activity 20

Activity • • • • • • • • • • • → 21

Reading, critiquing and questioning

STUDENT HANDOUT 1

Read the paper given to you. As you read, answer the following questions. Be prepared to discuss your critical appraisal in our next session.

1. Who is the author(s) of the paper?
2. Why do you think the author(s) has decided to publish this paper?
3. Is the source you are looking at the original source of data (is the study reporting primary or secondary data)?
4. Has the author(s) included a relevant background literature review? Is this adequate?
5. Is there a good, clear description of how the research was carried out? Can you understand how the research was carried out, from the description given? Do you think any information is missing?
6. What questions form in your mind as you read the paper? How can you go about answering these questions?

7. Can you understand the interpretations/findings presented in the paper? Has the author(s) explained results in a clear and succinct way?
8. Are all interpretations/conclusions backed up by evidence? Has the author(s) jumped to conclusions about anything, or made assumptions that are not backed up by evidence?
9. Is there anything in the paper that you don't understand? If so, what do you think the author(s) should have done to make it clearer?
10. Are all sources acknowledged and referenced properly?
11. Is the paper well-written? Can you make any suggestions for improvement?
12. Is the paper useful to other researchers and/or the general public? Does it tell us something important? If so, what does it tell us?

Learning outcome: By the end of this activity you will have a deeper understanding of what is involved in critical appraisal and will be able to apply this understanding to academic texts, and to your written work, as your studies progress.

STUDENT HANDOUT 2

Read the paper given to you. As you read, answer the following questions. Be prepared to discuss your critical appraisal in our next session.

1. Who is the author(s) of the paper and what are their credentials?
2. What is the reason for making data/research results public?
3. Is the source you are looking at the original source of data (is the study reporting primary or secondary data)?
4. Are research topic and purpose well-justified?
5. Is there a well-described conceptual or theoretical framework? Is it adequate and appropriate?

6. Is there a philosophical/epistemological discussion? Is it adequate and appropriate?
7. Is there a detailed description of methodology? Is it clear why this methodology was chosen and how it is the best way to answer the research question?
8. Are methods well-documented or described? Is there a description of sampling procedures, method(s) of data collection and method(s) of data analysis? Are methods and descriptions appropriate and adequate?
9. Do you think the correct procedures have been followed (this could include, for example, when forming

hypotheses, generating samples, conducting experiments, analysing data and reaching conclusions)?

10. Are all data reported (including those that weaken or contradict the results presented)? Do statistics apply to the point/argument that is being made? Have the figures been manipulated to fit the argument? Have data been interpreted correctly?

11. What questions are raised by data? Are these questions answered in the paper and, if not, how might you go about answering them?

12. Are visual data presented in a way that enables readers to draw their own conclusions and verify the assertions that have been made (if relevant)?

13. Have conclusions been investigated, tested and verified by other scientists? If not, would it be possible for others to do so?

14. Are assumptions and conclusions valid and backed up by evidence? Are results credible, dependable, authentic and trustworthy?

15. Have generalisations been made that are not based on careful experimentation and analysis?

16. Has bias been introduced into any of the information presented? Has the researcher(s) highlighted, and acknowledged, any bias that might be present in the research process? Is positionality discussed?

17. Are ethical considerations discussed and well-described? Are they adequate and appropriate?

18. Have all sources been acknowledged?

19. Is the report well-written and presented? Are all diagrams, charts, figures and graphs well-presented, complete and referenced in the text, if used?

20. Is the importance/impact of the research demonstrated clearly?

Learning outcome: By the end of this activity you will have a deeper understanding of what is involved in critical appraisal and will be able to apply this understanding to academic texts, and to your written work, as your studies progress.

Activity 21

Activity • • • • • • • • • • • ➜ 26

Structuring written work

STUDENT HANDOUT

Read the two assignments that have been given to you. Both assignments address the same question, which provides an example of the type of question that you will be required to answer during this course. One of these assignments provides an example of a well-structured assignment, the other an example of a badly structured assignment. Get together with your group members during independent study to read through and discuss the assignments. As you do this, start to think about why one is well-structured and why the other is badly structured.

Discuss these issues with your group members and develop a list of all the clues, issues and points that help you to identify the well-structured assignment and the badly structured assignment. Some of these points are obvious, whereas others are more subtle. Once you have done this, develop a checklist that will help you to produce well-structured assignments as your course progresses. We will discuss your work when we next meet. If you have any questions about how to structure assignments, make a list so that we can work through them during our discussion.

Learning outcome: By the end of this activity you will have a greater understanding of how to produce a well-structured assignment, which will help you to feel more confident and knowledgeable about producing assignments as your course progresses.

Activity •••••••••• ➡ 27

Editing and proofreading

STUDENT HANDOUT

This game provides an entertaining way for you to find out more about how to edit and proofread your written work. Produce, with your group members, a piece of written work that is under 750 words in length. The topic can be a group choice, but make sure that it is related to this course in some way. When we next meet your peers are going to edit and proofread your work, and you will edit and proofread their work.

There is a slight twist to this game. When you produce your piece of written work you must deliberately incorporate a number of errors and mistakes. These should be the types of errors and mistakes that students should look for when their work is edited and proofread. However, you should try to make some of these very difficult to spot so that your peers really have to concentrate on editing and proofreading. Count the mistakes and keep a list: other groups will try to find them so you need to keep a detailed record so that you can check that they have been spotted by other groups. The group that is able to spot the most mistakes in all pieces of written work will be deemed the winner.

Learning outcome: By the end of this activity you will have a greater understanding of what to look for when editing and proofreading your work and will feel more confident in carrying out these tasks as your course progresses.

Activity • • • • • • • • • • • → 28
Producing an effective argument

STUDENT HANDOUT

The following list provides guidance for those of you who are new to poster presentations.

- Poster presentations are used to share information with peers. They present complex material in a user-friendly, accessible form that should be laid out clearly and legibly. Close attention must be paid to both content and visual appearance.
- There are different styles of poster presentation (different templates are available, depending on the software used). Examples include:
  - one-piece posters that are produced in A3 or A4 size and enlarged at the print-out stage;
  - panel styles that incorporate a number of separately produced panels or pages that are printed and mounted on a background;
  - column styles that present information in columns arranged in a logical sequence;
  - digital posters that are projected rather than printed (static or dynamic).
- Before producing your poster consider the following:
  - know your audience and pitch content accordingly;
  - work out the specific point(s) you wish to get across;
  - keep focused on the topic and ensure that you concentrate on the specific point(s);
  - work out an explicit 'take-home' message, clear conclusion or summary of implications.

- When designing your poster consider the following:
  - keep words to a minimum and language simple and clear;
  - ensure the font is suitable and large enough to be read at a distance;
  - don't mix too many fonts and font sizes;
  - structure it well, with appropriate titles, headings and sub-headings and a logical flow (keep connected items together);
  - make it visually stimulating;
  - ensure there is plenty of open space (or white space);
  - make it colourful but don't mix too many colours and use bright colours sparingly;
  - high contrast helps text to stand out (notice that screen and paper may look different);
  - use charts, graphs, diagrams, illustrations or photographs, if possible (simplify them, remove non-essential information, crop and edit, adjust colour and contrast, where appropriate);
  - ensure all work is acknowledged and include references, when required.
- One of the most important aspects of poster presentations is the opportunity for creativity. Therefore, ensure that you produce a poster presentation that is exciting and creative, in addition to being interesting and informative.

Activity • • • • • • • • • • ➔ 29

Paraphrasing, quoting and summarising

STUDENT HANDOUT

Much of the work that you undertake as an undergraduate student involves reading the work of experts in your field and incorporating their ideas into your own assignments. You can gain information, ideas and evidence to help develop your argument or to back up your argument, for example. Three techniques that you can use to incorporate the ideas of other researchers and writers into your work are paraphrasing, quoting and summarising.

Work through the questions given below, answering each as fully as possible. These questions will help you to understand what is meant by paraphrasing, quoting and summarising, recognise the similarities and differences and work out how, when and why each should be used in your assignments. If you understand how to carry out these tasks correctly you will be able to produce better assignments, build well-structured arguments and avoid plagiarism (taking the words and ideas of others and passing them off as your own, either intentionally or unintentionally).

1. What is paraphrasing?
2. When should you paraphrase?
3. Why should you paraphrase?
4. How do you paraphrase? Think about issues such as how to identify and highlight the main points, key words and essential information; how to reword or rephrase the information (changes to grammar, sentence structure and word order, for example); how to identify and reproduce the point of view or attitude of the author.
5. How do you reference a paraphrase? What information do you need to record?
6. Can you think of any occasions when it might not be appropriate to paraphrase?
7. What is a quotation?
8. When should you use a quotation?
9. Why should you use a quotation?
10. How do you use a quotation? Think about issues such as quotation marks, length of quotation, what happens when words are omitted and what happens if words need to be added.
11. How do you reference a quotation? What bibliographical information should be included and in what format?
12. Can you think of any occasions when it might not be appropriate to use a quotation?
13. What is a summary?
14. When should you summarise?
15. Why should you summarise?
16. How do you summarise?
17. How do you reference a summary?
18. Can you think of any occasions when it might not be appropriate to summarise?
19. What are the main differences between paraphrasing, quoting and summarising?
20. Why should you integrate paraphrases, quotations and summaries into your assignment?

Learning outcome: By the end of this activity you will understand what is meant by paraphrasing, quoting and summarising and will know how, when and why to use these techniques in your written work.

Activity • • • • • • • • • • → 30

Citing, referencing and producing a bibliography

STUDENT HANDOUT

Work with your group members to research, prepare and practise a teaching session on citing, referencing and producing a bibliography. You will have 20 minutes in which to deliver your teaching session to your peers, when we next meet. There will also be some time available at the end of the session for discussion, questions and to evaluate each group teaching session.

Your teaching session must cover citing, referencing and producing a bibliography. However, the focus, structure, style and delivery method are a group choice and you can use any equipment, materials and props that you deem appropriate. Ensure that your teaching session is interesting, informative and creative. Your peers should learn from your session and should be engaged and interested in what you are teaching. You will also sit through teaching sessions delivered by your peers so you can learn more about the topic and will be able to ask questions based on what you already know.

Learning outcome: By the end of this activity you will understand how to cite, reference and produce a bibliography and will be able to apply this understanding during your course when producing assignments, projects and dissertations.

Activity • • • • • • • • • • • → 33

Engaging in reflective writing

STUDENT HANDOUT

This activity requires you to design or choose a tool or medium that will help you to engage in reflective writing as your course progresses. Reflective writing helps you to gather your thoughts and commit them to paper. It enables you to describe, summarise, translate and process experiences and learning, enabling you to break down, draw on and apply what you have learnt. This helps you to find solutions to dilemmas, leads to new insight and helps with decision making, judgement and reaching conclusions.

There is a variety of tools and mediums that you can use to record reflective thought and some of these are listed below. Find a tool that works for you. When we next meet you will need to give a brief description of your chosen tool and illustrate how you intend to use the tool for reflective writing as this course progresses. We will discuss your progress in reflective writing halfway through the course and then evaluate your reflective writing and the tool/medium that you have used at the end of the course, so ensure that you engage in reflective writing on a regular basis throughout your studies.

Examples of tools and mediums that you could choose are given below, but there are plenty of other methods available, so try to be inventive and creative (and you can use more than one method, if you wish). This is a personal choice, so ensure that you choose a method that works for you. If you find that one method is not working, you can change to another as your studies progress (your reasons and justification will be recorded in your reflective writing). If you do change your tool or medium, be prepared to discuss why you made this decision. Tools that you could consider include:

Personal learning journals

Personal diaries

Storytelling

Theatre performances/plays

Book chapters

Spreadsheets

Tables

Documentary style reporting

Teaching sessions (hypothetical or role play, for example)

Counselling sessions (third person, hypothetical or role play, for example)

Reflective interviews

Blogs

When you use your tool to engage in reflective writing, ensure that you move beyond the purely descriptive, to include comprehension, analysis, synthesis, evaluation, conclusions and action, for example. If you are unsure of what is meant by some of these terms, read around the subject and record your thoughts, action and reasons for action in your reflective writing.

Learning outcome: By the end of this activity you will have chosen, used and evaluated a tool or medium that has helped you to engage in reflective writing over the duration of your course, which will help to raise awareness of the value of reflective writing during your studies and beyond.

Activity • • • • • • • • • • • → 35

Introducing statistics

Work through the following tasks with your group members, spending five to ten minutes on each task. We will then hold a class discussion on the issues raised.

Task 1

Discuss what is meant by the word 'statistics'. What do you think about when this word is used?

Task 2

Discuss what you think is meant by 'descriptive statistics' and by 'inferential statistics'. Why do you think each of these is used? Give some examples of both types.

Task 3

Discuss specific instances where you feel statistics have been abused, misused or are unreliable and cannot be taken seriously.

Task 4

Draw up a checklist, or a list of questions, that will help you to evaluate whether statistics are reliable or unreliable and whether or not they can be trusted.

Learning outcome: By the end of this activity you will have a greater awareness of statistics, understand how they can be used and abused in the real world and know how to evaluate the reliability of statistics that are presented.

Activity • • • • • • • • • • • ➔ 37

Understanding graphs, charts and visual representations

STUDENT HANDOUT

Work with your group members to research, prepare and practise a teaching session on understanding graphs, charts and visual representations. You will have 20 minutes in which to deliver your teaching session to your peers, when we next meet. There will also be some time available at the end of the session for discussion, questions and to evaluate each group teaching session.

Your teaching session can cover any aspect of understanding graphs, charts and/or visual representations. The focus, structure, style and delivery method are group choices and you can use any equipment, materials and props that you deem appropriate. Ensure that your teaching session is interesting, informative and creative. Your peers should learn from your session and should be engaged and interested in what you are teaching. You will also sit through teaching sessions delivered by your peers so you can learn more about the topic and will be able to ask questions based on what you already know.

Learning outcome: By the end of this activity you will have a deeper understanding of graphs, charts and visual representations and will feel more confident when approaching and using this type of material during your studies and beyond.

Activity • • • • • • • • • • • → 38

Introducing data mining

STUDENT HANDOUT

You have been successful in obtaining a job as a data scientist. This is a new post within the organisation. Your employers feel that their organisation could benefit from the insights gained through data mining. However, the directors of the organisation know little about data mining and are unable to see how it works or how it can be of benefit and help their organisation to improve and expand.

As your first task within your new job you have been asked to produce a document that will help your directors to understand more about data mining. In particular, they need to know what it is, how it works and why it would be of benefit to their organisation. They are also concerned about ways that data mining activities could have a negative impact on their organisation (privacy, security and the misuse or abuse of data, for example). The style of document that you produce, and type, size and nature of the organisation for which you work, are your personal choice.

Upload your document onto the digital platform that has been set up for this purpose. Once this has been done, you will have the chance to read the documents produced by your peers and vote on the best one. This will be the document that defines, describes and explains data mining in a clear, succinct and user-friendly way. It should also be imaginative, creative and hold the interest of readers.

Learning outcome: By the end of this activity you will understand what is meant by data mining, know about the processes involved and understand the potential benefits and problems associated with data mining in the 'real world'.

Activity · · · · · · · · · · · · ➔ 39

Finding and using datasets

STUDENT HANDOUT

A 'dataset' is a collection of data (gathered by a survey, observation or investigation of a particular phenomenon, for example) that is usually presented in tabular form. 'Big data' refers to extremely large and complex datasets, 'small data' refers to datasets of a manageable volume that are accessible, informative and actionable and 'open data' refers to datasets that are free to use, reuse, build on and redistribute (subject to stated conditions and licence).

Find and use two datasets that are relevant to your dissertation. These could be datasets that help with your background research or datasets that help to explain emerging results, for example. As you use the datasets, answer the following questions. We will use these questions as a basis for discussion when we next meet.

1. Where did you find the datasets?
2. How easy were they to find?
3. Did you encounter any difficulties when searching for relevant datasets?
4. How well were the data presented?
5. Were they easy to understand?
6. What method(s) did you use to explore the data?
7. Did you encounter any difficulties when exploring the data?
8. What tasks did you perform (sort, filter, code, query or annotate, for example)?
9. How successful were these tasks?
10. Did you encounter any problems when performing these tasks?
11. How useful did you find the information? Is the information relevant to your research?
12. Did you find any datasets that weren't suitable or were inappropriate? If so, why was this?
13. What tips and advice would you give to peers who are thinking about finding and using datasets?

Learning outcome: By the end of this activity you will understand how to find, use and critique datasets that are relevant to your assignments, projects and research.

Activity • • • • • • • • • → 40

Becoming an active listener

STUDENT HANDOUT

Active listening involves one person listening carefully to the words of another and understanding, evaluating, interpreting and summarising what they hear. It is structured, responsive and focused. Active listeners are not distracted by the development of their own thoughts and arguments, but instead concentrate fully on the ideas being presented. Active listening helps us to learn, increases knowledge and understanding, helps to avoid misunderstandings and enables us to find solutions to problems.

Find a radio talk show or an audio podcast on a topic that is of personal interest. Listen actively to the presenter for at least 20 minutes (or for the duration of the podcast if this is shorter) using the description provided above as a guide. Be aware of when you become distracted. Jot down a brief note of what has distracted you and then return to your active listening.

Once you have listened for at least 20 minutes, or the podcast has finished, try to sum up the main points. You will find this easier to do if you have listened actively and have not been distracted. If you find it difficult to summarise the main points, think about why this is the case. Were you interested in the topic? Could you hear properly? Did you understand what was being said? What distracted you from listening actively? Possible distractions can include:

- the development of your own thoughts and arguments;
- external disturbances from other people or technology;
- predicting what is going to be said or finishing sentences for the speaker;
- feeling overwhelmed or confused by the subject matter;
- drifting mind;
- boredom;
- taking notes and jotting down distractions!

This exercise helps you to think more about how you listen and raises awareness of what can distract you from listening. As you encounter other situations, such as listening to lecturers, attending seminars, interacting with peers and undertaking group work, try to improve your active listening skills so that you really hear what the other person is saying. The following tips will help:

- be prepared;
- assume a positive attitude;
- focus on the speaker;
- listen willingly;
- listen for useful, important and salient points;
- hear what is being said rather than what you expect or want to hear;
- concentrate on the message, not on the delivery;
- avoid emotional involvement;
- become aware of, and reduce, distractions (personal or external);
- don't jump to conclusions;
- defer judgement;
- ask questions to clarify;
- probe for further information;
- summarise what has been said;
- review notes;
- practise as much as possible: it takes time to become a good active listener.

Learning outcome: By the end of this activity you will have an increased understanding and awareness of what is meant by active listening, which will help you to develop and use these skills as your course progresses and in life in general.

Activity • • • • • • • • • • • • ➔ 46

Learning through storytelling

STUDENT HANDOUT

Part 1

Think about stories that you have heard or read in the past. These could be stories told in a formal learning setting, or stories told in a less formal setting, but which are intended to convey some type of useful message to the listener/reader. Once you have done this, give a short summary of a story to your group members and then discuss the following questions.

1. What did you learn from the story?
2. What is the key lesson that the story conveyed?
3. Why do you think the story was memorable?

4. What did you like about the story?
5. What did you dislike?

Part 2

Produce a digital story with your group members that will enable you to tell your fellow students about something related to your course. You can use any technology or features that you wish. Try to make the story interesting, creative and useful. Above all, ensure that your story helps your fellow students to learn from it. When you produce your digital story, think about the following:

1. What is the key lesson that you wish your story to convey?
2. What do you want others to learn from your story?
3. How are you going to ensure that others learn from your story?

4. Will your story stimulate thought and reflection? Will it have emotional and intellectual impact on the listener/viewer?

Learning outcome: By the end of this activity you will recognise the potential for learning through storytelling, having reflected on stories from your past and having produced, presented and received feedback on your own story related to your course.

Engaging with lecturers and tutors

STUDENT HANDOUT

A student has paid £9,000 for her course and expects to pass and get a good degree. She fails her first assignment. What should she do?

- Visit the students' union to find out how to make an official complaint.
- Demand to see her tutor to argue for a mark increase.
- Vow to work harder on the next assignment.
- Seek and receive constructive feedback about how to improve her work.
- Google essay mills.
- Read up on how to produce better assignments.

A lecturer has received his mid-term student feedback. One student has written 'he dresses really badly, has smelly breath and is rubbish at his job'. What should he do?

- Take the student aside and tell him that the comments are offensive.
- Decide to mark the student down on his next assignment.
- Run a short session on how students can provide constructive feedback.
- Buy some mouthwash and new clothes and try to improve his teaching.
- Throw the comments in the bin and never think about them again.
- Become self-conscious, a little depressed and wonder whether he is in the right job.

An international student excelled in an education system where it was socially unacceptable to question elders, experts and doctrines. Rote learning and tutor-led sessions were the norm. The student is having difficulty adjusting to self-directed learning and critical analysis. What can be done?

- Her personal tutor should take action and recommend specific courses and training sessions.
- The student should take action and find out about specific courses and training sessions.
- The tutor and student should meet to discuss worries, concerns and ways forward.
- The student should seek out students from her country for mutual support.
- The tutor or student should do nothing, as the student will adjust naturally.
- The tutor should offer practical guidance about course requirements to all students.

A student comes to see his personal tutor and bursts into tears. What should his tutor do?

- Give him a tissue and tell him to pull himself together.
- Put his arm around him and comfort him the best he can.
- Try to find out the cause of the tears.
- Tell him to go to the student counselling service.
- Tell the student to come back when he's feeling better and they can get on with some work.
- Call in a female tutor who he thinks is much better at dealing with this sort of thing.

A student is panicking about her latest assignment. She wants to meet her tutor in the hope that he will give her some clues about what to include in the assignment. What should the tutor do?

- Find out the purpose of the meeting before agreeing to meet.
- Meet the student and provide a list of information that should be included in the assignment.
- Email the student, tell her to stop panicking and instruct her to find the information herself.
- Meet with the student, prompting, probing and encouraging her to find solutions to the problem at hand.
- Produce a Student Handout that provides more detailed information about the assignment and give it to all students.

A tutor has a reputation for being abrupt and concise with feedback. One of his students doesn't understand the comments that have been given on a recent assignment. What should the student do?

- Ask a friend if they can work out what the comments mean.
- Email the tutor for clarification.
- Post derogatory comments online about the tutor's useless style.
- Forget about trying to work out what the comments mean and move on the next assignment.
- Ask to meet with the tutor to discuss the comments.
- Drop the course so he does not have to deal with this tutor again.

A student notices that one of her tutors who she thinks is rather nice has turned up at a party. What should she do?

- Introduce herself and get to know him better.
- Leave him well alone. He is, after all, her tutor.
- Get drunk and make a pass at him.
- Don't make any plans: just see how the night progresses.
- Approach him and say she is having difficulty with the course or latest assignment.
- Have a brief chat, acknowledging that they are student and tutor.

A lecturer notices that a student has not been turning up to lectures. What should she do?

- Ignore the problem: she has too many courses to teach and too much work to spend time chasing up one student.
- Email the student to ask why he has not been attending.
- Find out if he has been missing any other lectures.
- Arrange a meeting to discuss why he has not been attending.
- Recommend that he be sent a warning about attendance.
- Ask some of his friends if they know why he has not been attending.

A student has received a poor mark and some very negative comments on an assignment that he worked hard to complete. He is extremely despondent. What should he do?

- Try to turn negative feedback into something positive so that he can learn from the feedback.
- Discuss the issues with his tutor, explaining how hard he worked and why he is feeling so despondent.
- Become active in the feedback process: seek other views and look to other sources of feedback.
- Don't bother working so hard: what's the point?
- Leave his course and get a job: he won't be in so much debt and perhaps university is not for him.
- Work with the tutor to illustrate that negative criticism is not constructive and does not help students to learn.

A tutor learns that one of his students has mental health issues through reading comments on her Facebook page. He is worried about her. The mental health issues have not been disclosed to him by the student. What should he do?

- Ignore the mental health issues unless the student discloses them to him.
- Arrange a meeting to discuss the mental health issues and provide information about support services at university.
- Speak to a university counsellor to find out what he should do.
- Join her Facebook group and try to address the issues subtly online.
- Ask her friends to keep an eye on her.
- Contact her parents.

Activity 47

Activity • • • • • • • • • • • ➜ 51

Using primary and secondary sources

STUDENT HANDOUT

Read the definitions of 'primary sources' and 'secondary sources' given below. Once you have done this, work together with your group members to compile two lists: one of primary sources and one of secondary sources. We will then hold a class discussion to talk about the issues raised by this exercise.

'Primary sources' are first-hand narratives, original documents, original objects or factual accounts that were written, recorded or made during or close to the event or period of time. They have a direct connection to a person, time, event or place. Primary sources have not been subject to processing, manipulation, analysis or interpretation by others.

'Secondary sources' interpret, analyse and critique primary sources. They provide a second-hand version of events, or an interpretation or critique of first-hand accounts, conditions or objects. Secondary sources tell a story one or more steps removed from the original person, time, place, event or object.

Learning outcome: By the end of this activity you will know what is meant by primary and secondary sources and will have a greater understanding of how to find, choose, use, cite, reference and manage both primary and secondary sources in your academic work.

Activity • • • • • • • • • • ➜ 53

Finding truth and fact in mass information

STUDENT HANDOUT

Imagine that you have applied for a job as a 'fact checker' for a national organisation. This is a person who is employed to check that the facts and assertions made in written text are correct and true.

As part of the selection process you have been asked to choose a piece of written text that has already been published (in print or online). You must go through the text meticulously to identify all the facts and assertions that have been made. Once you have done this, produce a plan of action that lists the methods you would use, if you got the job, to check each fact/assertion that you have identified.

This is your dream job and you are very keen to be selected. Make sure that you choose a challenging piece of text that needs you to work hard to identify facts and assertions, and check the claims that are made. Avoid text containing facts that are easy to confirm, verify, disprove or refute as your potential employer will not be impressed and will look to a more hard-working candidate. Hand your text and plan of action to me by the stated deadline.

I will play the role of potential employer and you will play the role of potential employee when we next meet. In my role I will be hiring the best candidate(s) for the job, so convince me that this is you by producing a detailed and comprehensive analysis and plan of action, and by contributing to the class discussion.

Learning outcome: By the end of this activity you will understand how to identify facts and assertions that have been made in written text and will know how to check facts and assertions to verify, confirm, disprove or refute what has been written.

Activity • • • • • • • • • • • • → 54

Recognising statistics, facts, arguments and opinions

STUDENT HANDOUT

Work through the following tasks and questions during independent study. Take your time. It is important that you understand the issues involved as it will help you to produce better written work, help you to develop effective arguments and make it harder for others to dispute or criticise your work.

1. Give a full definition of what is meant by 'statistics'.
2. Give some examples of the ways in which statistics can be misused.
3. How can you determine whether statistics are accurate?
4. If using statistics in your work, how can you convince the reader that your statistics are correct?
5. Give a full definition of what is meant by 'facts'.
6. How can you determine that a fact is correct and true?
7. If using facts in your work, how can you convince the reader that your facts are correct and true?
8. Give a full definition of what is meant by 'argument' (in relation to academic research and writing).

9. What do you think constitutes a weak argument?
10. How do you ensure that your arguments are strong and effective when presented in your work?
11. Give a full definition of what is meant by 'opinion'.
12. Is it ever appropriate to use opinion in academic writing? Justify your answer.
13. How can you differentiate between an argument and an opinion?
14. How can you detect when opinions are disguised as arguments?
15. How can you ensure that you don't mistake opinions for arguments in your work?

Learning outcome: By the end of this activity you will be able to recognise the difference between statistics, facts, arguments and opinions, understand how and when they are misused and know how to use them correctly in your academic work.

Activity • • • • • • • • • • • ➔ 55

Organising, managing and storing information

STUDENT HANDOUT

Choose a tool that will help you to organise, manage and store information collected for your coursework and assignments. This information can include references, quotations, evidence to help back up an argument, statistics, visual information and lecture notes, for example. There is a wide variety of tools available, including paper management systems, with pages, files and folders; apps that help you to organise and build references and bibliographies; or software that enables you to manage, sort and search information, for example. If you prefer, you can design your own tool, perhaps creating a useful spreadsheet or database that will help you to record, organise and search information. Once you have chosen, adapted, modified or designed a tool, test it by entering some information you have collected. This will help you to evaluate the effectiveness of your tool.

It is important that you choose a tool that works for you. It should assist in increasing efficiency, help with your studies and enable you to stay organised. It should help you to find information that you have collected when you need to, and enable you to identify and record useful references. It can also help you to store personal notes or important information from lectures. Your chosen tool should be an aid to study, not a distraction.

Once you have chosen, tested and evaluated your tool, prepare a five-minute presentation to give to your peers when we next meet. You will need to describe your chosen tool and discuss issues such as advantages, disadvantages, strengths and weaknesses. You can also offer advice about adopting and using this tool if your peers decide that it would be a more effective tool than the one they have chosen. Once presentations are complete you can continue with your chosen tool, or decide to modify, adapt or change tools as a result of the presentations given by your peers.

Learning outcome: By the end of this activity you will have chosen, tested and evaluated a tool that will help you to organise, manage and store information collected for coursework and assignments.

Activity • • • • • • • • • • • ➔ 56

Referencing, copyright and plagiarism

STUDENT HANDOUT

Craft a story with your group members that will enable your peers to learn about 'referencing, copyright and plagiarism'. Ensure that your story is entertaining, informative and memorable. Also, try to be creative and imaginative. The specific topic, style, structure, content and genre of your story are group choices. When you craft your story, think about the following:

1. What are the key points that you wish your story to convey?
2. What do you want your peers to learn from your story?
3. How are you going to ensure that your peers learn from your story?
4. Will your story stimulate thought and reflection?
5. Will your story have emotional and intellectual impact on your peers?
6. Will your story help them to learn and remember what they have learnt?

Prepare your story for our next session. Your group will be given up to 15 minutes to tell your story and a further five minutes for peers to ask questions and discuss your story. You will also be able to listen to the stories told by other groups. Questions that we will address after each story include the following, so think about these issues when you craft your own story:

1. What did you learn from the story?
2. What are the key points that the story conveyed?
3. Do you think you will be able to remember this story and the points it has conveyed? Why?
4. What did you like and/or dislike about the story?

Learning outcome: By the end of this activity you will have a greater understanding of what is meant by referencing, copyright and plagiarism, having crafted, told, heard and discussed memorable stories on this topic.

Activity · · · · · · · · · · ➜ 57

Developing thoughts and imagination

STUDENT HANDOUT

This activity is called 'developing thoughts and imagination'. Work with your group members during independent study to craft a story about 'Kim's determination to develop thoughts and imagination'. The age, gender, nationality and social situation of Kim and the context, content, style, structure and genre of story are group choices. Ensure that your story is entertaining, informative and memorable. Also, try to be creative and imaginative. When you craft your story, think about the following:

1. What are the key points you wish your story to convey?
2. What do you want your peers to learn from your story?
3. How are you going to ensure that your peers learn from your story?
4. Will your story stimulate thought and reflection?
5. Will your story have emotional and intellectual impact on your peers?
6. Will they be able to remember the key points you wish to convey, and remember the story?

Prepare your story for our next session. Your group will be given up to 15 minutes to tell your story and a further five minutes for peers to ask questions and discuss your story. You will also listen to stories told by other groups, so think of questions that you might like to ask about other stories you will hear.

Learning outcome: By the end of this activity you will have crafted, told and listened to stories about how to develop thoughts and imagination, which will provide a memorable way to help you to develop your own thoughts and imagination as your course continues.

Activity · · · · · · · · · · · ➜ 58

Reflecting, thinking and making connections

STUDENT HANDOUT

This exercise is called 'reflecting, thinking and making connections'. It is a self-guided individual exercise that will not be seen or assessed by your tutor, unless you would like to discuss the issues that have been raised.

Start to think about and reflect on your personal learning journey. Think about your past learning, your present learning and your future learning. When you think of this learning journey, consider connections that can be made with your personal and professional lives. The following questions will help to stimulate thought and reflection.

1. Has your personal learning journey helped you to develop and grow? If so, how has this development and growth helped you in your personal and professional lives, and how might it help you in the future?
2. What have you achieved in your life? When thinking about your life, what would you say you are proud of? Can you connect these achievements with your learning? With reflection (and perhaps with hindsight) what connections are you able to identify?
3. What connections can you make between growth and development, ideas, learning and life that may, at first, appear dissimilar?
4. Is there anything that you want to achieve in life and, if so, how can learning help? How can desired achievements be factored into your future learning journey? What connections can be made?
5. Learning can lead to cognitive reframing where we begin to see things differently. Has this happened in your personal learning journey? If so, has it helped in your personal and professional lives? Will it help in the future?
6. Learning can help with cognitive flexibility, enabling us to combine and connect the familiar and unfamiliar in innovative ways. Has this happened in your personal learning journey? If so, has it helped in your personal and professional lives? Will it help in the future?

Work through these questions or pose your own questions to aid thought and reflection, which will enable you to discover connections between learning and life. Write down your thoughts and reflections. It is useful to return to your notes later in your course so that you can reflect further, think more deeply and make additional connections as your learning journey progresses. Also, you might find that connections that were not obvious during your course become more obvious when you have completed your course and are continuing on with your personal and professional journey.

Learning outcome: By the end of this activity you will have taken time to reflect on, think about and make connections between your learning and personal and professional lives, which will enable you to gain a deeper understanding of the benefits and relevance of learning.

Activity • • • • • • • • • • ➔ 59

Learning how to question

STUDENT HANDOUT 1

Over the next week take note of questions that are asked. These could be questions that are asked by your tutor; questions that are asked by partners, family members or children; questions that are asked by TV reporters or journalists; questions that are asked on social media sites and questions that are asked by researchers, for example. When you hear or see a question jot it down so that you can build a list of different types of question that are asked.

As you build your list consider the following questions:

1. What is the purpose of the question?
2. Why was it asked?
3. How was it asked?
4. What is the question trying to do?
5. Do you consider it to be a 'good' or 'bad' question? Why?
6. Do you think the question will be successful or unsuccessful in doing what the questioner hopes it will do? Why?
7. Do you think the question could have been asked in a different way to make it more successful? If so, in what way?

Group the questions from your list into categories, if possible. These could include, for example, questions that introduce a problem, test existing assumptions or stimulate reflection, or questions that constrain thought, lead to a specific answer or are simple, irrelevant or patronising. This will help you to think more about whether questions can be considered 'good' or 'bad' and whether they are successful in what they are purporting to do.

Once you have done this, start to think about how questions can be used in your academic study. The following questions will help you to do this:

1. How can questions be used to stimulate thought and increase creativity?
2. What types of question constrain thought?
3. How can questions help to introduce and solve problems?
4. How can questions increase comprehension and knowledge?
5. How can questions help you to explore a topic?
6. How can questions be used to analyse and critique the work of others?
7. How are questions used in research?
8. What is the difference between open and closed questions and when and how are they used in research?

Develop a personal action plan that will help you to improve your ability to ask questions in your academic studies. Include within your plan action such as raising awareness, increasing understanding, practising, reflecting and developing skills.

Learning outcome: By the end of this activity you will have a raised awareness and understanding of the types of question that can be asked and will have developed a personal action plan that will help you to use questions effectively in your academic work.

STUDENT HANDOUT 2

Over the next week take note of questions that are asked. These could be questions that are asked by your tutor; questions that are asked by partners, family members or children; questions that are asked by TV reporters or journalists; questions that are asked on social media sites and questions that are asked by researchers, for example. When you hear or see a question jot it down so that you can build a list of different types of question that have been asked.

When we meet next week we will discuss these questions. In particular, we will think about the type of question that has been asked, the purpose of the question, whether it can be considered a 'good' or 'bad' question and think about how questions can be used effectively in our academic work. Once we have done this you will go on to develop a personal action plan that will help to improve your ability to ask the right questions in your studies and beyond.

Learning outcome: By the end of this activity you will have a raised awareness and understanding of the types of question that can be asked and will have developed a personal action plan that will help you to use questions effectively in your academic work.

Activity • • • • • • • • • • → 61

Hypothesising and theorising

STUDENT HANDOUT

You have been asked by the principal (head-teacher) of your local college to produce a video or podcast that explains what is meant by 'hypothesising' and 'theorising'. She wants to show the video/podcast to her students who are aged 16–18 and who are hoping to go to university. Some are thinking about careers as researchers or scientists. The principal thinks that it will be useful for her students to view videos/podcasts that have been made by university students who can provide good role models for her students and who can explain the issues in a creative, imaginative and informative way that will inspire her students to think more about their future learning and careers.

Prepare a short video or podcast about 'hypothesising and theorising' that is suitable for college students aged 16–18. Try to be as creative, imaginative and informative as possible. You must engage the students and keep them interested, as well as helping them to learn. Once you have produced your video/podcast, upload it onto the digital platform that has been set up for this purpose, by the stated deadline. Watch the videos/podcasts produced by your peers and comment on their work (remembering to remain constructive, supportive and encouraging). This will build a useful bank of videos/podcasts that can be accessed throughout your course, when required.

Learning outcome: By the end of this activity you will have a clear understanding of what is meant by hypothesising and theorising, having researched and explained the terms to others and having built a useful bank of videos/podcasts that can be accessed throughout your course.

Activity • • • • • • • • • • • → 62

Reasoning inductively and deductively

STUDENT HANDOUT

Find out what is meant by *inductive reasoning* and *deductive reasoning*. Once you have done this, find two research reports (journal papers, monographs or theses, for example), one that uses inductive reasoning and one that uses deductive reasoning. Choose any research reports that you wish, as long as they are relevant in some way to your subject of study. Describe how reasoning has been used in each research project and provide an analysis and critique of the reasoning methods and the way they have been reported. We will discuss your findings when we next meet.

Learning outcome: By the end of this activity you will have a greater understanding of what is meant by inductive and deductive reasoning, and will know how to recognise, analyse and critique their use in different types of research.

Activity • • • • • • • • • • ➔ 63

Analysing and critiquing

STUDENT HANDOUT

Work together in pairs to find a research paper from an academic journal that is relevant to this course. Once you have found a suitable paper, read through it, on an individual basis. As you read, answer the following questions. When you have done this, get back together with your partner to discuss, compare and contrast your answers.

1. Who is the author(s) of the paper?
2. Why do you think the author(s) has decided to publish this paper?
3. Has the author(s) included a relevant background literature review? Is this adequate? Has other research on this topic been explained clearly?
4. Is there a good, clear description of how the research was carried out? Can you understand how the research was carried out, from the description given?
5. Has the author(s) included everything you need to know about how the research was carried out? Do you think any information is missing?
6. Has bias been introduced into any of the information presented? Has the researcher(s) highlighted, acknowledged and taken steps to reduce or eliminate any bias that might be present in the research process?
7. Is there anything in the paper that you do not understand? If so, what do you think the author(s) should have done to make it clearer?

8. Are all interpretations/conclusions backed up by evidence? Has the author(s) jumped to conclusions or made assumptions that are not backed up by evidence?
9. Can you understand the interpretations/findings presented in the paper? Has the author(s) explained the results in a clear and succinct way? If not, what could be done better?
10. Are you convinced by the interpretations/conclusions? Why?
11. Are all sources acknowledged and referenced properly?
12. Is the paper well-structured and well-written? Can you make any suggestions for improvement?
13. Is the paper useful to other researchers and/or the general public? Does it tell us something important? If so, what does it tell us?
14. Has the importance/impact of the research been demonstrated?

Keep a copy of these questions as you will find it useful to refer back to them when you analyse and critique research papers as your course progresses and when you begin to write up your own research for your dissertation.

Learning outcome: By the end of this activity you will have a greater understanding of how to analyse and critique academic papers and will feel more confident and knowledgeable about undertaking these tasks as your course progresses.

Activity · · · · · · · · · · · · · → 65

Getting the most out
of group work

STUDENT HANDOUT

Work through the following exercise during independent study ready for when we next meet. We will discuss your responses in class before you are assigned your group project. Take time to work through this exercise as it will help you to get the most out of group work as your course progresses.

1. What do you think is meant by the word 'compassion'?
2. What do you think is meant by the word 'encouragement'?
3. What do you think is meant by the word 'respect'?
4. What relevance do these words have to group work?
5. Find two relevant references that offer useful advice about working in groups. These can be books, websites, journal papers or blogs, for example. Provide a short summary of the references you have found and explain why they are useful.
6. Sum up, in one sentence, a tip or piece of advice that will help you and your peers to work effectively in groups.

Learning outcome: By the end of this activity you will have a deeper understanding of how to work effectively in groups and will feel confident about getting the most out of group work as your course progresses.

Activity • • • • • • • • • • • • → 69

Surviving virtual group work

STUDENT HANDOUT

Discuss the scenarios given below with your group members, answering each question as fully as possible (spending about ten minutes on each scenario). After 40 minutes of group discussion we will hold a class discussion about the issues raised.

Scenario 1

A group of first-year students have been chosen by their tutor to work together on a virtual project. The students have never worked together before and only two of them have ever worked on a virtual project before. Some of the group members are very tech-savvy, whereas other members are nervous about using the latest technology for communication and study purposes.

1. How should these students plan and prepare for their virtual project?
2. What issues do they need to discuss before they begin their project?
3. What potential problems can you identify and how can these be overcome?

Scenario 2

Halfway into a virtual project some students within the group are unhappy. One student has not done any work and two others feel that they are doing all the work. Some are worried that they are not going to complete the project by the stated deadline.

1. What strategies can these students adopt to overcome this problem?
2. How can they work together to complete their project by the stated deadline?
3. Could anything have been done to prevent this problem from arising?

Scenario 3

A research professor wants to set up a global virtual team to work on a specific research project. She has the opportunity to choose team members for the project and wants to ensure that she chooses the right people so that the project is successful and grant money is well spent.

1. What skills, characteristics and attributes does she need to be a successful team leader?
2. When choosing team members, what skills, characteristics and attributes should she look for?
3. What issues should she consider in terms of technological requirements and communication?

Scenario 4

A local group of students has been set up to work on a virtual university project. A dominant group member believes there should be a team leader and has nominated himself, but he has never worked on a virtual project before.

1. How should the group handle this issue?
2. Does this group need a team leader?

3. How can this group move forward to work together successfully?

Learning outcome: By the end of this activity you will have a greater understanding of how to undertake virtual group work and will feel more confident about working on virtual projects, knowing how to recognise and overcome problems if they occur.

Activity 69

Activity • • • • • • • • • • ➔ 70

Working within international teams

STUDENT HANDOUT

Imagine that you are applying for a distinguished scholarship that will provide you with a good income for the next few years and help to advance your career. The scholarship will enable you to work within an international team on a specific project that is of great personal interest. Therefore, you really want to succeed in your application.

As part of the application process you have been asked to produce an essay (written assignment) of no more than 2,000 words that gives your account of 'best practice' when working within an international team. The structure, style and content of your essay are personal choices and you can also choose the type of team, your expected role within it and the nature of the research project. When you write your essay ensure that you concentrate on issues of 'best practice' when working within an international team.

The scholarship providers will make their award based on the best essay, so ensure that you produce an excellent piece of written work that will win you the scholarship.

Learning outcome: By the end of this activity you will have researched and produced an essay on best practice within international teams, which will help you to feel more confident and knowledgeable about working effectively within an international team as your course and career progresses.

Activity • • • • • • • • • • • → 71

Understanding group dynamics and avoiding conflict

STUDENT HANDOUT

This activity is an entertaining and light-hearted way to get you to think about group dynamics and avoiding conflict when working in groups. You must work with your group members to produce a video that illustrates problems with group dynamics and conflict. The focus, content (the problems you choose to highlight), structure and type of video are group choices. When we next meet we will view all the videos, discuss the problems you have illustrated and work together to provide solutions to the problems.

You will need to research what is meant by group dynamics and think about the problems that can occur within groups when group members interact and work on a project together. This can include individual behaviour, group processes, interaction and relationships, for example. You will also need to think about how problems with group dynamics can lead to conflict, which can include conflict in relationships, structures, processes and tasks, for example.

When you produce your video keep it light-hearted. We want viewers to be introduced to the issues so that we can discuss them in more depth and find practical solutions, but we do not want viewers to be upset or offended by what they are viewing. Be creative and imaginative. Introduce humour if you wish: often it is easier to remember what you have learnt if the information presented is entertaining, light-hearted and humorous.

Your video should be no more than ten minutes long. We will view each video in turn, and hold a discussion after each to talk about the issues raised and to find solutions to the problems that have been illustrated. Your peers will be encouraged to ask questions about your video, so be prepared to provide answers, when required.

Learning outcome: By the end of this activity you will have a raised awareness of problems that can occur with group dynamics and understand how to recognise, and address, these problems so that conflict can be avoided in group work as your course progresses.

Gaining confidence with IT for academic study

STUDENT HANDOUT

Consider the following real-life statements made by students who are new to using information technology (IT) for academic study. Discuss each statement with your group members and identify solutions to the stated problems, worries or concerns.

1. It might sound odd but I'm quite scared of using computers. I think I'm going to break them and get stuck and never be able to sort out the problems.
2. Those computer suites are really daunting. There are loads of youngsters all typing really fast, knowing what they're doing and probably thinking what's that idiot doing in here.
3. It all just moves too quickly. One minute you've learnt it and then it all changes and you've got to learn it all again. Sometimes it seems a bit pointless trying to keep up with it all.
4. My problem is I just switch off if a see loads of figures. I just don't understand them and don't know what they mean.
5. These days everyone knows everything about tablets and phones and stuff. Kids are brought up with it. I feel left behind and don't know what to do about it.
6. I know I should know how IT can help with my university course but if I'm honest I don't really know. Obviously, I can word-process my assignments and obviously there's the internet for research, but what else is there? What else should I know about and how do I find out?

Once you have discussed each of these statements and found solutions, work with your group members to develop an action plan that you can use to help you get the most out of IT as your studies progress.

Learning outcome: By the end of this activity you will feel more confident with the use of IT during your academic studies and will have developed an action plan that you can implement to help you get the most out of IT as your course progresses.

Activity · · · · · · · · · · · ➔ 77

Using data visualisation tools and software

STUDENT HANDOUT

This activity introduces you to data visualisation tools and software. It builds a useful, student-centred resource on which you can draw throughout your course, when required.

'Data visualisation' is a term that is used to describe the presentation of data in a visual format that helps us to better understand the data, see patterns and recognise trends. It provides insight into data and helps us to develop hypotheses to explore further. Large datasets can often appear overwhelming: data visualisation tools and software help to make them more manageable.

This activity asks you to find a data visualisation tool and/or software that you must then test using suitable data. Information about how to do this is provided below. Once you have carried out your test you will need to review and critique the tool/software and post your thoughts on the digital platform that has been set up for this purpose.

Finding visualisation tools and software

Choose one of the data visualisation tools listed below or, if you prefer, find your own tool to use. It is useful to visit a few sites first, so that you can get an idea of the types of tool or software that are available. Some tools are more complex than others, requiring code-writing and programming skills, for example. Ensure that you only use tools that are free to use (those that are available through your university or those that offer a free trial, for example). Once you have done this, test your chosen tool. You will need to find suitable data that can be used for your test (see below).

Data visualisation tools and software (in alphabetical order):

- Chartblocks (http://www.chartblocks.com)
- Datawrapper (https://www.datawrapper.de)
- Dygraphs (http://dygraphs.com)
- Excel (https://products.office.com/en-GB/excel)
- Gephi (https://gephi.org)
- Paraview (http://www.paraview.org)

- Plotly (https://plot.ly)
- R (https://www.r-project.org)
- Raw (http://raw.densitydesign.org)
- Tableau public (https://public.tableau.com)
- Visualize Free (http://visualizefree.com)

Finding data to test the tool or software

You can find suitable data by using the Google Public Data Explorer (www.google.com/publicdata/directory) or by visiting the following websites.

- The UK Government's open datasets can be found at www.data.gov.uk. This site brings together data from all central government departments and a number of other public sector bodies and local authorities.

- The Economic and Social Research Council (www.esrc.ac.uk) in the UK has published details of almost 1,000 datasets generated by ESRC-funded grants. The data are free to access and use.

- The US Government's open datasets can be found at www.data.gov. Data are provided by a wide variety of organisations, including Federal agencies, the US Geological Survey and the National Aeronautics and Space Administration (NASA).

- World Bank Open Data can be found at http://data.worldbank.org. This site provides free and open access to global development data.

Alternatively, you can use your own data to test the tool, if you have generated suitable data from your research.

Testing, reviewing and critiquing your chosen tool or software

Once you have found suitable data, test your chosen tool or software. When you do this consider the following questions as these will help you to review and critique your visualisation tool/software:

1. Is the tool/software easy to use? Are clear instructions available?
2. Did you encounter any difficulties when using the tool/software? If so, what were they? How did you overcome these difficulties?
3. What do you consider to be the strengths and weaknesses of your chosen tool/software?
4. What tasks were you able to perform? How successful were these tasks?
5. Are the visualisations clear and easy to understand? Do they help you to recognise patterns or trends?
6. Are there any ways in which the tool/software could be improved?
7. What advice would you offer to your peers who may be thinking about using this tool/software?

Posting your review and building a useful resource

Once you have tested, reviewed and critiqued your chosen tool/software post your review on the digital platform that has been set up for this purpose. The aim is to provide a comprehensive, practical and useful resource that you and your peers can access throughout your studies. Therefore, be as detailed and informative as possible. Review the posts given by your peers and ask questions, pose dilemmas, answer questions and help to solve problems. Upload links and sample visualisations, if you feel it will be of benefit to your peers.

Learning outcome: By the end of this activity you will have tried, tested and critiqued a data visualisation tool and/or software and will have developed a useful student-centred resource on which you can draw throughout your course, when required.

Activity 77

Activity • • • • • • • • • • • • ➔ 78

Copyright infringement and plagiarism of electronic material

STUDENT HANDOUT

Work with your group members to produce a video or podcast that teaches about copyright infringement and plagiarism of electronic materials to your fellow students. You will need to carry out detailed research and hold a focused discussion with your group members to reach agreement on what is meant by copyright infringement and plagiarism of electronic materials. The focus, structure, style and method of presentation are your choice, but make sure that you produce an interesting, creative and informative video or podcast from which your fellow students can learn. You can use any recording equipment, materials and presentation software that you deem appropriate. Take care not to infringe copyright or plagiarise electronic materials when you produce your video.

Your video/podcast should be uploaded on the digital platform that has been set up for this purpose by the stated deadline. Once you have uploaded your video/podcast, take some time to view, discuss and provide feedback on the videos and podcasts uploaded by your classmates. This activity will provide a useful resource on which you can draw to help you understand what is meant by copyright infringement and plagiarism of electronic materials. This will help you to recognise when others have breached copyright or plagiarised and enable you to avoid these problems in your personal academic work as your course progresses.

Learning outcome: By the end of this activity you will know what is meant by copyright infringement and plagiarism of electronic materials, recognise when it might have occurred in the work of others and understand how to avoid it in your own academic work. You will also have a useful collection of videos/podcasts on which to draw, when required.

Activity • • • • • • • • • • • ➔ 83

Running focus groups

STUDENT HANDOUT

This activity helps you to think about the focus group method and find out more about how to run a focus group. This is a collection of interacting individuals, with common characteristics or interests, holding a discussion that is introduced and led by a moderator. This person ensures that the discussion stays on topic, while controlling breakaway conversations, dominance and disruption. The aim of a focus group is not to reach consensus: instead, it is to gain a greater understanding of attitudes, opinions, beliefs, behaviour and perceptions (with the focus on interaction as part of the research data). Focus groups can be used in an exploratory way to help inform a questionnaire, or they can be used towards the end of a project to help explain emerging themes, for example. In some projects, researchers use focus groups as the only data collection method. Participants are chosen from the study population, using a variety of sampling techniques (depending on methodology).

Search online for two focus group demonstrations. Watch the demonstrations carefully, taking notes as you do so. Think about what the moderator is doing, how questions are asked and how participants are encouraged to speak. Think about the purpose of the focus group and decide whether or not you think it is generating the kind of information that is required. You can also think about the wider picture: how focus groups are used in research, problems that could occur (and perhaps have occurred in your chosen demonstrations) and how these can be overcome, for example.

Now imagine that you have been asked to write a review of both of these demonstrations for your university magazine (you can write one review to discuss both demonstrations, perhaps to compare or contrast, or write two separate reviews, depending on preference). The editor wants you to make sure that reviews are interesting, informative and help the reader to understand more about how focus groups are run (and perhaps the focus group method in general). The structure, style, length and content of review are a personal choice, but make sure that your peers are able to learn from what you have written. Ensure that links to your chosen demonstrations are provided, all material is referenced correctly and that you are not in breach of copyright when using any online material.

Hand your review(s) in by the stated deadline. I will compile all reviews into a PDF that will be sent to all students on this course. You will be able to read each other's reviews and access the resource later in your studies, if you decide to use focus groups in your research.

Learning outcome: By the end of this activity you will have a greater awareness of the focus group method and understand more about how focus groups are run. You will have produced a collection of focus group reviews that can be accessed if you decide to use focus groups for your research project.

Working with supervisors and personal tutors

STUDENT HANDOUT

Draw a Venn diagram on your piece of card. This consists of the universal set (a large box drawn around the edge of the card), which is to be named 'roles and responsibilities'. In the box draw two sets (these are two large overlapping circles). Name one set 'personal tutor' and the other set 'student'. The overlap is called the intersection and includes both personal tutor and student.

Once you have done this work through the list below, placing each item somewhere on your Venn diagram. Think about each item, discuss it with your group members and reach agreement about where it should be placed on the diagram. For example, do you consider it to be the role or responsibility of the personal tutor, the student or both? Or do you think that it is not the responsibility of either and, therefore, must be placed outside both sets? As you work through the list you might think of additional roles and responsibilities that have not been included. If so, add them to your Venn diagram. Once you have placed all the items on the diagram we will hold a class discussion on the issues raised.

Possible roles and responsibilities

prepare for meetings

show up on time

initiate conversation

develop a meaningful relationship

listen actively

act on what is said

explore academic goals

explore personal goals

develop study and learning skills

provide learning resource information

give useful book references

comment on work

encourage personal development and growth

provide support and encouragement

make specialist referrals

work towards goals

set boundaries

remain motivated

display enthusiasm

explore expectations

encourage independence

encourage peer networking

encourage joy of learning

stimulate intellectual thought

challenge arguments

share worries and concerns

disclose sensitive information

provide feedback

develop a good working relationship

act on feedback

provide refreshments

act on advice

respect boundaries

seek help

commit to work requirements

complete work on time

provide careers advice

Learning outcome: By the end of this activity you will have a greater understanding of roles and responsibilities when working with personal tutors and supervisors, which will enable you to work effectively together and build a good working relationship as your course progresses.

Activity · · · · · · · · · · · · ➜ 87

Understanding the reasons for assessment

STUDENT HANDOUT

Discuss the following questions with your group members. Once you have done this we will hold a class discussion on the issues raised.

1. What do you think is meant by the term 'assessment'? How is this term used in higher education?
2. What, in your opinion, is the purpose of assessment in higher education?
3. How can the assessment of students help tutors?
4. How can assessment help students?
5. How can the assessment of students help course leaders/administrators and universities?
6. Provide a list of the different methods of assessment that might be used on a university course. Discuss, with your group members, the effectiveness of the methods you have mentioned.

Learning outcome: By the end of this activity you will have a raised awareness about the meaning and purpose of assessment in higher education and will understand the relevance to teaching, learning, performance and personal development.

Activity • • • • • • • • • • • • → 90

Preparing for an exam

STUDENT HANDOUT

Discuss the following questions with your group members. Once you have done this we will hold a class discussion on the issues raised.

1. How can you prepare academically for exams?
2. How can you prepare psychologically for exams?
3. How can you prepare physically for exams?
4. How can you prepare practically for exams?

Learning outcome: By the end of this activity you will have thought about, and discussed, how to prepare for exams academically, psychologically, physically and practically, which will help you to be prepared for, and feel more confident about, taking exams as your studies progress.

Activity • • • • • • • • • • • → 91

Taking an exam

STUDENT HANDOUT

Think about useful tips and pieces of advice that you can offer to your peers that will help them to take exams. Discuss these issues with your group members and come up with a list of useful, snappy and creative tips and pieces of advice about taking exams. You have about 20 minutes to develop your list.

Once you have done this you will need to share your list with the rest of the class during a class 'brainwave'. This is a variation on the brainstorm technique and will require a member from each group to stand up, in turn, and give one tip or piece of advice, taking care not to repeat what has already been said. This method enables you to share information, while listening to others, thinking quickly and memorising what has come before. Each answer is given quickly, without judgement or criticism, even if you disagree with what has been said. The aim of the brainwave is to help you to discuss, share and remember useful information and advice about taking exams in an entertaining and creative way.

Learning outcome: By the end of this activity you will feel more prepared, knowledgeable and confident about taking exams, having discussed and shared tips and advice with your peers.

Activity • • • • • • • • • • • → 94

Recognising and avoiding academic malpractice

STUDENT HANDOUT

Work with your group members during independent study to develop three scenarios that illustrate three different types of academic malpractice (one in each scenario). The structure, content, style and context of scenario are a group choice as long as you ensure that each scenario illustrates one different type of academic malpractice. You can make the malpractice obvious and easy to spot, or you can choose to make the malpractice well-hidden and difficult to detect in your scenarios.

  When we next meet we will discuss each scenario. Your peers will identify the type of academic malpractice that you have illustrated and will then discuss possible ways to avoid, rectify, reduce or eliminate the type of malpractice that has been illustrated in your scenarios. Ensure that all scenarios are plausible and try to be inventive and creative: it is important that we have a wide coverage of different types of malpractice and that the ensuing discussion will interest, inform and enlighten your peers.

Learning outcome: By the end of this activity you will understand more about what is meant by academic malpractice, will know about specific types of academic malpractice and will understand how to avoid, reduce, rectify or eliminate academic malpractice.

Activity • • • • • • • • • • → 95

Recognising ethical issues and dilemmas when using the internet

STUDENT HANDOUT

Discuss the scenarios given below with your group members, answering each question as fully as possible. After 40 minutes of group discussion we will hold a class discussion to talk about the issues raised.

Scenario 1

A student is sent an email from a friend about a course assignment. The email contains a string of emails from other students that include suggestions for information to include in the assignments, useful references, research reports and text that has been cut and pasted from a variety of websites, journal papers and blogs. The student finds the information extremely useful so she emails it to a couple of her friends.

1. Could this student have infringed copyright? If so, in what way?
2. What do you think is, and is not, protected by copyright?
3. What should the student have done to ensure that copyright was not infringed?
4. What can you, as students, do to ensure that you do not infringe copyright?

Scenario 2

A student has found an essay on the internet that is in the public domain. One section is of particular relevance to his latest assignment so he copies and pastes the section into his assignment. He changes a couple of words here and there so that it reads better and fits his writing style.

1. This student is guilty of intellectual dishonesty. But what, exactly, is his crime?
2. What is the difference between plagiarism and copyright?
3. How would you define plagiarism?
4. How can you, as students, avoid plagiarising the work of others?

Scenario 3

A student keeps a blog about her experiences at university. She wants the information to be freely available to anyone who wants to read, use, publish, quote or pass on the information to other people. However, she understands that, once her blogs have been written, they are protected by copyright.

1. What can this student do to make her work freely available for anyone to use, publish, quote or pass on to others?
2. How can you tell whether or not you can use the work of others without infringing copyright?

Scenario 4

A student is concerned about how to use the internet ethically. He doesn't want to be accused of intellectual property theft, nor does he wish to act unethically when using social media, emailing and joining chat groups. He feels it would be useful to have a simple 'Code of Ethics' when using the internet that would help him to act responsibly.

1. What issues would you include in a 'Code of Ethics' for using the internet?

2. How would you ensure that students are able to access, and abide by, your Code of Ethics?

Learning outcome: By the end of this activity you will have a raised awareness of ethical issues and dilemmas when using the internet and know how to recognise, avoid or overcome such issues as your course progresses and in life in general.

Activity 95

Activity · · · · · · · · · · · → 96

Knowing about subjectivity and objectivity

STUDENT HANDOUT

Prepare three questions that you can ask your peers about subjectivity and/or objectivity. You can ask about subjectivity, objectivity or both in each question and this can relate to your studies, your research, academia, politics, journalism or any other part of life. Ensure that you develop meaningful and searching open questions that will generate in-depth discussion, stimulate thought and enable your peers to learn something new or gain deeper insight about subjectivity and/or objectivity.

When we next meet you will pose your questions in turn, one at a time, to the rest of the class. Your peers will discuss possible answers to your questions (there may not be a right or wrong answer, which does not matter: the goal is to generate discussion and stimulate deeper thought about the topic). You should also prepare answers to your own questions so that you can join in, or lead, the discussion, where appropriate. Your answers should be clear, concise, thorough, informative and enlightening.

Learning outcome: By the end of this activity you will have gained a deeper insight into what is meant by subjectivity and objectivity, and will be able to relate and apply this understanding to your studies, research and life in general.

Activity • • • • • • • • • • • → 97

Detecting and addressing bias

STUDENT HANDOUT

Work with your group members during independent study to produce a short video or podcast (no longer than five minutes in length) on a topic related to this course. Your presentation should be interesting, entertaining and informative, helping your peers to learn something new. However, within your presentation you must incorporate some type of bias. This could be one type of bias or several types of bias, depending on group preference. Also, you could make some types of bias very obvious, whereas other types can be more subtle, obscure or hidden. To be able to do this effectively you must first understand what is meant by bias and then find out about the different types of bias that are present.

Once you have produced your video or podcast upload it onto the digital platform provided. When we next meet your peers will view your video and try to detect bias that has been incorporated. You will also be asked to detect bias that has been incorporated into the videos produced by your peers: some will be easy to detect, whereas others will be much harder. Once you have detected bias we will discuss how it might be addressed (reduced, acknowledged or eliminated, for example). This will help you to think about how bias is presented in speech and text and will help you to develop strategies to deal with bias when encountered in the work of others and in your own work.

Learning outcome: By the end of this activity you will understand what is meant by bias, have a greater awareness of when it occurs and understand how to recognise and address bias in the work of others and in your own work.

Activity •••••••••• ➜ 98

Collaborating and cooperating ethically

STUDENT HANDOUT

Work with your group members during independent study to develop three scenarios that illustrate unethical practice when collaborating and cooperating with others in academia (your peers or research colleagues, for example). The structure, content, style and context of scenario are group choices as long as you ensure that each scenario illustrates a different type of unethical practice. You can make the unethical practice obvious and easy to spot, or you can choose to make it well-hidden and difficult to detect in your scenarios. Ensure that all scenarios are plausible and try to be inventive and creative in your scenarios: it is important that we have a wide coverage of unethical practice and that your scenarios are able to stimulate thought, generate in-depth discussion and help your peers to learn something new.

We will discuss each scenario when we next meet. Your peers will identify the unethical practice that you have illustrated and will then discuss possible ways to prevent, avoid or rectify the unethical practice that has been demonstrated.

Learning outcome: By the end of this activity you will know how to recognise, prevent, avoid and rectify unethical practice when collaborating and cooperating with others, which will help you to collaborate and cooperate ethically as your studies progress and in future careers.

Activity • • • • • • • • • • → 100

Knowing about data protection

STUDENT HANDOUT

Imagine that you have applied for a job as a data protection and compliance manager for a global finance company. You must prepare thoroughly for the interview, which you will role play with a partner when we next meet. This involves finding out all you can about data protection and compliance issues, and thinking about the tasks that will need to be performed by a data protection and compliance manager in a global finance company. You will need to convince your partner that you are a suitable person for the job, so ensure that you prepare well for the interview.

Once you have found out all you can about the role of data protection and compliance manager, develop a list of questions that you can ask your partner when the roles are reversed in the role play. One of you will be allocated the role of interviewee, and the other allocated the role of interviewer. After 20 minutes you will swap roles with your partner and be allocated a further 20 minutes to play the opposite role.

This is an interesting, entertaining and memorable way for you to learn about data protection and compliance. This activity helps you to apply and reinforce your learning through playing the role of both interviewer and interviewee in a real-world context (you can be inventive and creative in these roles and have fun in the role play). When you have completed the role play we will hold a class discussion to talk about the issues raised and relate these issues to your research.

Learning outcome: By the end of this activity you will have a deeper understanding of data protection and compliance issues and will be able to apply this understanding to your own research, when required.